NEVER STRAIGHT

It is said the shortest distance between two points is a straight line. But at sea, charting any course comes with a slew of uncontrollable factors. The winds, the currents, the swell… Only the strongest will, the keenest experience and a sharp intuition can overcome such overwhelming powers. Only by keeping the highest expectations and harnessing the deepest resources can one chart a course between where one is and where one aims to be. There is very little chance it will ever be a straight line. **Yet more often than not, it will be the right one.**

#Perpetual

OYSTER PERPETUAL
YACHT-MASTER 42

ROLEX

SANTOS

DE

Cartier

Will the world always be this unpredictable?

Will my investments weather the storm?
How can I be sure?

For some of life's questions, you're not alone.
Together we can find an answer.

ART INSPIRES TECHNOLOGY
TECHNOLOGY COMPLETES ART

Reflecting a spiraling staircase, the LG SIGNATURE OLED R takes you to higher levels of Art & Technology,
revealing an unprecedented narrative about what a TV means today.
The LG SIGNATURE OLED R, rolling out a new perspective.

LG SIGNATURE has revolutionized the way we view TV through three modes of the OLED R.
In Full View, the OLED screen is entirely visible to amplify your entertainment experience
with vivid color and perfect black through millions of self-lit pixels.
In Line View, the TV rolls down to only partially reveal the screen, allowing you to set the mood
with music, clock, frame, mood lighting & sounds, or home dashboard.
In Zero View, the screen is completely concealed inside the speaker,
creating space to immerse yourself in the beauty of the interior and captivating sound.

LG SIGNATURE
OLED R

BVLGARI

ROMA

OCTO
finissimo
THE THINNEST

July/August
Contents

Ⓜ

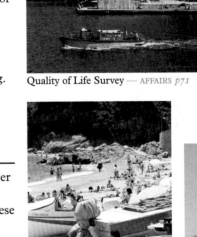

Quality of Life Survey — AFFAIRS *p71*

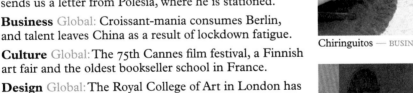

Chiringuitos — BUSINESS *p123*

Marseille — CULTURE *p153*

Pietro Porcinai — DESIGN *p168*

Summer specialists — FASHION *p194*

❸ Inventory & Expo: *Where to go, buy & eat*

Baden — INVENTORY *p215*

On the cover:
PHOTOGRAPHY:
Rodrigo Cardoso,
Nathalie Mohadjer,
Felix Odell, Andrea
Pugiotto, Trisha Ward,
Dan Wilton

Laurent-Perrier

Cuvée Rosé, chosen by the best.

Illustrated by Quentin Blake

The Ritz London

MAISON FAMILIALE INDÉPENDANTE

Monocle Films
What's on

Broaden your horizons with this month's thought-provoking selection of films by Monocle, which spans a report on slow living and longevity in the Aegean, a visit to an electric flight school in Sweden that's leading the way in forging a green future for aviation, and a conversation with a photographer about his memories of shooting a dramatic sports event for Lusophone nations. We also explore a farm in the mountains above Nice that is making environmental responsibility a pleasure.

NEW FILM

Meet the Photographers: John Balsom

The *Jogos da Lusofonia* are an Olympics-style event for people from the world's Portugese-speaking nations. To celebrate the release of our latest longform publication, *The Monocle Book of Photography*, shutterbug John Balsom revisits his trip to the 2009 event in Lisbon.

Why Greeks live longer HEALTH

Nestled in the heart of the Aegean, the island of Ikaria is a secluded spot with a humble, unhurried way of life. Today a third of the island's population lives to be more than 90 years old. We venture to its *kafeneios*, beaches and allotments to meet the bronzed seniors.

Inside an electric flight school MOBILITY

A new electric flight school in Skellefteå, northern Sweden, is inspiring a future of emission-free aviation. We take to the sky in the first electric-powered planes approved for use by European flight regulator EASA to learn what it takes to nab a green pilot's licence.

Escape to la campagne: Côte d'Azur TRAVEL

Permaculture farm and hotel Casa Sallusti was created to show that you can enjoy the good things in life while still respecting the planet. We visit its founder, Isabella Sallusti, and meet the young people who work at the farm in search of a slower, more nourishing, way of life.

Fine lines

The Monocle Minute On Design is our handsome weekly newsletter that highlights the work of the best architects, product designers, graphic artists and urban planners. Sign up for free now at *monocle.com/subscribe/newsletters*

WE ARE ALL CONNECTED

Connecting more countries
than any other airline.

TURKISH AIRLINES

July/August
Radio contents

An optimal quality of life requires a perfect soundtrack. Get your fix of award-winning daily news shows, smart weekly magazine programmes and top tunes on Monocle 24, our 24/7 radio station and podcast platform that offers the best in culture, design, business, urbanism and more. Find your favourite show at *monocle.com/radio* or wherever you get your podcasts.

Positive outlook:
MONOCLE ON SUNDAY
Join Tyler Brûlé as he hosts a lively review of the past seven days and sets the agenda for the week ahead. A special guest panel joins him around the mics at MONOCLE's Zürich HQ for a morning missive.

Fresh thinking:
THE BULLETIN WITH UBS
Hear the finest minds cut through the hype and get to the heart of the big stories in finance. Listen for sharp insights into the people, places and products shaping the week ahead.

Choice cuts:
THE CURATOR
Our editors and producers introduce the best of the past seven days on Monocle 24, with standout news clips, special features and reports from our network of global correspondents.

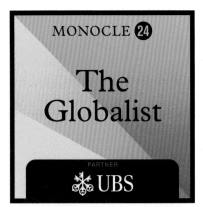

Leading lights: THE GLOBALIST
Stay on top of the international news agenda with our current affairs and business show, which features a smart review of the latest international newspaper front pages. Stories that matter, wherever you are in the world.

Well turned out:
KONFEKT KORNER
Join editor Sophie Grove and style director Marcela Palek from our sister publication *Konfekt*, and Gillian Dobias as they discuss ideas and reports from the worlds of fashion, food and travel.

World's best:
THE FOREIGN DESK
Our award-winning, global-affairs show is hosted by Andrew Mueller and features smart thinkers, expert guests and in-depth discussions on the big issues of the week – and some smaller stories too.

Better business:
THE ENTREPRENEURS
This weekly tour of the most inspiring people, companies and ideas in business – from start-ups to heritage brands – brings you the stories behind the best in hospitality, design, fashion and retail.

(M)(24)

Monocle 24

Unrivalled radio and perfect podcasts. See the schedule at *monocle.com/radio* or listen via Apple Podcasts, Spotify or wherever you get your audio.

1. *Up to date:* Listen live and stay in the moment.
2. *Or up to you:* Download your favourite shows.
3. *Total coverage:* Business, culture, design, media, news and more.

Paul Smith + ē **DePadova**

MONOCLE: Issue 155

July/August
Masthead

GROUP

Editorial Director
& Chairman
Tyler Brûlé
tb@monocle.com

MONOCLE

Editor in Chief
Andrew Tuck
at@monocle.com

Creative Director
Richard Spencer Powell
rsp@monocle.com

Editor
Josh Fehnert
jaf@monocle.com

Production Director
Jacqueline Deacon
jd@monocle.com

Chief Sub Editor
Lewis Huxley
lh@monocle.com

Photography Director
Matthew Beaman
mpb@monocle.com

Executive Editor
Nolan Giles
nsg@monocle.com

Culture Editor
Chiara Rimella
chr@monocle.com

Business Editor
David Hodari
dho@monocle.com

Fashion Editor
Natalie Theodosi
nt@monocle.com

Deputy Design Editor
Nic Monisse
nm@monocle.com

Associate Editor
Alexis Self
as@monocle.com

Style Director
Marcela Palek
mp@monocle.com

Fashion Director (Paris)
Daphné Hézard
dhz@monocle.com

Senior Correspondent
Robert Bound
rb@monocle.com

Senior Correspondent
Sophie Grove
sgr@monocle.com

Fashion Markets Editor
Kyoko Tamoto
kt@monocle.com

Researcher
Carolina Abbott Galvão
cag@monocle.com

Researcher
Grace Charlton
gc@monocle.com

Editorial Assistant
Jack Simpson
jms@monocle.com

Interns
Monica Lillis
Annabel Martin

DESIGN

Art Director
Sam Brogan
sbr@monocle.com

Designer
Jessica North-Lewis
jnl@monocle.com

Assistant Photography Editor
Amara Eno
ae@monocle.com

Junior Designer
Oli Kellar
ok@monocle.com

Junior Photography Editor
Kamila Lozinska
kl@monocle.com

BUREAUX

Bureau Chief & Senior
Asia Editor (TOKYO)
Fiona Wilson
fw@monocle.com

Associate Bureau Chief
(TOKYO)
Junichi Toyofuku
jt@monocle.com

Bureau Chief & Asia
Editor (HONG KONG)
James Chambers
jch@monocle.com

Writer/Researcher
(HONG KONG)
Naomi Xu Elegant
nxe@monocle.com

Europe Editor at Large
(MILAN)
Ed Stocker
ejs@monocle.com

US Editor (LOS ANGELES)
Christopher Lord
cl@monocle.com

Production Co-ordinator
(ZÜRICH)
Carlo Silberschmidt
cs@monocle.com

SUB EDITING

Deputy Chief Sub Editor
Genevieve Bates

Senior Sub Editor
Yo Zushi
yz@monocle.com

Sub Editor
Sarah Cohen
sco@monocle.com

Sub Editor
Sonia Zhuravlyova
sz@monocle.com

ONLINE

Senior Digital Designer
Rogerio Mota
rmm@monocle.com

Senior Web Developer
Juan Muñoz
jmh@monocle.com

Web Developer
Valentina Labib
vl@monocle.com

Digital Content Manager
Bill Whitehouse
bw@monocle.com

Assistant Digital
Content Producer
Emilie Wade
ew@monocle.com

CONTRIBUTING EDITORS

**Jessica Bridger, Ben
Davis, Alicia Kirby,
Tristan McAllister,
Andrew Mueller, Sheena
Rossiter, Saul Taylor**

CORRESPONDENTS

Liam Aldous (MADRID) *la@monocle.com*
Aarti Betigeri (CANBERRA) *aab@monocle.com*
Lars Bevanger (OSLO) *lab@monocle.com*
Michael Booth (COPENHAGEN) *mb@monocle.com*
Kimberly Bradley (BERLIN) *kab@monocle.com*
Petri Burtsoff (HELSINKI) *pbu@monocle.com*
Ivan Carvalho (MILAN) *ic@monocle.com*
Annabelle Chapman (WARSAW) *abc@monocle.com*
Guy De Launey (LJUBLJANA) *gdl@monocle.com*
Gaia Lutz (LISBON) *gsl@monocle.com*
Zach Dundas (PORTLAND, OREGON) *zd@monocle.com*
Lucinda Elliott (LATIN AMERICA AFFAIRS) *le@monocle.com*
Mary Fitzgerald (NORTH AFRICA) *mfi@monocle.com*
Mary Holland (NEW YORK) *mho@monocle.com*
Sasha Issenberg (US POLITICS) *si@monocle.com*
Daphne Karnezis (ATHENS) *dk@monocle.com*
Alexei Korolyov (VIENNA) *ako@monocle.com*
Gabriel Leigh (TRANSPORT) *gl@monocle.com*
Tomos Lewis (TORONTO) *tle@monocle.com*
Liv Lewitschnik (STOCKHOLM) *ll@monocle.com*
Charlotte McDonald-Gibson (THE HAGUE) *cmg@monocle.com*
Leila Molana-Allen (BEIRUT) *lmo@monocle.com*
Anastasia Moloney (BOGOTÁ) *anm@monocle.com*
David Phelan (TECHNOLOGY) *dwp@monocle.com*
David Plaisant (ROME) *dmp@monocle.com*
Lyndee Prickitt (NEW DELHI) *llp@monocle.com*
Henry Rees-Sheridan (NEW YORK, RADIO) *hrs@monocle.com*
Gwen Robinson (BANGKOK) *gr@monocle.com*
Sarah Rowland (SOUTHERN STATES, USA) *sr@monocle.com*
Laura Rysman (CENTRAL ITALY) *lr@monocle.com*
Janek Schmidt (MUNICH) *js@monocle.com*
Olga Tokariuk (UKRAINE) *ot@monocle.com*
Annick Weber (LUXEMBOURG) *aw@monocle.com*
Benno Zogg (SECURITY) *bz@monocle.com*

BOOKS

Head of Book Publishing
Joe Pickard
jp@monocle.com

Deputy Editor,
Book Publishing
Molly Price
mpr@monocle.com

Assistant Editor,
Book Publishing
Amy Van Den Berg
av@monocle.com

Production Manager,
Book Publishing
Sarah Kramer
sk@monocle.com

FILM

Senior Producer
Megan Revell
mr@monocle.com

EDITOR AT LARGE

Hidetoshi Nakata
hn@monocle.com

MONOCLE 24

Head of Radio
Tom Edwards
te@monocle.com

Executive Producer/Presenter
Markus Hippi
mh@monocle.com

Senior News Producer
Rhys James
rj@monocle.com

News Editor
Christopher Cermak
cc@monocle.com

Senior Producer/Presenter
Carlota Rebelo
cr@monocle.com

Producer & Senior
Correspondent
Fernando Augusto Pacheco
fp@monocle.com

Producers
Emma Searle
es@monocle.com

Charlie Filmer-Court
cfc@monocle.com

Associate Producer
Sophie Monaghan-Coombs
smc@monocle.com

Researcher
Lilian Fawcett
ljf@monocle.com

Researcher (ZÜRICH)
Désirée Bandli
dfb@monocle.com

Head of Production
Sam Impey
sji@monocle.com

Senior Studio Manager
David Stevens
djs@monocle.com

Studio Managers
Christy Evans
ce@monocle.com

Mae-Li Evans
me@monocle.com

Nora Hoel
nh@monocle.com

Steph Chungu
sc@monocle.com

Chris Ablakwa
cka@monocle.com

Sound Editor
Jack Jewers
jj@monocle.com

Presenters
Guy De Launey
Nancy Durham
Georgina Godwin
Andrew Mueller
Emma Nelson
Paul Osbourne

Because you give your dreams the love you deserve.

Experience now the drēmər® bed at your nearest Hästens store.

HASTENS.COM

Hästens

since 1852

July/August
Masthead

PUBLISHING

Publisher
Anders Braso
ab@monocle.com

Associate Publisher
Luke Courtier
lc@monocle.com

Creative Solutions Director
Kate Parkinson
kp@monocle.com

Advertising Director – Asia
Guido de Boer
gb@monocle.com

Advertising Manager –
Europe
Antje Petzold
anp@monocle.com

Creative Solutions Executive
Emma Croft
ec@monocle.com

Publishing Account Assistant
Cameron Walters
cw@monocle.com

ADVERTISING OFFICES

Milan (ITALY)
MIA
mia@miasrl.it

Bangkok (THAILAND)
Nartnittha Jirarayapong
noo@njintermedia.com

Taipei (TAIWAN)
Keith Lee
leekh@ms4.hinet.net

Seoul (SOUTH KOREA)
Seo Jin-Mahn
jinmahnseo@doobee.com

USA
Sam Jones
swj@monocle.com

CIRCULATION AND
SUBSCRIPTIONS

Circulation & Brand
Partnerships Director
Holly Anderson
han@monocle.com

RETAIL

Head of Retail & Hospitality
Philippa Cooper
pc@monocle.com

Senior Operations Manager
for Retail & Hospitality
Raffael Lienert
rl@monocle.com

E-Commerce &
Merchandising Manager
Rosie Croft
rc@monocle.com

Supply-Chain &
Logistics Manager
Mathilde Felter
maf@monocle.com

Product Development
Manager
Diego Lopez De La Fuente
dl@monocle.com

Intern
Eleonora Frattini
ef@monocle.com

EVENTS

Head of Brand,
Communications & Events
Hannah Grundy
hg@monocle.com

Events Producer
Paige Reynolds
pbr@monocle.com

CUSTOMER SERVICE

Director of Customer
Experience
**Lina Constanza
Mendez Saenz**
lcms@monocle.com

Customer Relations
& Insights Executive
Benson Batty
bb@monocle.com

Customer Relations Associate
Jenny Lam
jla@monocle.com

FINANCE

Chief Operating Officer
Anna Nunziata
an@monocle.com

Group Treasurer
Pauline Ho
pho@monocle.com

Finance Director
Poppy Cocoracchio
pkc@monocle.com

Finance Manager
Joe Shafi
jsh@monocle.com

Junior Management
Accountant
Farzana Ali
fa@monocle.com

Credit Controller
Kiran Ladwa
kla@monocle.com

Accounts Assistant
Danica Fernandes
df@monocle.com

THE BOARD

Directors
Richard Atkinson
Tyler Brûlé

Chairman
Tyler Brûlé

EDITORIAL DIRECTOR'S
SUPPORT

Executive Assistant
Julia Klavins
jik@monocle.com

HEAD OFFICE

Monocle
Midori House
1 Dorset Street
London W1U 4EG
TEL: +44 (0)20 7725 4388
FAX: +44 (0)20 7725 5711
info@monocle.com
customerservice@monocle.com

FRONT OF HOUSE

Brenda Tuohy
bt@monocle.com

ZÜRICH HQ & BUREAUX

Zürich
90 Dufourstrasse,
CH-8008, Zürich
TEL:+41 44 368 7000

Toronto
776 College Street,
Toronto, ON M6G 1C6
TEL: +1 647 694 2626

Tokyo
1F, Luna Rossa,
1-19-2 Tomigaya,
Shibuya-ku, Tokyo 151-0063
TEL: +81 (0)3 6407 0350

Hong Kong
1–4 St Francis Yard,
Wan Chai, Hong Kong
TEL: +852 2804 2323

Los Angeles
Platform, Unit 105,
8820 Washington Boulevard,
Culver City, 90232
TEL: +1 310 982 2966

SHOPS

London
34 Chiltern Street
London W1U 7QH
TEL: +44 (0)20 7486 8770
londonshop@monocle.com
Fabio Forin:
ff@monocle.com

Hong Kong
Shop 1, Bo Fung Mansion,
1–4 St Francis Yard, Wan Chai,
Hong Kong
TEL: +852 2804 2626
hkshop@monocle.com
Harry CK Wong:
hw@monocle.com

Toronto
776 College Street, Little Italy,
Toronto, ON M6G 1C6
TEL: +1 647 694 2626
torontoshop@monocle.com
Catalina Posada: *cp@monocle.com*

Tokyo
1F, Luna Rossa, 1-19-2
Tomigaya, Shibuya-ku, Tokyo,
151-0063
TEL: +81 (0)3 6407 0845
tokyoshop@monocle.com
Nanako Sato:
nas@monocle.com

Merano
25 Via Dante, 39012, Merano
meranoshop@monocle.com
Linda Egger: *ge@monocle.com*

Zürich
90 Dufourstrasse, Seefeld,
CH-8008, Zürich
TEL: +41 44 368 7001
zurichshop@monocle.com
Raffael Lienert: *rl@monocle.com*

Los Angeles
Platform, 8820 Washington
Boulevard, Culver City, 90232
TEL: +1 310 982 2966
lashop@monocle.com
Sam Jones: *swj@monocle.com*

TRAVEL RETAIL

Hong Kong
Hong Kong International
Airport, Gate 61, Terminal 1
TEL: +852 2116 5530
Harry CK Wong:
hw@monocle.com

MONOCLE CAFÉS

London
18 Chiltern Street
London W1U 7QA
TEL: +44 (0)20 7135 2040

Zürich
90 Dufourstrasse, CH-8008,
Zürich
TEL: +41 44 368 7001

MONOCLE KIOSK

Zürich
Seidengasse 1, Zürich
zurichkiosk@monocle.com
TEL: +41 44 368 7005

Receive the full print and digital line-up

Our subscriber
offer: £160. Sign up
now and receive:

1. 10 issues
2. Four specials
3. Exclusive digital
   travel guides
4. Tote bag
5. 10 per cent discount
   at The Monocle Shop

Subscribe at
monocle.com

*Monocle (ISSN 1753-2434) is
published 10 times a year by Winkontent
Limited, Midori House, 1 Dorset
Street, London W1U 4EG. Registered
no. 05265119 England. Printed by
Neef & Stumme, Schillerstrasse 2,
29378, Wittingen, Germany. Colour
reproduction by Rhapsody Media, 1
Phipp Street, London, EC2A 4PS. All
rights reserved, reproduction in whole
or in part without written permission is
strictly prohibited. All prices correct at
the time of going to press but subject to
change. Monocle subscriptions: monocle.
com or email subscriptions@monocle.
com. All paper used in the production of
this magazine comes from well-managed
sources. Annual subscription price £100
(£80 equivalent BAR). The US annual
subscription price is $135. Airfreight and
mailing in the US by Worldnet Shipping
Inc, 156-15, 146th Avenue, 2nd Floor,
Jamaica, NY 11434, US. Application
to mail at periodicals postage prices is
pending at Worldnet Shipping Inc. US
Postmaster: send address changes to
Monocle and Worldnet Shipping Inc.
Subscription records are maintained
at Winkontent Limited.*

BURJ AL ARAB™

Jumeirah

DUBAI

EXCEPTIONAL DUBAI ESCAPE
DISCOVER THE WORLD'S MOST ICONIC HOTEL

Wake up to views of the sparkling Arabian Gulf, with your private butler on hand,
Dubai as your playground and a Hermès scented bath to retreat to. Make the
most of our Exceptional Summer Escapes package to enjoy up to 20% off and
complimentary USD 100 resort credit to enjoy during your stay.

Refresh your routine in extraordinary surroundings.

jumeirah.com/BAAEscapes

July/August
Contributors

The magazine you're holding could not have come together without the tireless efforts of our global network of creative folk. Find out about a few of the writers, illustrators and photographers we called on to report for Issue 155.

Haeryun Kang
Writer
— BUSINESS *p117*

Kang was born in Busan, South Korea, and has called Turkey, China and the US home. She first got a taste for journalism while reporting for her high-school newspaper in Shanghai and at an internship during college at *The Gleaner*, a daily in Kingston, Jamaica. For this issue she wrote for our Quality of Life survey (*see page 71*) about Seoul and reported on Rolling Korea, a language school that integrates K-pop dance and vocals into its curriculum. She remains tight-lipped about any singing and dancing that might have taken place.

What would make your city more liveable?
I don't think even the president of South Korea can fix this but I wish Seoul had better air quality. Air pollution is a severe issue here, caused by multiple factors, including South Korean coal plants and fine dust from China.

Fiona Ma
Writer
— FASHION *p194*

Ma hails from Hong Kong but now lives in London. With a focus on fashion, she began her career at *Women's Wear Daily,* an industry trade journal. Thanks to her fashion know-how, we dispatched her to Arles in France to peruse the rails of Summer, a cosy shop offering a sharp mix of Japanese, French and Californian skate and surf brands, and to meet its charming owners.

What would improve your city?
I would love to see more green spaces with a communal sense of caring for them. I would also like to see more safety measures that would greatly improve the lives of women and children so that they can access these spaces at any time of day.

Key to writers:
(CAG) Carolina Abbott Galvão.
(LA) Liam Aldous.
(CPB) Catherine Balston.
(DBA) Désirée Bandli.
(AB) Aarti Betigeri.
(LB) Lars Bevanger.
(GBI) Georgia Bisbas.
(MB) Michael Booth.
(KAB) Kimberly Bradley.
(TB) Tyler Brûlé.
(PBU) Petri Burtsoff.
(IC) Ivan Carvalho.
(JCH) James Chambers.
(ABC) Annabelle Chapman.
(GCH) Grace Charlton.
(JDA) Jonna Dagliden.
(ADC) Alexandra de Cramer.
(LE) Lucinda Elliott.
(JAF) Josh Fehnert.
(CFC) Charlie Filmer-Court.
(MFI) Mary Fitzgerald.
(NSG) Nolan Giles.
(FG) Ferdinand Godinez.
(DHO) David Hodari.
(HK) Haeryun Kang.
(DK) Daphne Karnezis.
(AKO) Alexei Korolyov.
(KKR) Karen Krizanovich.
(SLA) Sarah Lang.
(ALV) Arik Levy.
(TLE) Tomos Lewis.
(LL) Liv Lewitschnik.
(CL) Christopher Lord.
(FMA) Fiona Ma.
(AMM) Annabel Martin.
(LMO) Leila Molana-Allen.
(SMN) Sophie Monaghan-Coombs.
(NM) Nic Monisse.
(MMO) Murdo Morrison.
(AM) Andrew Mueller.
(FP) Fernando Augusto Pacheco.
(DMP) David Plaisant.
(MPC) Molly Price.
(SQ) Samia Qaiyum.
(CR) Carli Ratcliff.
(CCR) Carlota Rebelo.
(SRO) Stella Roos.
(JSC) Janek Schmidt.
(GRS) Gregory Scruggs.
(HLS) Hannah Lucinda Smith.
(EJS) Ed Stocker.
(NT) Natalie Theodosi.
(JT) Junichi Toyofuku.
(HU) Hester Underhill.
(AW) Annick Weber.
(CWE) Clarissa Wei.
(FW) Fiona Wilson.
(YX) Yvonne Xu.
(NXE) Naomi Xu Elegant.

Alana Paterson
Photographer
— AFFAIRS *p71*

Paterson lives about an hour north of Vancouver. Photojournalism came naturally to her "when I realised I was OK at photography and advertising wasn't fulfilling. I found ideas and stories much more interesting." For us she photographed Vancouver at its best. After a long day of shooting she realised that she'd locked her keys in her truck – but a coat-hanger and a few nimble moves saw her unlock the doors in no time. "I even got a round of applause from the café I was parked in front of," she says.

What would improve your city?
More affordable housing would allow Vancouver to flourish. It would mean a more healthy, stable and flourishing population all the way to better culture, arts and music scenes.

Prasad Ramamurthy
Writer
— AGENDA *p58*

Based in Mumbai, Ramamurthy has worked as a journalist for more than 20 years. He started out in news broadcasting but has recently embraced a slower pace of life, focusing on the stories of people and places, "which I find eminently more fascinating". For this issue, he reported on a popular running club. "I was meant to run with them but ended up with heatstroke and had to watch them do their thing from the sidelines." We're sure he will join in next time.

What would improve your home?
Mumbai could do with more green spaces, even though the part of the city I live in has a fair amount of them. My own home has about 60 plants – edible, ornamental and flowering – making it a refuge from the city within the city.

Peter Zhao
Illustrator
— DESIGN *p178*

Beijing-based Zhao was a designer at a computer-game company when a friend asked him to help with some illustrations. "The images turned out to be good and I found my true calling," he says. For this issue, he applied his considerable talents to our urbanism advice story, sketching everything from buses and kiosks to parks and city farms.

What does quality of life mean to you?
Thinking about quality of life, more and more young people are choosing the kind of life that suits them best and I am happy to see this happen. When it comes to cities and neighbourhoods, there are more gourmet cafés and restaurants, which means that we can truly relax and unwind, and this helps us work and live better. Also bike-sharing schemes help to make our cities cleaner and healthier.

Eir™
Intelligent Toilet

An artful approach to
design and technology.

The Eir™ Intelligent Toilet exemplifies the art of innovation with its flowing
lines and personalized finish detail. It pairs a high-performance flushing
platform with the latest inpersonal hygiene. Finish details are available in
rose gold or polished chrome.

StudioKOHLER.com

marset-store.com

Editor's letter
Key to the city

The world's urban centres are flourishing once more despite pandemic-related predictions of their demise. Editor in chief Andrew Tuck celebrates our cities' resilience, vision and innovation, as evidenced in Monocle's Quality of Life survey.

The city is back. For believers in urban living, the past few years have been a testing time as think tanks, columnists and handwringers have talked up the exodus to the 'burbs and beyond, predicted the decimation of all retail, said that the WFH movement will derail attempts to revive pandemic-punched downtowns. We've also had to endure the soothsayers and futurologists who have railed against grand urban visions for new infrastructure (surely, they say, cargo bikes and ride-shares are all you need?), investing in new offices (because that Wework story really worked out how they predicted).

But it turns out that our cities have a resilience that allows them to adapt and change – and come roaring back. Not the same but not diminished either. Ask anyone apartment-hunting in Paris or London if demand for urban living has left it a renters' market and you'll soon understand that demand is buoyant. The trouble is that too often we extrapolate a vision of the future from just a few troubled spots, a few headline-grabbing reports. It's more mixed and interesting than that.

Yes, our cities have come back to life after the pandemic at different speeds, but they remain as hothouses for social change, innovators in sustainable architecture and design, and places where magical things can occur. Of course, some people have left the city permanently for greener pastures but that's nothing new and the gaps that they have left are being snapped up by a new generation of people who understand that a great city lets you come of age surrounded by supportive peers; dare to embrace your dreams.

This passion for cities is why I loved reading the proof pages for this Quality of Life issue, which unpacks the shifts reshaping our hometowns. In the US, for example, Chris Lord travels to Miami to see how the city has gained a new generation of entrepreneurs moving from the chillier north because of its mix of business-friendly policies and a quality of life also improved by its very sunny disposition. For the nomadic worker, Miami – along with a host of southern sunshine-belt outposts such as booming Dallas – has become a huge draw.

But Europe has its own sunbelt. In Lisbon our correspondent Gaia Lutz meets the recording artists from across the Lusophone world who are using the city as an incubator for rich musical experiments that forge sounds from Africa to Brazil. It's a scene that is making Lisbon reassess its cultural landscape and hopefully leave it richer and more diverse. Something similar is happening in Marseille where a few key metrics – affordable rents, those hours of sunshine and a cacophony of cultural influences – are making the city the go-to place for a new generation of French artists – read Julia Webster Ayuso's report on page 153.

And in Palma de Mallorca we meet Jaime Oliver and Paloma Hernaiz from the architectural practice Ohlab who understand that all those hours of Mediterranean sun also come with a challenge: how to make buildings that can stay cool without you cranking up the air-con. You can see their new Passivhaus apartment block on page 184.

Yet urban inventiveness is not limited to sunny outposts. Writing his debut story for MONOCLE, Tom Vanderbilt visits Oishii, a vertical farm in New Jersey that's growing Japanese mountain strawberries that sell at $50 for just eight fruit. The Oishii venture is a luxury player in the urban farming story but it's one of many tech-driven projects attracting huge interest and investment as people wonder how cities will best feed themselves in the future – and as the technology becomes cheaper and more widespread.

And then, of course, there's the survey of the best cities to call home – we always send this to newsstand and then duck for cover as people wonder why their hometown failed to rank. But that's the joy of this survey: it starts debate, makes people look around and wonder what would make their city better. Anyway, I am sure you will let us know your thoughts. But despite any jostling among fans of particular cities, how great that there is so much excitement about the future of the city in general, about how it shapes and changes our lives. And how, done well, it can deliver a better quality of life for all its citizens.

Thank you for reading – and I hope subscribing to – MONOCLE. Feel free to email me at *at@monocle.com*. — Ⓜ

ILLUSTRATOR: Matiejus Vaura

AT *the* FRONT

HOW TO LIVE: HOTEL ETIQUETTE

The list

Even a fantasy hotel needs house rules. These would be ours, writes Tyler Brûlé.

Though MONOCLE gets more than its share of offers to open a hotel in an emerging city, a resort in a far-flung destination or a members' club in one of our key markets, we have resisted the temptation. But we do think about who we'd hire to oversee a renovation (did I hear you say Studio KO or Studioilse?), run the bar or design the uniforms (Sofie D'Hoore, please). We also think about the house rules that would keep things civil and serene. Welcome to the Auberge Monocle.

1. Make an entrance. We worked hard on our fine fittings and flattering lighting, so get dressed up and turn a few heads.

2. Don't photograph other guests. You know perfectly well why.

3. Light a candle. The restaurant is dim for a reason. If you can't read the menu, we'll bring you an extra candle.

4. Take it back to your suite. We used to say this when a couple were getting too frisky on the lounger; today we ask that you take your conference call in your room.

5. You might make friends for life by sending a bottle of rosé to the people across the terrace. It's a nice thing to do. If they refuse, let the front desk know and we'll ensure that we're fully booked should they want to return.

Finally, keep your phone on silent or, better yet, leave it in your room. You'll be surprised how much your stay improves. *Merci!* — Ⓜ

THE INTERROGATOR

Jennifer Musisi
Uganda

A lawyer by trade, Jennifer Musisi never had plans to lead a city. But her work at the Uganda Revenue Authority, where she helped stabilise an organisation dealing with crippling corruption and systemic dysfunction, meant she was perfectly placed to head up a public authority. So when the Ugandan central government established the Kampala Capital City Authority in 2011, Musisi was a natural choice to be its first executive director, a position equivalent to mayor. She stayed in the job until 2018 and now serves on the board of c40 Cities and as a UN ambassador for sustainable development – roles where she helps to improve the lives of urban dwellers. Here, she tells us about issues facing mayors across the globe and why she loves living in Kampala. — NM

To start, tell us about your work at the Uganda Revenue Authority.
I was tasked with bringing down corruption and building up the country's revenue base. In Africa the tax base is small and businesses try to evade paying it. Part of my job was convincing people that the government wasn't going to squander it but use it to build better roads and improve healthcare.

How did you end up at Kampala Capital City Authority?
My plan was to take early retirement, do some consulting and work on my art. But the president requested I come and help transform Kampala.

That's a significant change of plans. What did you learn about local government in Kampala?
A lot of what happens in cities eventually ends up affecting the rest of the country and, as a result, local governments in urban areas offer a template for development purposes for the rest of the country. In Uganda, for example, everything begins and ends with Kampala. Here, there's a lot of rural to urban migration, with the population growing exponentially every day. This means that there are challenges in terms of providing jobs and infrastructure, and dealing with unplanned development. But if we sort out these issues in the country's biggest city and test solutions here, we can create templates that can be replicated in smaller urban centres.

What are some of the most pressing issues facing cities across the globe?
The big thing is working out where the money is going to come from to implement solutions. Almost every city I know is stretched financially, so national governments have to come in to support cities in their mandates. Urban areas are the financial, political and industrial centres of nations. They are everything, so they need to be prioritised by national governments.

Finally, what do you love about your home city of Kampala?
The people and the climate. The weather and wildlife are lovely. It's paradise as far as I'm concerned.

Reporting from...

Monocle's global team of writers bring news of rogue beavers storming Zürich, exciting regeneration projects in Los Angeles and Tokyo, and Hong Kong's superstar boy band.

ZÜRICH
Eager beavers

In recent months wild beavers have been steadily advancing from the Swiss countryside towards Zürich's urban climes. And they're earning celebrity status. One of them, which locals have nicknamed "Bucky", has become a big draw for urban wildlife spotters. — DBA

LONDON
When in London...

Cancel your holiday in Italy: the City of London is investing £2.5m (€2.9m) to encourage tourists to visit its unheralded Roman ruins. The goal of this drive is to invigorate the somewhat soulless financial and business district outside working hours. — GCH

Holy fail

Few typographical errors are as legendary as a glitch in a 1631 British edition of the *King James Bible*. The text omits the key word "not" from the seventh commandment, thereby instructing readers, on the highest authority, to commit adultery.

Perhaps 20 copies of the so-called "Wicked Bible" are still intact and have, inevitably, become more coveted than any neighbour's ass, fetching five-figure sums at auction. One has now surfaced in New Zealand and is being cared for by the University of Canterbury in Christchurch.

The perpetrators of the error received worse punishment than most sub-editors who miss a trick: they were stripped of their printing licence on the order of King Charles I of England. Anyone who has worked in publishing will have been party to a misprint – they're easily done, if rarely as amusing as this one. That could be why the Almighty carved his edicts into stone. — AM

First flush of film-making

What do German film-maker Wim Wenders, Japanese architect Tadao Ando and one of Japan's most celebrated actors have in common? The answer: public toilets. Wenders has announced that he's making a film about The Tokyo Toilet, a project that saw Ando and a host of other starry Japanese architects design beautiful, clean public loos in Shibuya. The film's hero, a toilet cleaner, will be played by Kôji Yakusho, an appealingly self-effacing actor who starred in *Babel*. With a global release expected in 2023, we're hopeful that Wenders' film might encourage other cities to build cinematically inspiring toilets of their own. — FW

New releases

A new state-run programme in Bolivia is offering early release to prisoners who improve their literacy while behind bars. Which other countries are easing pressure on their penal system by offering similar incentives? — AMM

1

Brazil
In Minas Gerais state, prisoners can pedal stationary bicycles that charge nearby street lights. The bright idea sees sentences reduced with three eight-hour shifts in the saddle.

India
At Yerwada Central Prison, cons can take part in a yoga programme to get months taken off their sentence. How's that for a flexible release?

3

Thailand
Thai inmates can fight for their freedom in a Muay Thai match against foreign opponents. If they win, they can earn an early release date.

Hot potatoes

The US-Mexico border is one of the world's most fraught, thanks largely to conservative American politicians inflaming fears of immigration across it. But it is not widely appreciated that Mexico has concerns about what travels in the opposite direction – specifically, potatoes. In May a shipment of American spuds crossed freely into Mexico for the first time in more than 25 years. Due to Mexican pettifogging, US potatoes had previously only been allowed to be sold within 16 miles (26km) of the border. But following a decision by Mexico's Supreme Court, American taters can now be sold everywhere. — AM

ILLUSTRATOR: *Leon Edler*. IMAGES: *Alamy*

TOKYO
Japanese garden

Regeneration work has begun on the outer edge of Yoyogi Park, near MONOCLE's Tokyo bureau, where an unloved chunk of land is set to be transformed by 2024. The area will have a new skatepark, running station and, most importantly, plenty of greenery. — FW

HONG KONG
Mirror ball

In July there will be anthems galore when Hong Kong's government marks the anniversary of its return to China 25 years ago. However, we expect more passionate singing at the Coliseum when boy band Mirror perform 12 sold-out shows at the Cantopop arena. — JCH

TORONTO
Sobering news

It'll be a dry summer in Toronto – and not due to warm temperatures. The council has, once again, refused to lift a ban on drinking alcohol in parks. But public pressure is growing and city hall might not be able to bottle making a change to the law for much longer. — TLE

LOS ANGELES
On the waterfront

A scheme to put the Los Angeles river to better use has been approved. For inspiration, city planners should look to the Frogtown neighbourhood, where a cycle café and small businesses have already given their stretch of the river a fresh lease of life. — CL

CORRESPONDENT'S VIEW:
Quality of life
Simple pleasures

I have a go-to walk on summer nights in Paris that always leads me to the same place: La Palette. On rue de Seine, in the heart of Saint-Germain-des-Près, this bar has long been popular among the staff and clientele of the neighbourhood's galleries. Its painting-lined interior spills out onto a buzzing terrace. I sit down in my usual spot with a good view of the entrance. Sometimes I read; sometimes I write. Mostly, though, I people-watch: the most entrenched of Parisian pastimes.

But why La Palette? Well, this is a place to linger. It's where the *beau monde* – France's fashionable set, from artists to politicians – gather and debate late into the night over bottles of wine; former president Jacques Chirac was a regular. Here, business meets pleasure as local gallerists exchange gossip about recent finds at estate sales and auctions. Couples clink glasses and friends share a *planche* laden with cheese and charcuterie under the evening sky.

In his essay "Les vraies richesses" ("True Riches"), French author Jean Giono praised the simple life of fresh air, food and wine shared with friends, objects made with care, and time in nature. Although Giono was writing in the 1930s, some things have not changed: our quality of life is still largely shaped by our ability to eat well, laugh among friends, relax outside after a long day's work and, in Paris, people-watch too. As dusk falls over La Palette, I will raise a glass to that. — ABC

ΞLΞTRΞ

The CV

1974: Born in Pittsfield, Massachusetts
1996: Graduates in history from Amherst College, magna cum laude
2001: Begins pilot training in Oxford
2003: Pilots his first commercial flight with British Airways
2007: Pilots first long-haul flight from London to Hong Kong
2015: Publishes first book, *Skyfaring: A Journey with a Pilot*
2018: Begins piloting Boeing 787 aircraft
2022: *Imagine a City: A Pilot Sees the World* is published

Ⓜ THE VIEW FROM: Mark Vanhoenacker

Dreams take flight
London

The pilot and author on how he fulfilled his childhood ambitions and why he is fascinated by cities as well as the view from the sky.

WRITER
Carlota Rebelo

PHOTOGRAPHY
Max Miechowski

For Mark Vanhoenacker, it all began in his childhood bedroom: as he stared at the paper globe perched on his desk, next to a model aircraft, dreaming of cities and places far from his hometown in Pittsfield, Massachusetts. "I was very drawn to the names of cities. When you're spinning a globe, a name is almost all the information you have," he says.

Now a veteran British Airways long-haul pilot, he has recently written a travelogue-cum-urbanism memoir called *Imagine a City* – a follow-up to his hugely popular *Skyfaring: A Journey with a Pilot* – reflecting on his relationships with metropolises across the globe and how they have changed over the course of his nearly 20-year aviation career. But, he explains, there was turbulence on arriving at this point.

Growing up gay, in a small town, meant that the hustle and bustle and freedom of big urban settlements was just the stuff of dreams. "Like a lot of kids in that situation, I looked at cities as a way of going into another place and imagining my own future – a future that might be more comfortable than how I felt at the time," he tells MONOCLE.

As he moved through his adolescent years, Vanhoenacker's fascination with names on the globe turned into a curiosity over airline route maps. "You would see these two names that were only connected by this curving, perfect line. I knew that all of those places were impossibly complicated and intricate, with rich histories, and yet they were connected in this deceptively simple way by aeroplanes."

Today, Vanhoenacker recognises cities by silhouettes, co-ordinates, or the particular way the streetlights shine at night from above. And while it's not uncommon for passengers to stare out of the window and wonder what lies below – especially when crossing a part of the world for the very first time – Vanhoenacker confirms that the view really is better from the flight deck. "With those fast forward windows, it really is an extraordinary sight. As we're descending you can see how cities are steered by geography, by the rivers or mountains around them, how they lie by the harbour or the way a railway line crosses its entirety."

This, Vanhoenacker explains, is one thing that anyone – pilot, urbanism enthusiast or otherwise – can learn about observing cities from the sky: how the grid, when viewed from above, can tell us about our likely experiences on the ground, leading to an unexpected appreciation of a place. For proof, he points to his own relationship with Salt Lake City. "I saw it first from the air, which drew me to spend time there. It's in an extremely striking location, ringed by mountains in the east, which gives way to a desert. So when I visited as a traveller, I was much more excited about going there, because I already had the sense of the city from seeing the grid above."

When MONOCLE meets Vanhoenacker, he's just about to take his routine pilot exams, where every six months he has to go into a flight simulator to practise all kinds of scenarios (even the most unlikely ones). His favourite aircraft is the now-retired Boeing 747 – the same as the model aircraft he had as a child.

And as for his favourite view when he makes the approach into a city? "I really love flying into Los Angeles, especially in the last hour and a half of the flight. You get the sense of these vast deserts transforming into a ring of mountains, which are often snowcapped, and then beyond them you have this bowl of light lying on the edge of the Pacific. It's an extremely dramatic approach. And I really recommend that you get a seat by the window on the right side of the aircraft." — Ⓜ

Knoll

Matic Sofa Piero Lissoni, 2020
Photo: Gionata Xerra

Modern Always®

Celebrate 80 years of iconic design, from pioneering
modernist vision to bold contemporary designs for home
and office. Always timeless. Always true.

www.knolleurope.com

Showroom Knoll: London, Milan, Paris, Tokyo

Above water
Hong Kong

An exciting, high-inducing watersport that helps you escape the lockdown blues has finally arrived in Hong Kong.

WRITER
James Chambers

PHOTOGRAPHY
Jimi Chiu

Hong Kongers are said to have descended from a mythical half-human, half-fish creature called Lo Ting. I have it on good authority that this is not true but Cantonese folklore does help to explain the city's close ties with the sea: a source of prosperity, nutrition and endless fun. Naturally, when the pandemic shut down travel in 2020 and political events on dry land turned up the heat, the water became a vital place for all Hong Kongers to go wild and connect with their inner Lo Ting.

When I arrive at Tai Tam harbour on Hong Kong Island's sandy south coast, an Aussie expat called Hugh is towelling off after his fourth wake-surfing lesson as a student. A hybrid of wakeboarding and surfing, it's a popular pastime right now but there's always a new watersport on the horizon. I'm here to try my hand at the latest, e-foiling: stubby surfboards with a single propeller underneath that can sail through the air.

As residents flock to the beach every weekend, or go out on their boats, these flying surfboards are running rings around the usual flotilla of banana boats, inflatable unicorns and other water toys.

"It's easy to get started but difficult to master," says Kenny Wan, an instructor from Island Wake. Wan is in the driving seat as we head out to sea aboard a Mastercraft speedboat and pass by a dragon-boat team practising for a race. The 30-year-old is a picture of tranquillity with his long, bleached blonde hair fluttering in the breeze.

Wan cuts our engines in Turtle Cove bay and ties a rope to a yellow buoy just beyond the shark nets. Moving to the back of the craft, he inserts a battery into my beginner's model e-foil and offers a crash course in the controller, which I must carry in my hand: press the trigger to start the motor and the buttons to adjust speed. That's it. Just jump on and away you go. It all sounds too simple for piloting a flying machine, which can reach up to 40km/h; I've never accepted the offer of a life jacket and helmet so willingly.

I jump into the water, lay on the board, pull the trigger and I'm off – then I'm up. Wan was right: standing is easy. I go up a few gears and can feel the board lifting off the water.

"Did you see that?" I ask Wan, after circling back to the boat to hand in my helmet. I must have been flying.

"Barely – just a few inches," he says, before issuing a few more instructions. "Shift your body forward, lean back more and move your front foot up and down."

I set off again, go up a few more gears and this time my board lifts fully off the water. Free of drag, I pick up more speed and soar over the waves. Then a gust of wind blows, there's a wobble – and panic sets in. My propeller hits the water, followed by my board, and I go crashing into the sea, face first.

My right temple stings but I emerge from the water raring to go again. The real appeal of e-foiling is the ease of getting back in the saddle and I can now see why it's taking off in Hong Kong. Surfers have to paddle out to catch every wave but there are no sore arms with e-foiling. Next time I can try the pro model, says Wan, as we return to the harbour. E-foiling might not keep me fit but, after two years of being stuck in Hong Kong, it has certainly given me a huge lift. — Ⓜ

I should be in Baywatch

Ona Collection

Simple as Nature

Inspired by the Mediterranean. Natural colours, pure lines and soft shapes.
This is Ona: a timeless, versatile and sustainable collection. www.roca.com/ona

Hit the bar
Copenhagen

Inspired by Québec, taking Denmark by storm: this special bar and shop is a social hub that plays a unique role in its neighbourhood.

WRITER
Nic Monisse

PHOTOGRAPHY
Jan Søndergaard

Mike Wittrup and Daniel Rørbaek met while studying advertising at Copenhagen's Danish School of Media and Journalism in 2010. "We found a good chemistry and good balance working together and decided to move to Montréal in 2013 to work as a creative team," says Rørbaek. It was here that they fell in love with the *depanneur*. A staple in cities across Québec, these small corner shops serve snacks, beer and coffee; their offering and owners playing an integral role in day-to-day neighbourhood life.

"In Montréal, the guy who ran the one near us was quite a character," says Rørbaek. "He was funny – a legend in the neighbourhood." Returning to Copenhagen, the duo set up their own creative studio, Barkas, but they also took inspiration from this "legend": when a vacancy at a small shop in the Nørrebro neighbourhood came up, they set up their own take on his establishment.

Called (you guessed it) Depanneur, it started as a small shop and bar serving beer and cocktails, and soon grew to include a line of products designed by Wittrup, Rørbaek and the Barkas team – beer first, then soft drinks, juice and coffee, and now a range that includes ceramics and clothing collaborations.

"At Barkas, we work with so many amazing brands from all over the world," says Wittrup. "But for us, this is a playground, where we can do things that we think are

interesting as a brand, without having to ask for permission." Outgrowing its original space, Depanneur moved to a bigger location just around the corner in 2020.

"We know of eight couples that have met each other at Depanneur and now have children," says Rørbaek. "When we opened, it was a place where we, the Barkas office and our friends went. Then, all of a sudden, there was a big group made up of lots of different people – that's always been the atmosphere of Depanneur." It's an atmosphere that certainly lifts the mood on the streets in Nørrebro, offering the perfect model of a well-designed and design-minded neighbourhood shop and bar. — Ⓜ

1. **Mads Ostenfeldt Højgaard**
Sales manager
"Goes by the name OH."

2. **Eske Viuf**
Shop manager
"Host with the most."

3. **Adam Simony**
Managing director
"The one in charge."

4. **Mimi Rørbæk Mølholm**
Daniel and Kathrine's baby
"Youngest member of the team."

5. **Kathrine Mølholm**
Finance director
"Miss Moneypenny."

6. **Mads Henriksen**
Operations director
"Makes sure everything runs smoothly."

7. **Anders Bergsbo**
Event manager
"Taking care of all external and internal parties."

8. **Mathias Torp**
Logistics manager
"Mr A to B."

9. **Laura Jones**
Design director
"Ensures that everything looks good."

10. **John Hunt**
Oberkellner
"Head waiter and longest-serving employee."

11. **Visti Poulsen**
Delivery driver
"Always on time."

12. **Kaiu Meiner**
Designer
"Visualises everything from labels to menus."

13. **Christian Kier**
Sales director
"Knows all the kiosk owners in Copenhagen."

Mike Wittrup and Daniel Rørbaek
When Mike Wittrup (*on left*) and Daniel Rørbaek began working together in 2014, they always knew that they wanted to start a creative studio that did more than hit targets. "With Barkas, our concept was to start our own projects," says Wittrup. Depanneur – which saw the duo joined by Mads Henriksen and Kathrine Mølholm as co-founders – is a case in point.

60 Years of Defining Tomorrow

LS60 Wireless – Shaping the future of High-Fidelity

Designed by Michael Young in collaboration with the KEF product design team, this contemporary design addition to the KEF family defies the limits of audio performance with its iconic slim structure. The LS60 Wireless is a celebration of 60 years of sound innovation with a clear eye on the future high-fidelity experience.

AirPlay2, Chromecast, Spotify, Tidal, MQA, HDMI eARC, and more.

WHAT HI·FI?
★★★★★
KEF LS60 Wireless
05/2022

Listen and believe

KEF 60 YEARS

The AGENDA

The stories you should be paying attention to – and the ones you might have missed.

CITIES —— ATHENS

In the hot seat

Athens is the hottest capital city in mainland Europe, a place where heatwaves that send the mercury up to 40C are an all-too regular occurrence. That's why Eleni Myrivili's job exists. Last summer she was appointed as the city's (and continent's) first chief heat officer, tasked with helping to build resilience against rising temperatures.

MONOCLE meets Myrivili (*pictured*) on Philoppapou hill on a late spring evening. There is a cool breeze blowing but the balmy heat reminds Athenians of what's to come. A 2018 report by Newcastle University showed that among 571 cities worldwide, Greece's capital will be one of the hardest hit by heatwaves and drought in the coming decades.

That portentous warning was proven correct almost immediately: devastating wildfires in the Attica region north of the city later that year became the second deadliest of the century, killing 102 people. Then last year, following Myrivili's appointment, Greece experienced its worst heatwave since the late 1980s, with temperatures reaching a record 45C. "On a basic level, heat causes serious health problems to the most vulnerable, increases the frequency of wildfires and even affects a country's productivity and economy," says Myrivili, gesturing animatedly.

Her background is in anthropology, in which she received a PHD from Columbia University in 2004, before becoming a leader of Greece's Green party in 2007. From 2017 to 2019, she served as a deputy mayor of Athens, promoting urban growth and climate-change resilience in her hometown. Myrivili's new role is similarly multi-faceted: she must employ her anthropological knowledge of communities alongside her political nous and climate activism in order to bring about change.

In a place like Athens, this will be no mean feat. The city suffers from a number of disadvantages, both man-made and natural. It is densely populated and surrounded by mountains, with few public parks. "The challenge here is to introduce nature-based solutions," says Myrivili. "We don't have the luxury of vast open space or large pavements. The battle against heat is really a battle to reclaim public space, especially from cars." She has backed plans to introduce more no-traffic zones, electric buses and metro stations, though progress is slow.

Myrivili's appointment reflects a realisation by mayor Kostas Bakoyannis that something has to change. "Athens has made big steps towards being greener, which is a major part of the cooling puzzle," says Myrivili. In the past few years, a number of pocket parks have been created in built-up areas and formerly disused water fountains renovated. Her mission is to find and implement more far-reaching solutions.

"My goal is to create more 'green and blue' infrastructure," she says. "Bringing water back to the city is so important, restoring our streams and rivers that we buried underground." One of the more recent initiatives is a plan to create "green corridors" connecting different neighbourhoods. "The idea is to pedestrianise those streets, plant more trees on either side and ban parking."

She insists that though city hall can do more, it's imperative that individuals also step up. "When we're redesigning the city, it also comes down to the materials we build with." Athens is largely made from concrete and asphalt, materials that absorb and store heat, which they then radiate at night.

"We need to go back to retrofitting buildings with thermal efficiency. We need to look back at traditional architecture and how people found ways to cool their homes before we started using fossil fuels."

Gazing across the whitewashed metropolis, she speaks hopefully of an irreversible sea change in public opinion, "Athenians are demanding more from their leadership. One of my aims is to try and unite all the different advocates for a greener Athens. That's the only way to make the city green and blue." — DK

IMAGES: Félix Odell, Eirini Vourloumis

URBANISM —— FRANCE

Off the road

Hugging the Mediterranean for 5km, Marseille's famous corniche is a crucial part of the city's life. No surprise then that a decision in 2021 to shut the road to motor traffic on at least one Sunday a month has proved hugely popular.

On designated *La voie est libre* ("The way is free") days, the road is filled with locals and tourists walking, running, biking and rollerblading. Food trucks – many of them selling *panisses* (chickpea fritters), a local speciality – punctuate the route. Cafés, bars and gelato stands do a roaring trade. Usually the corniche would be choked with traffic on a Sunday. "It feels like we can finally breathe," one resident tells MONOCLE. "It's about reclaiming the most beautiful part of our city, even if it's just for a day."

This inspired initiative is one of several efforts to transform the city by the Green-Left coalition – known as Printemps Marseille (Marseille Spring) – that swept the municipal elections in 2020. Before that, France's second city had a rather ignominious environmental record. According to rankings collated by the Clean Cities Campaign, it is the most polluted city in France; the new administration is determined to change that. Parts of downtown have been fully pedestrianised. There are long overdue plans to expand and improve the city's creaking public transport system. More cycle paths are also in the pipeline.

This year Marseille was chosen to participate in an EU project gathering 100 cities aiming to be carbon neutral by 2030. Local officials note that nearly half the city's emissions are caused by motor vehicle use. Getting more of Les Marseillais out of their cars, even if it's just on a Sunday, can only be a good thing. — MFI

POLITICS —— LEBANON

Independents day

Najat Aoun Saliba is the kind of politician that Lebanon has not seen in living memory. She trained in analytical chemistry in the US before returning to her homeland to take up a professorship at the American University of Beirut. Air pollution became her chief concern. For Saliba, Lebanon's environmental woes are symbolic of its government's criminality. She didn't get involved in politics until circumstances compelled her. During the garbage crisis of 2015, when government incompetence led to tonnes of rubbish piling up in Beirut, she took to the stinking streets.

"After seeing the situation deteriorating I started feeling that scientific publications alone aren't going to make a difference," says Saliba. By the time the 2019 mass movement – "the *thawra*" – came about she was part of a network of activists. It was the 2020 Beirut port explosion that propelled her into politics. "Waking up the day after the explosion and feeling the city devastated, the smell of death everywhere, the ground shaking under our feet, we really felt that the government had abandoned us," she says.

Saliba and a group of like-minded reformists launched Taqaddom, a radical party that ran two independent candidates in this May's parliamentary elections. Both won, unseating long-serving MPs who had

ANDREW MUELLER ON...

The Australian election

In Australian politics, a theme recurs of charismatic Labor leaders returning their party to power after long periods of governance by conservative Liberal-National coalitions: Gough Whitlam in 1972, Bob Hawke in 1983, Kevin Rudd in 2007. Anthony Albanese, Australia's new Labor prime minister, is not of this ilk – although he has never claimed to be.

It is plausible to think of Albanese as Australia's Joe Biden – a timeserver whose party agreed on him because they couldn't agree on anybody else; whose election victory owed more to weariness with a divisive and shambolic incumbent government than to enthusiasm for the alternative. But a win is a win – and this win could prove important.

The end of Scott Morrison's premiership is – or so it must be hoped – the end of equivocation about climate in Australian politics. Morrison and similar fatalists insisted that Australia could not fix a global problem alone, which is true enough. But though Australia is a smallish country by population, it commands disproportionate space on the world stage. Therefore, it could, and should, take a lead.

Albanese arrived in office pledging an emissions reduction target of 43 per cent by 2030. His victory also adds to worldwide hopefulness for those who prefer government by unfussy centre-left types who'd rather improve the lives of their fellow citizens than conduct inane culture-war bun-throwing. Australia suddenly seems less a natural ally of Boris Johnson's UK than it does of Biden's US, along with Canada, Spain, Germany, Portugal, Slovenia, New Zealand and all five Nordic countries.

Another former Labor prime minister, Paul Keating, cited historian Manning Clark's theory of the country's history as a contest between "enlargers" – those with an upbeat vision of what Australia might be – and "straiteners and punishers" who are the spiritual heirs of the cops who arrived with the convicts in the 19th century. In Australia, Labor has traditionally enjoyed depicting itself as the party of the enlargers. Though it might run counter to his cautious instincts, Albanese should think big. — Ⓜ

dominated the Chouf-Aley region. Saliba is one of only eight women in the new crop of MPs – the highest number a Lebanese parliament has had. More than a dozen other independent candidates won.

While they are only a small group within the 128-person parliament, Saliba believes that they can make a big difference in changing the culture of a government that has ignored its people for decades. "Other politicians here come for power or money but we are coming as servants of the people," she says. "We are presenting ourselves as honest, transparent and inclusive. And I want the people to watch what we do and hold us to account." — LMO

Three essentials in new Lebanese MPs' in-trays

Justice for the victims of the Beirut blast
Establishing an independent judiciary that's able to hold corrupt officials to account is a vital first step.

The healthcare system
Lebanon once had the region's best hospitals but in the past two years the healthcare system has collapsed.

Restoring depositors' rights
When Lebanon's financial system crashed, the biggest losers were small depositors, many of whom lost their life savings and pensions.

SOCIETY — USA
Clean streets

Bruce Harrell campaigned to be Seattle's mayor on a platform to clean up the streets of a city that, until recently, scored high in liveability rankings (since the pandemic and 2020's protests, graffiti and illegal refuse dumping have proliferated). This resonated with voters, who elected him last November with 62 per cent of the vote.

Six months into the job, Harrell and his administration have cleared homeless encampments that had become frequently unsafe magnets for drug trafficking and crime, referring those in need to shelters and housing.

Abandoned vehicles are getting the boot. And the mayor has committed to hiring 125 extra police after the force, demoralised by "defund" rhetoric, lost officers in droves amid a spike in gun violence.

In May he asked Seattleites to return the favour. On a Saturday in that month, several thousand turned out for the first One Seattle Day of Service, which Harrell's team organised as a collective effort to roll up sleeves citywide. Civic associations, charities, garden clubs and community groups welcomed their neighbours to pitch in on everything from painting over graffiti and picking up litter to ripping up weeds and planting flowers.

While Harrell appealed to the public's sense of civic pride, he also added a carrot: volunteer hours could be used to pay off $50 (€47) of parking fines, traffic camera violations and other minor municipal infractions. When helping a city get back on its feet, the ends justify the means. — GRS

DIPLOMATIC SPAT
Port in a storm

Who *vs* who:
Hungary *vs* Croatia

What it's about:
The landlocked nature of Hungary and tactless related remarks by the country's combustible prime minister Viktor Orbán (*pictured*). Asked why Hungary was opposed to a complete ban on Russian oil imports, Orbán explained that such an embargo was an easier threat to make for EU countries with sea access. Not an unreasonable point but Orbán followed it wistfully with, "We would have had ports too, if they hadn't taken them away from us." Croatia heard this as provocative nostalgia for the days when it and its Adriatic coast were part of the Austro-Hungarian empire and accordingly summoned Hungary's ambassador for one of those meetings at which biscuits are not proffered.

What it's really about:
Borders in the Balkans have been historically prone to violent alteration and therefore remain a touchy subject. Though Croatia's foreign ministry issued a thunderous denunciation of "territorial claims against foreign states", an attempt by Hungary to recapture lost Habsburg realms can be safely assessed as unlikely. It is hard to know whether this specific indiscretion was deliberate, instinctive or a slip of the tongue but it is pretty much standard Orbán.

Likely resolution:
Relations to be restored to a low simmer until the next time Orbán says something belligerent and/or obnoxious. On form, it shouldn't be a long wait. — AM

1

The COMMENT

HORTICULTURE —— ALMERE

Going green

Josh Fehnert visits an expo for greenery that's trying to change our cities – and perspectives.

"It's about how to make cities healthier and nicer to live in," says Frank Cornelissen, commercial director of the Floriade Expo 2022 horticultural fair. He's standing in the shadow of a 20 metre-tall sculpture of a parent and child made from Cor-Ten steel bees. "We need bees, we need pollinators," he adds. It's a bright, cloudless day and we're in Almere, a planned city 30km east of Amsterdam. Here, amid the drifts of tulips and grey-haired flower fanciers, organisers are selling Dutch horticultural chutzpah to the world.

Founded in 1960, Floriade took root as a once-a-decade garden jamboree for all things flowery, leafy or green. Spread across a 60-hectare site around an artificial lake, this year's edition is stuffed with organic oddities, from huts made from mycelium to swathes of unkempt woodland and immense greenhouses containing the wares of some 200 green-fingered firms. There are also 33 national pavilions where artists, architects and curators have created spaces and exhibitions that riff on this year's theme: Growing Green Cities.

The UAE pavilion yields a latticed structure riffing on the nation's modernist-inspired 1960s sha'bi houses. The crunch of salt crystals underfoot and the sound of trickling water give way to an exhibition focused on the UAE's geographical position between the desert and ocean. "We have mangrove forests that grow in the sea, we have meadows of seagrass and many other salt-tolerant plants," says Angela Migally, executive director of the Salama Bint Hamdan Al Nahyan Foundation. She worked with Amsterdam studio Tellart and architecture firm Pragma to respond to Floriade's city-focused brief, which takes in topics from food security to water scarcity.

"Human beings *are* nature," says Herman Kossmann, co-founder of Amsterdam-based Kossmanndejong. He helped to shape Amsterdam-Almere's wooden exhibition space, which aims to give nature a voice and nudge onlookers to listen to what it's saying. "Amsterdam has 800,000 inhabitants. But you could say that we have trillions if you count animals, plants and bacteria." A pleasant idea but it's hard to know what to do with it. As I wander out, past the selfie space, I ponder how the high-minded messages touted by many of the pavilions might take root elsewhere.

One definite legacy of the show will be the site itself, which is slated to become 20,000 housing units as part of a nationwide plan to build a million new homes. Rotterdam-based MVRDV is overseeing the plan for a leafy rethink of the garden suburb, to be dubbed Hortus. For now, it's hard to imagine such calm amid the furore of the fair.

Before I leave, and as the sun sets, I take a few moments to visit Utopia Island. This is the wildest part of Floriade, where a handful of gardeners and artists have been left to create spaces to sit, stroll and enjoy the nature. Blissfully there's no-one around to hammer home the "concept" either – no small text to take in or statistics to quote. It's here, under a beech tree by the waters of an artificial lake, that city planners might learn most about the virtues of greening our urban landscapes. — Ⓜ

Hear more on 'The Urbanist' at monocle.com/radio.

3

1. Qatar's national pavilion
2. Bloom with a view within the greenhouse complex
3. Volunteer logs her time
4. Community garden on the shores of Weerwater

2

4

PHOTOGRAPHER: *Alex Crétey Systermans*

SCHRAMM
home of sleep

SCHRAMM ORIGINS Paio – Design Urte Stöcklein

Handmade in Germany

schramm-werkstaetten.com

The COMMENT

SOCIETY —— USA

Death of the salesman

Henry Rees-Sheridan From 'inspirational and educational hubs' to online sales only, as electric-vehicle manufacturers begin to eschew tradition, are we about to witness the end of the car showroom?

The shimmering forecourt. The windscreen price tags. The grim rictus of the crumpled salesman. An instantly recognisable fixture of the US suburban landscape, the car dealership brings together two prominent features of the nation's culture: entrepreneurial capitalism and automobile ownership.

Dealerships – and dealers – loom large in the national imagination. From *The Simpsons'* Gil Gunderson to *Fargo's* Jerry Lundegaard, no figure more poignantly conveys the predatory desperation at the frayed edges of the US economy. Indeed, the stigma attached to the profession has even touched the life of the current president. When Joe Biden became a senator in 1972, his father quit his job as a car dealer because, according to the president's sister Valerie Biden Owens, he "didn't want a United States senator to have a used-car salesman for a dad".

It would take a strange sort of masochist to enjoy a trip to the outskirts of town to be upsold mudflaps. So why haven't alternatives to dealerships emerged? One reason is that innovation within retailing has been stymied by regulation. In the early 20th century, car dealers were at the mercy of manufacturers, who could undercut their own

franchisees by endorsing a new dealership down the street. In the 1940s and 1950s, laws were adopted to protect them. There was a limit placed on the number of franchisees a car-maker could license in a given area and the direct sale of cars by manufacturers was prohibited. In most states these laws still apply but the industry is changing rapidly.

Electric vehicles (EVs) accounted for all of the net growth in global car sales in 2021. Several prominent EV manufacturers are young companies that are not locked into the legacy dealership model. They're taking advantage of this freedom by developing new ways of using physical spaces to sell their cars.

> Events held here often have nothing to do with cars. They include bicycle maintenance workshops and tending the edible garden

One of them is Rivian, a company specialising in off-road EVs. Its flagship bricks-and-mortar location is Venice Hub in Los Angeles, where there are two display vehicles that visitors can sit in. The rest of the facility looks like a modern community centre with a library, communal hall and open-air spaces. Denise Cherry, who designs Rivian's facilities, describes the Hub as a "space designed to inspire and educate people". The events held there often have nothing to do with cars and include bicycle maintenance workshops and tending the Hub's edible garden.

Polestar, a performance EV manufacturer owned by Volvo, has taken another approach. In buildings that resemble the lair of a discerning Bond villain, colour and material samples are displayed in chrome drawers and the walls are adorned with artfully framed photos of the cars' components. The company's website describes its spaces as like "an art gallery where the cars are the exhibits".

What Rivian and Polestar's very different buildings have in common is an absence of salespeople. Polestar's website boasts that "product experts are on hand to share their knowledge and enthusiasm with you. Selling just isn't in their job description." The truth is that, in many states, franchise laws mean that they couldn't have salespeople even if they wanted to. Instead, if a visitor wishes to buy one of the vehicles on display, they must do so online. Other EV manufacturers, such as Tesla and Lucid, also offer such an option.

EV makers still have major hurdles to overcome. The new technology presents manufacturing challenges. Rivian's stock, for example, fell sharply this year after the company failed to meet its 2021 production target. But the sector will inevitably grow. If companies eschewing dealership models continue their ascent, the traditional car showroom could slide into obsolescence within this decade.

What would that mean for our retail – and cultural – ecosystems? We can surely find a better use for the land that dealerships currently occupy. But the psychic energy that car dealers are avatars of has to manifest somewhere. Virtual currencies seem to be the new epicentre of contemporary American legerdemain. But it just doesn't feel the same being hustled online. — Ⓜ

IMAGE: *Alamy*

CHANEL
CONNECTS

THE ARTS & CULTURE PODCAST

KENNEDY YANKO

Soldiering on

In the February issue of MONOCLE, Ukrainian novelist and former soldier **Artem Chekh** wrote a dispatch from his hometown, Kyiv. He spoke of his latent dread of a war he hoped would not happen. Since then, his worst fears have been realised. His wife and son have moved west to Lviv and Chekh has re-enlisted in the army. He writes for MONOCLE from Polesia, near the border with Belarus, where he is stationed with a company of the Ukrainian Territorial Defence Forces in the thick, battle-scarred woods that surround the infamous town of Chernobyl.

Music is my saviour. The same music as before: Leonard Cohen, The Beatles, The Cranberries, Morcheeba. I have some basic ideas about other people's private boundaries. That's why I listen to music using headphones and keep things under my folding bed, not scattered all over the house. I don't interrupt when someone speaks. I don't shout when someone is asleep. I share cigarettes with my comrades. I'm a good boy.

Three months ago all my private boundaries were protected. I was working on a novel; I had a glass of wine in the evening and pizza delivered to my front door. But I am a soldier now. I live with 20 combatants, all recruits in Ukraine's Territorial Defence Forces, in an old house in Polesia, a wetland region north of Kyiv. We are former truckers, music producers, shop owners – they are my family, my home comforts and my pizza couriers now.

Yesterday I was in Gostomel and I stopped by to look at the townhouse where my friends used to live. I wrote about them in my previous article for MONOCLE (*see issue 150*). Those friends with whom I drank wine and talked a lot. I looked at their mutilated house and cried. Then I got back into the car and drove on.

If you set out from our base in the morning you will be in Chernobyl by lunchtime. This was a desolate area, even before the war. The 30km radiation zone, put in place after the nuclear disaster in 1986, has made it a region of half-empty villages, poor infrastructure and dense forest. It's scarred by a different, more devastating, disaster now. Everything is ringing with the heavy echo of hostilities. The columns of Russian troops aiming for Kyiv passed through here. Every family can tell you horrors from the occupation.

One of the local women offered us the house of her dying mother. We found walnuts on the windowsill, a 2013 calendar hanging on the wall, religious icons, plastic flowers, holey curtains, hand creams, candles, mosquito spray in the cupboard. On the bedside table is a guide to radiation safety.

The locals help us with food: milk, eggs, venison. We help them with gasoline and our presence. They are calmer with us, they say. If we are here, then there is no enemy.

A month ago we were guarding strategic sites in Kyiv. First the famous TV tower which was hit by a Russian missile on 1 March. We moved to the area three days after the strike. Kyiv looked like London from Danny Boyle's *28 Days Later*: empty, rubbish-strewn streets, military police in SUVs. We were conducting drills, waiting for the Russians, securing the ravine of Babyn Yar, where 33,771 Jews were massacred by the Nazis in two days in 1941.

In late March the Russians were forced to turn back from the capital and my unit was moved into the woods near the border with Belarus. Our first task was the inspection of one of the houses. The owner's son was in the army, so the enemy buried an anti-tank mine in the front garden. While we were looking for it, we heard stories of murder and looting, mined cemeteries, raped girls and boilers stolen from houses. Eventually our interlocutors all moved onto one inevitability of Russian occupation: the shit.

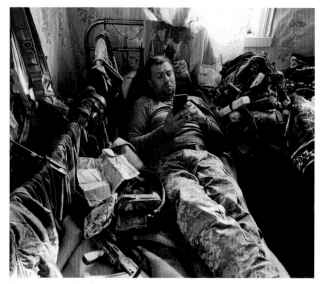

Rare opportunity for rest

Faeces on the beds, on the pillows, on the kitchen tables, left as a sign that the Russians were here. The Polish writer Stanislaw Jerzy Lec called this "excremental fierceness".

On our fifth day in Polesia, the medical service brought our neighbours their son's car. The car was all shot-up but its owner was nowhere to be seen. Locals claimed that the Russians were being redeployed from the area and that some of them were apologising and saying that they were only "following orders". When the Buryats and Chechens were deployed to the village the real terror began. Violence, looting and public executions.

When we entered a new village, the local women would surge towards us, hugging, crying and thanking us. But we were embarrassed. We didn't liberate these lands; we didn't chase the Russians away. My unit moved here to prevent a new attack on Kyiv, to build defensive ditches, dugouts and bunkers while more armed units are fighting in the east and south of Ukraine. I read obituaries every day, recognising familiar names. My acquaintances and friends. Former journalists, public figures, normal people.

In the trenches

Artem Chekh warms up

Frontline discussion

The day the invasion began I thought about my possible destiny. It seemed that life was over and I mentally said goodbye to everything, thanking the universe for the wonderful years it had given me. Did I imagine myself as a soldier digging trenches in the centre of Kyiv or hugging and comforting an old babushka who was crying like a child? Did I think that I would be driving a used pickup truck with a machine gun on its roof? What was I thinking when Russia launched its attack? I don't remember. It was so long ago.

In the first days of the invasion, I tried to join the battalion I had served with in 2014. Despite the fact that I was in the priority reserve, I was not registered. In desperation, I agreed to my former commander's suggestion to go to the battalion's headquarters without registering. "We'll find a solution," he said. But nothing was decided. My former comrades went south and I was left alone in the barracks, confused and unhappy. It seemed to me that I was of no use; everyone around was fighting and I had nothing to offer. After a few days I joined the Territorial Defence Forces. As for my former comrades, it's difficult to stay in touch. I know that one of my commanders was killed but I don't know how many others are still alive.

Several difficult lives have been lived. Many things that seemed impossible to ever imagine have happened on roads I used to drive down on trips to the countryside. Meanwhile, the trees have bloomed, nature has woken up – it has its own schedule to keep to. After the liberation of the Kyiv region, my city is also coming back to life. There is tension, there is the pain of war but the streets are crowded, the roads are congested, the cafés, gyms and dry cleaners are open, the supermarkets are full of groceries. Only the anti-tank checkpoints and sandbags remind us that, until recently, this was the front line. And, just a few kilometres beyond the suburbs, you can see the ruined cities whose names now ring out in infamy: Bucha, Irpin, Borodyanka.

From time to time I visit Kyiv. Not everyone is so lucky. I go to my empty apartment to wash my clothes, have a hot shower and lie on my orthopaedic mattress. Then I jump back in the car and return to the forests that have become my new home. The forests that halted my enemy.

We have come to terms with the fact that the war will be long and we will have to reconquer our territories one at a time. This is a great and terrible war. But I know we will win. We have no other option.

I'm lying on an army couch; I haven't taken off my shoes because I'm on patrol in half an hour. We are preparing to go somewhere closer to the fighting in the east or south. I'm glad because, right now, the stoves in our house are so hot that I can't breathe. It's like being in an office here: we argue over how hot to have the room. Sometimes it gets tense. I use such brutal curses that I surprise myself. But now I am tired and I have no strength to quarrel. A long night of patrolling the woods is ahead of me. So Radiohead are in my headphones, a 120kg soldier is playing Angry Birds on his phone next to me, the windows are shaking because de-mining is taking place in the village. I'll lie down for a while, then I'll make myself a coffee, fill my flask and go out into the dark woods hoping finally to meet a deer. I have never seen a live one before. — Ⓜ

SUNSPEL

ENGLAND 1860

THE CLASSIC T-SHIRT   HANDMADE IN ENGLAND FOR OVER 100 YEARS FROM SUSTAINABLE SUPIMA COTTON

PHOTOGRAPHER: Felix Brüggemann

F&B —— BERLIN

Buttering up Berlin

Every four weeks, a delivery truck filled with four tonnes of French flour parks on Maybachufer in the Kreuzberg district of Berlin. Across the street, at La Maison bakery, Parisian-style brasserie tables and chairs spill out over a canal-facing terrace while a buttery scent hangs in the air. In a small room at the back, pâtissiers knead, roll and bake up to 1,000 croissants a day. On a sunny weekend morning a Berliner vying to grab one might have to wait an hour in a queue that snakes around the block.

"I lived in France for a while and when I came back to Berlin, I was pretty shocked by how few places made their own croissants," says Andreas Altmeyer, who opened La Maison in 2019. "German bakers don't really learn how to make them." Altmeyer can take some of the credit for the city's current pastry craze: since long lines began forming outside La Maison, at least half a dozen new artisanal bakeries have opened in the city to serve the booming demand. Today it's possible to get a morning bun made from croissant dough rolled in spiced sugar with orange, ginger and black pepper at Sofi in Mitte, or a rye and buckwheat croissant served with cascara syrup and a ball of burrata at Prenzlauer Berg's Café Frieda.

"When we started out it was a different landscape," says Anders Alkaersig, co-owner of Albatross, another popular bakery in Kreuzberg. "Luckily the cohort of people interested in buying artisanal products has grown." A croissant gets its delicious, flaky texture from lamination, a process of folding dough and a slab of butter into a flattened rectangle with paper-thin layers that puff up in the oven. Passersby are able to peek into Albatross's production facility, which is kitted out with blast proofers and a laminator the size of a dinner table. Here, bakers knead, laminate, freeze, ferment and bake the croissants in a delicate three-day process.

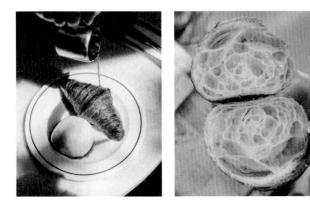

The specialist machinery is no small investment for a fledgling business but the reward is pastries that are the polar opposite of the dark-grained and dense bread typical in Germany. "It's nice that there are more places opening because it broadens the market," says Alkaersig. "You can go around and see that there are ways of making a croissant that are in the same tier but just different."

Morey Talmor and Guy Kenneth, two friends soaking up the sun outside Albatross on a Friday morning, become animated when describing the texture of the croissants they have just eaten. "By some way of magic, you have a cube of butter that went 'puff!' and expanded into a pastry just like popcorn," says Kenneth. "It's so light that you have one and it leaves you wanting more."

Berlin's bakery queues have become almost as notorious as the ones outside its nightclubs. "I really don't like the culture of big queues," says Altmeyer. "I've heard people say that they are good for business but my goal has always been to speed up the process as much as possible." — SRO

China is set to lose tens of thousands of executives, entrepreneurs and their families as conditions have become intolerable and quality of life eroded

EMPLOYMENT —— CHINA

The great escape

If you're running the HR division of a major multinational and thinking about releasing office space because you've been stuck with implementing a hybrid workplace policy, you might want to hit pause before giving up too many desks.

On a recent visit to Paris, the CEO of a major French luxury group tells MONOCLE that his biggest management concern isn't the conflict in Ukraine, the state of the markets or stalled supply chains, it is the impending talent exodus from China. "No one wants to stay after the school year finishes," he says. "Everyone wants to come back to Paris or be reassigned somewhere else in the world. And, of course, I owe it to these colleagues to find them new positions, even if I don't have any, given all that they've been through."

As China approaches three years of on-off lockdowns, Beijing is struggling to contain the steady stream of horror stories that have accompanied its "dynamic" approach to containing the pandemic. From families separated because a mother or father has been shipped off to a quarantine centre hundreds of kilometres away to managers who have moved from running shops to becoming trauma counsellors, China is set to lose tens of thousands of executives, entrepreneurs and their families as conditions have become intolerable and quality of life eroded.

"It's not just Western staff who want to leave, it's also our Chinese staff," says a Spanish vice president of a global retail group. "It's become increasingly uncomfortable to host conference calls with most of our company able to travel and do their jobs while our Chinese teams are locked up at home. It raises many questions about what business in China will look like in the medium term."

While multinationals are unlikely to exit the market, there's the looming challenge of how they're going to oversee a region that's tricky to manage at the best of times. Do they start offering hardship or danger pay because working in Shenzhen will be seen as unsavoury? Or, like so many shifts that occurred during the pandemic, will things settle back to something that resembles normal?

"I doubt it. Staff are leaving and memories aren't that short," says the French CEO. "When you're sent into quarantine, separated from your pet and then told it had to be put down for reasons unexplained, you realise you're in a country with values too far removed from your own." — TB

AVIATION —— GLOBAL

Flights of fancy

Can an industry that transports the rich and powerful at speed ever be sustainable? If a Mediterranean-bound Boeing with 180 holidaymakers on board is environmentally culpable, what of a €60m Gulfstream G650 carrying six bankers and three crew from Zürich to New York?

That private aviation can be green is a tough sell. Yet the journey to carbon elimination was a key theme at this year's European Business Aviation Convention and Exhibition, which is held annually in Geneva. On the surface, it was business as usual at the city's Palexpo, with ultra-wealthy clients and window shoppers mingling with trade visitors.

Gulfstream and Bombardier have long been battling for the title of longest-range and fastest business jet. This year Bombardier took the initiative, announcing the relaunch of the 15,000km-range-nudging Global 8000.

Business aviation is booming. Lockdowns, border restrictions and the grounding of much of commercial aviation during the pandemic saw those who could afford it turn to this reliable and safe way to travel, whether owned or chartered.

France's Dassault had its newest intercontinental offerings on show – the Falcon 6X and, in mock-up, the larger 10X. Airbus Helicopters displayed a limited-edition ACH130 with an Aston Martin-styled interior. Shared – or fractional – ownership operator Flexjet is beefing up its European fleet with five more aircraft this year.

The sustainability message was very much present, with biofuel seen as a way to offset emissions and new forms of propulsion, such as hybrid electric, a longer-term solution. The sector is convinced it can become carbon-neutral by 2050. Watch this airspace. — MMO

IMAGE: 3 Kaveria, Alamy

BOOKSELLERS —— FRANCE
School of thought

"We have a global responsibility for the métier of the bookseller," says Alexia Dumaine, standing in front of a digital whiteboard. "If people have a good experience in the bookshop we run, other bookshops will benefit." It's 09.00 on a Tuesday morning in Dumaine's class at the École de la Librairie, the oldest bookseller school in France, based in the Parisian suburb of Maisons-Alfort.

While the school's most popular course is the two-year post-baccalaureate bookseller diploma (aimed at 16-to-29-year-olds), it also offers shorter training courses for adults who want to change careers. Among today's group is Marjolaine Petillon, a web developer who wants to start selling books in the Basque country. Other classmates work in administration and banking. All are united in their dream of becoming bookshop owners. "There is a bit of a pattern among our mature students," says the school's director, Caroline Meneghetti. "Most of them are between 35 and 50 years old and are in lucrative jobs but they are longing for more purpose in their professional lives."

Though the job is not like that of a pharmacist or lawyer, which require a diploma to practise, the school's activities are rooted in the belief that in order to become a good *libraire*, you need more than a passion for books. The École teaches students three key facets of the profession: stockkeeping, customer relations and management. There's a classroom where students learn to create window displays, another with computers for teaching stock control and the Librairie La Ruche, its public-facing bookshop for practical classes. The aim is to have graduates leave with a fully fledged business plan. Alumni have gone on to open Francophone bookshops abroad, boutiques selling secondhand titles and book-cafés. Perhaps the most unusual venture to come out of the school is La Flânante in Brittany, a bicycle-bookshop opened in 2020 by Robin Ranjore that pops up at local markets and delivers orders to customers on two wheels.

Only in France could an institution like this really exist. "We're a country where the profession of the *libraire* is still very much alive," says Meneghetti, referring to the fact that every town or neighbourhood has at least one independent bookshop. A 1981 law establishing a fixed price for books sold in France has been instrumental in protecting small shops from chains such as Fnac as well as online

"At the school, we nurture this close, almost intimate, relationship between the vendor and the buyer"

retailers including Amazon. Meneghetti believes that "if you have a bookshop with a carefully chosen selection and helpful staff near your home, you'll always prefer going there to buying a book for the same price on Amazon. At the school, we nurture this close, almost intimate, relationship between vendor and buyer."

Dumaine, who used to manage Librairie Folies d'Encre in Montreuil and is now one of the school's 40 or so specialised tutors, agrees that an attentive, knowledgeable seller is integral to the survival of the bricks-and-mortar bookshop. "We might not have the same presence as Amazon but on some levels we win – curation, conviviality and advice."

After the class MONOCLE visits Librairie La Ruche, which operates like a normal business. We are greeted by manager Isabelle Gagnon, who gives a quick rundown of its inventory and a couple of suggestions. Something Meneghetti said comes to mind: "They say that the bookseller has an intellectual and managerial role but there's a third point that's just as important: you have to love people." — AW
lecoledelalibrairie.fr

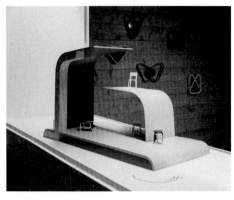

PHOTOGRAPHERS: *Stephanie Füssenich, Juho Kuva.* IMAGE: *Swalif Publishing House*

Countryside views

The village of Fiskars is an unusual backdrop for an international art and design festival. With its 17th-century former ironworks, the place is said to be the birthplace of Finnish industry. Today its ancient brick and wooden buildings stand in stark contrast to the glossy modern halls at Milan's Salone del Mobile or Art Basel. But it's here that the country's latest major cultural event has set up shop: the Fiskars Village Art & Design Biennale will occupy buildings across town for the summer.

"History lends this space a feel that cannot be replicated," says Anniina Koivu, co-curator of one of the biennale's three main exhibitions, U-Joints: Knots and Knits. "It's easy to imagine a craftsman knotting away or sculpting a piece of wood here hundreds of years ago," she says from inside the gallery space, an old granary set by a placid river. To be fair, choosing Fiskars as a location isn't that peculiar. Plenty of galleries have experimented with rural locations recently and the village is home to hundreds of artists and craftsmen as well as galleries, design brand Nikari and ceramics art museum Kwum.

The biennale pairs architecture shows with installation-led exhibitions. A show called *House by an Architect* is a collection of wooden mini houses laid out in a vast grassy field. Visitors to the biennale can book a night's stay in any of them, including a modern treehouse by Kristian Talvitie. "The way we live is undergoing a transformation and people's demands are changing," says biennale curator Kari Korkman.

The biennale's third main exhibition displays artworks by Fiskars-based co-operative Onoma. *Hidden* presents artworks exploring the limitations and possibilities afforded by our senses. "There is something hidden in all art," says participating artist Petteri Masalin. "The way we engage with artworks reveals different things to different people." — PBU
Fiskars Village Art & Design Biennale runs until 4 September; fiskarsvillagebiennale.com

Yes we Cannes

At the 75th Festival du Film in May, big-money bling made way for old-fashioned glamour. Julia Roberts dazzled in her understated all-black Louis Vuitton suit, while Rebecca Hall and Lashana Lynch went with a tutti-frutti Gucci gown and a mirrorball Dolce & Gabbana dress respectively. Gossip, as ever, was not in short supply: actor Vincent Lindon (cast member of last year's Palme d'Or winner *Titane*) acted as jury president but was rumoured to be a last-minute replacement for Penelope Cruz and George Clooney. The $1,000 (€930) membership-only American Pavilion attracted opprobrium when interns said they had paid up to $4,000 (€3,725) to work there.

There were plenty of memorable titles: director Ali Abbasi's *Holy Spider* is based on the true story of an Iranian serial killer. Swedish director Ruben Östlund's *Triangle of Sadness* is a funny and daring social satire set on a cruise ship and George Miller's imaginative *Three Thousand Years of Longing* is a big-budget take on an Arabian nights fantasy featuring Idris Elba as a *djinn* in a bottle.

> "Cruise said he makes films for people to enjoy on the big screen in the company of others"

The festival also had an abundance of sincerity. The opening ceremony featured an impassioned plea from Volodymyr Zelensky. Still, that seriousness didn't inhibit some spectacular presentations: Tom Cruise brought US show-stopping to another level by announcing *Top Gun Maverick* as eight French fighter jets flew above the Croisette trailing smoke in red and blue. Declaring that *Top Gun Maverick* would never premiere on a streaming service, Cruise reiterated that he makes films for people to enjoy on the big screen in the company of others. He has become a leading advocate for such entertainment; cinephiles all over the world will be hailing his Cannes-do attitude. — KKR

Talking books

Salem AlSuwaidi is always up for a debate. That's why the half-Emirati, half-Moroccan founded Swalif: a publishing house that aims to redefine the way young Arabs exchange ideas (*swalif* is Arabic for "informal conversations"). This UAE-based collective provides space and funding for creatives across the MENA region to propose book projects and then turn them into reality. Swalif's first release is *Encapsulated Volume 1: Photoessays on Khaleejiness*, a hardback exploring what being Khaleeji (from the Arabian Peninsula) means for a younger generation.

Swalif's aim is to publish a new book every quarter, to partner with galleries, offer artist residencies and facilitate new conversations between young Arab creatives. — SQ
swalif.store

1. TRANSFORMING THE EVERYDAY.

Unlimited Tomorrow creates prosthetics quickly and cost-effectively that allow those with limb loss and limb difference to live a relatively normal life. Here's how it does it.

We take many tasks for granted. Sweeping, cooking, brushing our teeth – tasks that require the full use of our limbs. But for millions globally, such tasks present a daily challenge. There are 57 million people in the world today with limb loss and limb difference. And though prosthetics have a history going back at least as far as Ancient Egypt, only 5 per cent of individuals who require it currently have access to the care and technologies that allow them to live a relatively normal life.

Far from the wooden appendages of the past, modern prosthetics, which are meant to return a certain level of functionality to

their users, can be expensive. But there's a company with a mission to change that – one that's using data, digital twins and additive manufacturing to fundamentally revolutionise the prosthetics industry.

In 2013, Easton LaChappelle hadn't yet founded Unlimited Tomorrow, a company based in New York State. He was 17 and tinkered with 3D printers around the house to explore his passion for robotics. Having received some notoriety for a transformer-like arm capable of throwing a baseball and shaking hands, he met a seven-year-old girl at the Colorado State Fair who wore a prosthesis – the first he had seen.

Unlimited Tomorrow's prosthetic limbs are made to suit various skin tones

TRANSFORMING THE EVERYDAY.

SIEMENS

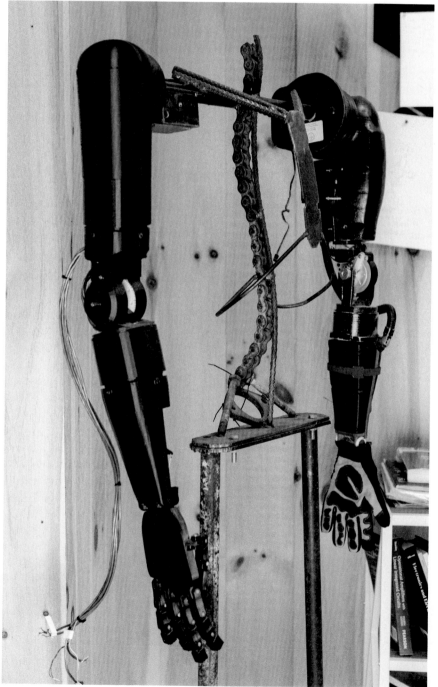

Prosthetic limbs in production

He spoke with the girl and her parents and learned that it can be cost-prohibitive. It only had an open-and-close function, had taken months to create and the girl would soon outgrow it. How could this be, he asked himself, when he was able to create his robotic arm for just $300 (€285)? It was a lightbulb moment. What started as a futuristic passion soon became a life's calling: to not only make prosthetics more user-friendly but to provide access to the millions of people who can't afford what was available on the market.

"I quickly realised that I didn't want to make technology to help one person," says LaChappelle. "There was so much need beyond this one little girl at a science fair. This is a global problem and from day one I looked at how I could create accessible and affordable prosthetic technology that could make an impact around the world. That was the vision early on, and is still the vision today."

The next year he received start-up capital from motivational speaker Tony Robbins, who had attended a TEDx talk LaChappelle had given in Denver, Colorado. Unlimited Tomorrow was born. His team knew that making prosthetics affordable at scale and at the necessary speed would not be easy. Added to that was the challenge of reducing their weight. A typical child's arm prosthetic is too heavy for some children, many of whom refuse to wear them as a result. Beyond utility, there is a psychological aspect to prosthetics. Children want to fit in – and LaChappelle

Recreating a user's residual limb in the digital space was a boon for the company, which today is achieving the unthinkable in the prosthetics industry.

Easton LaChappelle, founder of Unlimited Tomorrow

realised that prosthetics should match a child's opposing limb as closely as possible.

"There are no set sizes," says LaChappelle. "Every prosthetic is unique. We make a mirror image of the opposing limb, which is unheard of in the industry. We're making an extension of someone, both the prosthetic and opposing limb should match perfectly. We offer 140 skin tones and we are now even developing non-skin tones with cool designs, such as silvers and golds."

Fast-forward to 2020, when Unlimited Tomorrow introduced TrueLimb. Relying on additive-manufacturing technology, it's the industry's first lightweight, affordable, multi-articulating prosthetic limb with a realistic appearance. Weighing in at ½kg, TrueLimbs are lighter than a typical pediatric prosthetic arm and are personalised for each user, down to size, skin tone and fingernails. And starting at $8,000 (€7,600), they're much less expensive than conventional alternatives. Best of all, they arrive in weeks, not months.

But perhaps the biggest challenge was the socket that attaches to a user's residual limb – the most important piece of a prosthetic. Not only does it contain the sensors to activate grips but it is also critical to prosthetic comfort. Unlimited Tomorrow engineers were having trouble designing their sockets for the personalised fit that their users needed. With their previous workflow, the engineers would get a 3D scan of a user's residual limb, load it into their CAD tool and combine it with a generic socket model. But the process was too slow and it was hard to modify the results.

Easton had a chance encounter at a conference with a Siemens AG executive, who claimed he had something that might help. Easton was sceptical: the task was too granular and specific. The suggested NX™ Product Template Studio software gave the team much greater control of the socket geometry and caused a ripple effect throughout the company. Suddenly they were able to make prosthetics much more quickly than before – and they fit their users like a glove.

"I knew how hard a challenge this was." says LaChappelle. "I didn't think Siemens could help us achieve our goals in a scalable way. But they proved me wrong and we have been using the software every day to produce probably the highest number of sockets of any company in any given month. Siemens' expertise has allowed us to develop a really robust solution."

As a result, they're able to more accurately simulate digital models of the prosthetics, fine-tuning the variables to ensure not only a proper fit but that the sensors that allow users to move their hands are placed correctly.

"Intellectually, I understood what to expect when I received my TrueLimb in the post, but that was it," says Abby, a congenital amputee who is one of LaChappelle's customers. "The sensation and emotion in the feeling of a physical set of fingers moving somewhat independently of each other for the first time was something I couldn't have imagined or prepared for. I was shocked, excited, flabbergasted, really."

Unlimited Tomorrow's TrueLimbs are remarkable and show that, when coupled with a strong vision, digital technologies can make a real difference. By using them in the right way, we can transform entire industries and open up a world of opportunity for millions.

Find the full series at
monocle.com/content/siemens

PUBLIC SPACE —— ITALY

No place like home

The buildings that line the piazzas of Italian cities are as important as the public space itself. They define the space, serving as the backdrop for residents to sip their *caffè*, meet friends and watch the world go by. These buildings should, as such, be home to businesses and operations that serve the needs of local people. This is not the case in Venice, where St Mark's Square is more tourist trap than civic heart.

It's a situation that has been made more difficult by the fact that the Procuratie Vecchie building, with its iconic arched colonnade on the northern side of the square, has been closed to the public since it was built in 1538. But a newly completed renovation of its interiors by David Chipperfield Architects Milan (DCAM) looks to – in Chipperfield's words – "return the building to the people as a place to love and a font of inspiration."

Mostly vacant since the 1980s, Procuratie Vecchie was built as a home for senior Venetian government officials and is now owned by Generali, the insurance company that commissioned DCAM to revitalise the structure's interior. With the exception of striking new staircases, a rooftop pavilion and a new auditorium, the architects opted for a soft touch, seeking to reveal the various architectural interventions that have taken place over the building's 500-year life. Historic terrazzo flooring, timber ceilings and frescoes have been revealed and original brick walls whitewashed to tie the spaces together.

Every change was finished in partnership with local craftspeople, using traditional methods – an expensive and timely process. "We went a long way beyond strict commercial decision-making. It's much easier to cover up a wall and much easier to put some plasterboard somewhere," says Chipperfield. "What we've done is uncover everything and bring everything back. That takes patience, not just from the architects and the craftspeople but also from the client to understand that restoring something in this way is a noble cause."

The building's first and second floors have also been transformed into offices, a move that returns daily work to the centre of a city dominated by tourists and museums. Even more significant is the creation of the auditorium and new exhibition spaces, a café and rooftop terrace – all open to the public and managed by Human

> "This project has needed patience – from architects, craftspeople and the client; restoration in this way is a noble cause"

Safety Net, a global foundation supporting people living in vulnerable circumstances.

"Of course, in Venice, it's expected that international visitors will come and discover this space," says Emma Ursich, Human Safety Net's executive officer. "But the people of Venice will benefit too. They have a new space to be, where they can come for brunch on Sunday morning or listen to a concert."

The transformation of the building will allow locals not only to enjoy new views across the rooftops of St Mark's but new ways of experiencing Venice. It points to a more hopeful future – one where Venetians are invited to reclaim their city. — NM

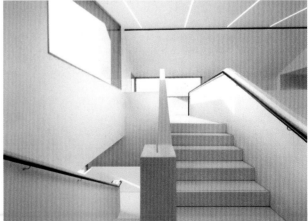

NOLAN GILES ON...

Engaging citizens

Westfield shopping centre in east London isn't the type of place you would imagine to hear a compelling conversation around urban planning. But tucked in to an out-of-use retail space, crowds gather around a miniature version of the local area plotted out on a table. They're here to learn about a corner of London that is being developed through a 2012 Olympic Games legacy project, which aims to improve quality of life. Too often in city developments the public isn't engaged with what's going on in the place it calls home. Exercises like this suggest that citizens are excited about shaping the place they live in and want to take part in the conversation.

People want to hear stories about what inspired a development, and how it will improve their lives

It's an idea that Spanish architect and curator Javier Peña Ibáñez has fostered in his home city of Logroño, where he hosts the Concéntrico festival each year (*see page 178*). Here the generally dry topic of urbanism is examined through beautiful, playful installations, which are temporarily constructed across the city. Beyond being a gathering point for a global community to debate building better cities, the event educates locals from all walks of life about the positive effect of good urban design. The result is an informed population engaged in this small city's progression.

So what initiatives can be implemented in cities that don't have the luxury of festivals? First, private developers and government bodies need to drop the jargon and level with those whose lives are going to be affected by their grand projects. Words such as "placemaking" and "densification" aren't fun or engaging. People want to hear stories – not just about how a development will improve their lives but what inspired it and how the history of their neighbourhood informed its future. They also want to imagine themselves in said future – photo-realistic renderings are OK, but more creative approaches to providing this are welcome. "Storytelling" is another overused expression in design but in the case of making urban development a palatable topic, it's a valuable tool. — Ⓜ

ARCHITECTURE —— UK

Competitive nature

The winners of architectural competitions face a lot of scrutiny around the worthiness and quality of their design. But no such grumblings have greeted Herzog & de Meuron's newly completed Royal College of Art (RCA) building in London's Battersea. Named the Rausing Research and Innovation Building, it was completed to a 2016 competition-winning design by the Swiss practice.

"It was a unanimous decision that they would be the winner because they were the only entrant that proposed a concept that looked beyond the site," says Paul Thompson, the RCA's vice-chancellor. "They didn't present a singular building but rather a vision that referenced the immediate streetscape and other RCA buildings."

It's a vision they have executed to perfection, with the new structure opening up to the neighbourhood around it. Located a short walk from the RCA's flagship Dyson building, the Rausing, as it's known, is composed of a ground floor with workshops (with full-height windows in some, allowing passers-by to look in) with two distinct wings on the floors above; one houses research spaces for subjects from robotics to manufacturing, while the other has dedicated design studios with balconies that enjoy views of the street and the Dyson building beyond.

"It felt natural to include all these balconies and give students the ability not just to open a window but to be able to get outside, look down and get a perspective [on the campus]," says John O'Mara, Herzog & de Meuron's UK studio director.

At the centre of the building is The Hangar, a double-height exhibition space with vast doors at either end that open out onto the street and connect to walkways intersecting the site. The result? Easy access for locals and students alike to the building's leafy courtyards. "What we wanted to do was make it feel very much a part of Battersea," says O'Mara of the building's openness to the public. "We wanted to root it down here and cement the neighbourhood for the RCA." And that's just what they've achieved – bricks and mortar justification for scooping that gold. — NM

"We wanted it to feel very much a part of the neighbourhood"

1

1. Cooling down after a run
2. Deepak Oberoi, co-founder of Bombay Running
3. Runner Gaurav Bangera
4. Club member Mukund Vedpathak
5. Runners out on the street

The COMMENT

FITNESS —— MUMBAI

Running the city

Prasad Ramamurthy on the joggers stretching their legs in congested Mumbai.

It's 05.30 on a Thursday. The sky starts to turn purple and Mumbai begins to stir. In a carpark in the coastal suburb of Bandra, a group of nearly 50 people, ranging in ages from 21 to 73, stand chit-chatting, high-fiving and back-slapping. All are members of Bombay Running, one of a growing number of running clubs in a city not well known for such pursuits. Today's run will follow a stretch of seafront called Bandstand. It's one of those rare spots in this city of 20 million souls where residents can come to open their lungs and stretch their limbs.

Over the past 10 years there has been a steady increase in the number of Mumbaikars taking up running. Their city has been slow to adapt: Mumbai has been ranked 27th of 30 in a survey of pedestrian-friendly Indian cities. This is unsurprising when you consider that only 30 per cent of the city's streets have pavements. Add to this a traffic density of 2,150 vehicles per kilometre, very poor air quality and an astronomical construction boom and it doesn't seem like a runner's paradise.

What the city does have going for it are pockets of respite – residential neighbourhoods with green cover, large public parks, seaside promenades – and a growing population of hardy joggers. "The city could

2

3

have better infrastructure and dedicated lanes for runners," says Bombay Running's Deepak Oberoi, who has been pounding the city's streets for almost 20 years. "But when life gives you lemons, you learn to adjust." That means timing a run to coincide with less traffic and lower temperatures: early mornings and late evenings. Runners also vary the length of their runs based on the season – shorter through the summer and monsoon, longer in winter.

Another factor is the day of the week. Shops and commercial establishments in different areas shut on certain days, which gives Mumbaikars a chance to run undisturbed. Puspamitra Sahu likes to go on Sunday jogs through the downtown financial district, home to her office at India's central bank as well as two Unesco World Heritage sites. "When you're at work, you don't have the bandwidth to look around," she says. "At the weekend, streets are empty. We can appreciate the area's art deco and Indo-Saracenic architecture at our own pace."

Becoming more aware of her surroundings is a by-product of her runs, says Shweta Bhalerao, who uses the time to explore Khar, the suburb where she lives. "I might have passed a shop or a beautiful bungalow and not noticed it because I was inside a car," she says. "But now, because I'm running, I've learned to appreciate my neighbourhood more." Lifelong Mumbai resident Gaurav Bangera agrees. "When you're running, your body is at work," he says. "But your mind is free to observe and remember. Running past public parks, I've remembered how my parents would take us there on picnics. That makes this city feel even more like home." — Ⓜ

4 5

Meet the new generation of makers

On the eastern outskirts of Paris stands Chanel's le19M, a showcase of the fashion house's commitment to the savoir-faire of the finest French artisans. Step inside.

le19M

CHANEL × MONOCLE

At the edge of the French capital, Chanel's le19M stands as a five-storey testament to the enduring importance and wonder of French couture's craft traditions.

Less than a year ago, Chanel opened the doors to *le*19M at the border of Paris's 19th arrondissement and Aubervilliers. The elegant building is home to 11 ateliers owned by Chanel and more than 600 artisans and experts. The maisons d'art that have taken up residence here include embroiderer and tweed-maker Lesage, embroiderer Montex, architectural embroidery studio MTX, boot-maker Massaro, pleating specialist Lognon, feather and floral decoration-maker Lemarié, goldsmithing studio Goossens, milliner Maison Michel and *grand flou* couture studio Paloma. Maison Eres, which specialises in lingerie and swimsuits, is also a resident.

Set across 25,500 sq m and wrapped in a giant exostructure, the building stands as a powerful symbol of the value of craft in a world of fast manufacturing. But this is nothing new for Chanel, which has always put craft at the centre of its collections and began acquiring applied-arts workshops in 1985.

"It's a question of offering the best working conditions for these artisans," says Bruno Pavlovsky, Chanel's president of fashion and president of *le*19M. "Years ago they used to be based in the centre of Paris, which was charming but it made it difficult to imagine a development." Almost a year on, not only has the move improved the artisans' working lives but it has also telegraphed a message of optimism about industries whose future has often been questioned.

Crucially, this isn't merely a matter of preserving the crafts of yesteryear. Inside *le*19M these days, you're just as likely to spot as many twentysomething apprentices as master artisans. Thanks to initiatives such as public workshops and partnerships with nearby schools, the volume of applications is only increasing.

The choice of location is part of Chanel's formula for success, says Pavlovsky, who describes it as full of youthful energy and potential. "We've been working with the mayors of Paris and Aubervilliers and local associations to connect ourselves with the area," he adds. "I love this idea of being half in Paris and half in Aubervilliers and being connected to this ecosystem of cities, associations and schools. There's so much that we can learn by being here."

With the opening of a new café next to its 1,200 sq m gallery and the launch of a series of artist workshops, all planned for this summer, the next step is to start attracting the wider public to *le*19M and create a true hub for the exchange of ideas and skills. "This building is financed by Chanel but what we're doing is not about Chanel," says Pavlovsky. "It's about these applied arts."

CHANEL

MONOCLE

TOP LEFT. Hatter Shariff Hisaund of Maison Michel moulding felt on a wood stock **TOP RIGHT.** Fabrics at pleating specialist Lognon **BOTTOM RIGHT.** Artisans at Montex embroidering by needle **BOTTOM LEFT.** Inside an atelier in *le*19M, where work stations are arranged to optimise natural light

CHANGE MAKERS

2

French architect Rudy Ricciotti worked closely with Chanel to deliver a building that could both embody and further the forward-looking ideals of le19M.

It's impossible to miss *le*19M as you drive north, not just because of its grand scale but also because of its striking design, which features windows encased in a canopy of snaking white rods, created using high-performance, fibre-reinforced concrete. This was the vision of award-winning French architect Rudy Ricciotti, who wanted to echo the intricacy of hand-woven textiles in his design of the exoskeleton.

"I was drawn to Chanel's desire to give artisans a comfortable home and make them feel protected," says Ricciotti. "We share so much with these artisans, from passion to expertise and an interest in passing down knowledge." Just as a sketch by Chanel's creative director, Virginie Viard, will go on to be interpreted by Lognon's pleating experts,

before being embellished by Lemarié's embroiderers, Riccioti's initial drawings went through a journey. After creating the design, he entrusted his engineer son to develop the technical side. The 24-metre strands of woven concrete were then cast in moulds, transported by trucks and craned onto the site. "It was crazy but I'm very devoted to this journeyman spirit," he adds.

Wanting to enhance working lives through architecture, Ricciotti studied the light coming in from every façade

of the building to achieve optimal levels of visual and thermal comfort. "Both Chanel and I put a lot of emphasis on this," he says. "Under these conditions entrepreneurial life can thrive and ateliers can keep attracting people."

Equally important was that the building wasn't divorced from its surroundings. For Ricciotti, it is a symbol of unity, linking Paris with Aubervilliers. "It is a chance for the area to be revitalised by a new space for work and culture," he says.

ABOVE. The entrance of *le*19M
RIGHT. The view from the building's top terrace

MAISON MICHEL

*Three decades ago, discovering the joy of making transformed Shariff Hisaund's life.
Now a key figure at Maison Michel, he passes on his knowledge to young craftspeople.*

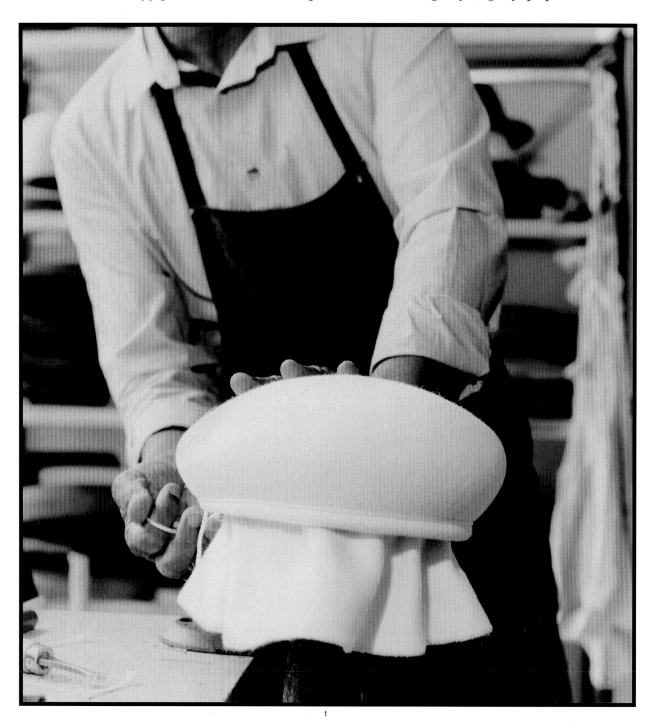

When mechanic and Mauritius native Shariff Hisaund arrived in Paris in the early 1980s he was just looking for a job that would pay the bills and give him shelter, safe from the cold European winters that he wasn't used to. He came across milliner Maison Michel by chance. During a trial, he quickly discovered his natural talent for hat-making and was hired by its founder, Auguste Michel.

Some 34 years later, he is one of the leading figures at the Maison Michel atelier and works with young hatters who have backgrounds as surprising as his own – such as 35-year-old Romain Clery, who studied chemistry and electronics before taking on Maison Michel's hat-making course seven years ago.

Hisaund, who has an encyclopaedic knowledge of the house's more than 4,000 woodblocks, skilfully moulds felt fabrics on his bench, before baking them

2

3

in what looks like a pizza oven. "There are always new models, new collections, partnerships with high-profile people," says Hisaund, who keeps a newspaper cutting featuring a picture of himself and the late Karl Lagerfeld near his desk. "That's what keeps me going." As he irons the edges of a felt beret, he turns his hands around to reveal palm lines shaped like the letter M. "I was really born to do this," he says. "There hasn't been a day in the past 34 years that I haven't felt joy coming into work."

4

5

---

1. Shariff Hisaund working on a felt hat design **2.** Maison Michel artisans at their work benches **3.** Hisaund shows his palm lines, shaped like the letter M **4.** A Maison Michel woodblock **5.** Hats from the the atelier's archive

4

LES ATELIERS LOGNON

Pleating underpins so much of haute couture yet has long been unheralded by the wider public. Marion Moinier at Lognon, however, sees its endless possibilities.

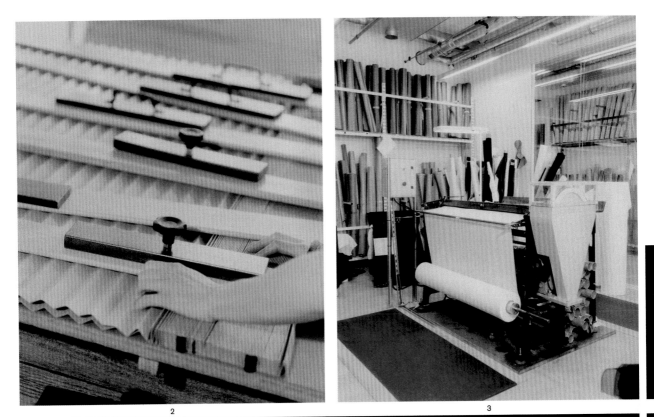

1. Marion Moinier **2.** Lognon's artisans creating pleating patterns
3. Inside Les Ateliers Lognon **4.** A pair of scissors from Moinier's work station

The fine craft of pleating that Lognon exemplifies is perhaps among the less-understood disciplines under the roof of *le*19M. Yet it provides the base of so many of the textiles seen on haute couture runways and beyond, according to 30-year-old pleating-mould designer and maker Marion Moinier.

Moinier, who trained as a fashion designer, found herself on an apprenticeship at Lognon because she was always incorporating pleats in her student collections. "I just wanted to see how it's all done – and here I am seven years later," she says.

At the time, her peers at fashion school saw more value in careers as stylists or designers than becoming artisans but Moinier was drawn to the sense of precision that comes with

4

working with your hands. Today, she remains just as passionate about the art of pleating, which was initially developed by founder Émilie Lognon in 1853. Moinier's eyes light up when she speaks about the "endless possibilities"

of developing patterns and discovering new techniques. There also seems to be a real resurgence of interest in craft, allowing Moinier and her colleagues to practise another major aspect of their jobs: passing down knowledge to the younger generation.

"Our craft isn't taught in schools, so we can only train new artisans in these ateliers," she says. "But I'm positive about the future. There's better communication around our craft and the next generation will come in and mix it up with new technologies." With momentum growing, it's only a matter of time until she reaches her goal of growing her team and expanding her work on larger-scale interiors projects too. "Working on a wall made of pleated cork? That would be truly exciting."

5

ATELIER MONTEX

*A young company in comparison to many of le19M's storied ateliers,
Montex is free to invent its own history of innovative craft.*

2

1. Victoria Funchs, embroiderer at Atelier Montex
2. Inside the atelier 3. Embroiderers at their work benches
4. A hand-made embellishment 5. All in the details

3

Montex was founded in 1949 and until the early 2000s it was known for selling embroidered fabrics by the metre to some of Paris's most renowned fashion houses. Today it maintains its modern outlook by being in constant search of new materials and designing innovative embroidery patterns – which is perhaps the most positive outcome of not having the kind of vast, historical archives as some of its older peers do.

Its team of 50 is the other major driving force behind the atelier's dynamic, forward-thinking ethos. Young embroiderers are coming on board with a real appetite for mastering their craft and contributing to keeping it alive.

Among them is Victoria Funchs, who has a background in costume design and now specialises in the use of the hand-guided Cornely machine. "I enjoy fully applying myself to something," she says. She didn't know about Cornely embroidery until she visited the open day of Parisian high school, Lycée Octave Feuillet, the only school that still offers this type of training. While she recognises that hers isn't a well-known vocation, she never hesitated in immersing herself in the craft. "There's just something so satisfying about driving the handle of that machine and creating new patterns," she says.

4

5

ASKA YAMASHITA

For Yamashita, the move into le19M has shifted her perceptions of her industry and the world around it, while affirming the importance of her craft to fashion.

Aska Yamashita joined Montex's drawing department more than 30 years ago and instantly formed a bond with then art director Annie Trussart, who encouraged her to look beyond drawing to embroidery and client relations. Five years ago, Yamashita succeeded her mentor and now leads the atelier.

How has your role evolved?
I see myself as a conductor, translating clients' briefs to the team and managing people. The work that we do with Virginie Viard always keeps us alive. She encourages us to try different designs. Chanel is the only house where you get to work with the creative director directly. It's a special relationship.

Has there been more interest from young apprentices lately?
Yes, we're starting to have more boys in the studio. In the past, girls would take up embroidery if they weren't doing well at school. Now, people come in because they're passionate about it. The communication around our work is evolving. Just being in *le*19M shows that what we do has value in fashion.

How has the move to le19M changed your everyday life?
For 29 years we were based in an old building in central Paris, across different floors. I was at the top and on some days I wouldn't even see parts of the team. Coming here brought us into the 21st century. It was like turning a page. This area also gave me a new perspective. Yes, we work in luxury but there's another reality outside our world.

CHANEL ✕ MONOCLE

Metropolis now: the world's most liveable cities

Monocle's 15th annual Quality of Life Survey charts 25 outposts on the up and ranks the best places to put down roots. Did your city make the cut?

EDITOR: Josh Fehnert

As MONOCLE's editors met to pore over the research that underpins our annual ranking of the world's most liveable cities the mood was rosier than it had been for a while. Let's be clear: all of that guff about the death of cities was wildly overstated. The more we read, the more we were cheered by our correspondents' reports on the optimistic turns that their cities had taken: Zürich is extending opening hours and street-side dining, and Stockholm is putting the brakes on its scooter problem, while most places fessed up to the need to recycle more, add bike lanes and prioritise pedestrians. Kyoto and Barcelona have had time to reflect on how to balance the interests of tourists and local residents, while Vancouver and Vienna were reconnecting with their leafy fringes. Lisbon's plan to put 48,000 empty city homes to better use was a good example of a fix that should give other cities pause for thought.

Cities are here to stay. They drive the national economy even in countries whose leaders appear to be asleep at the wheel. What's more, they remain exciting places where people rub shoulders, shop, eat, live and seek out surprises. The bored souls who moved out to the sticks and work from home might disapprove but that won't stop cities housing two-thirds of the world's population by 2050.

Some of the challenges facing cities today have been around for decades: crime, transport, housing, ambulance response times. We faithfully factor these into our metrics, as we have done since our first annual survey in 2007. We have also added newer nudges, criteria and considerations. How suitable is your city to the newer rhythms of work? Can you take a lunchtime dip, travel abroad easily or saunter down a high street filled with independent businesses, rather than "to let" signs? Is your city working to make cycling and walking more pleasurable? Is it creating public spaces to mingle? Is your mayor seeking carbon neutrality or giving gas guzzlers the right of way? It all matters more than ever. Finally, did your city trust you when the pandemic hit or overly threaten you if you broke the rules?

This year's shakedown takes into account retail and hospitality, access to green spaces and fresh air. We have added weight to better weather, a city's cultural clout, the cost of living and access to affordable housing. Cities should be for everyone after all.

This year's survey is the most qualitatively informed rundown that we have ever published. We scrutinised employment figures, population numbers and Gini coefficients but found ourselves needing to rely more heavily than ever on feedback from our correspondents on the ground. Living in cities is an experience, not a series of graphs to decode.

As such, Lisbon shoots up our ranking just as some long-closed-off Asian and Australian cities needed to be adjusted down. The Nordics have got the mix right and there are reasons to be hopeful about Tokyo's reopening, Seoul's urban investments and Milan's mammoth ambitions. We have also included ideas from Dakar, Buenos Aires, Istanbul and other cities.

What follows here is the product of months of data-gathering, long discussions and the sincerely held belief that understanding cities is crucial to how we live and build a better future. Whichever way the political, cultural or economic winds are blowing, we have sought out reasons to be optimistic about how they're run and where they're heading. Read on for our 2022 ranking. — Ⓜ

I.

Copenhagen

The best – and getting better.

Copenhagen's decision to gear its city planning towards cyclists and pedestrians has resulted in cleaner air and reduced congestion, and has helped to improve the health and wellbeing of its residents. But there's always more ground to cover: Nordic weather also demands a public transport system for days when the sleet feels like needles. So the Copenhagen Metro is still expanding, connecting previously distant neighbourhoods.

And the C-word? It's as if the dreaded virus never happened. The Danish capital's residents reverted to normality without a fuss, which reflects the sense of collective responsibility and togetherness that the city has fostered. Great new restaurants are opening almost every week (most have moved beyond the New Nordic dogma), culture has never been more vibrant and the economy is booming.

The city also scores well on safety, runs smoothly and has a generous welfare system and support for new parents (though inequality is nudging up). The whole country is undertaking the move towards carbon neutrality by 2050 but there are shorter-term advantages to living here – the proximity of the harbour for a lunchtime swim, for one.

A significant challenge for the city is finding space for all those who want to move here. The current solution – the artificial island of Lynetteholm at the southeastern harbour entrance, planned to house 35,000 people – is not without its critics. — MB

Adopt: More kiosks.

Drop: Rude cyclists. The city needs a polite-biking campaign.

Population: 646,812 (city), 1,370,131 (metropolitan area).

Newspapers: 13 (two local, 11 national).

Chain test: Seven Starbucks in the city.

Electric-car charging points: 1,225.

Commuters who cycle: 62 per cent.

Places to swim: Eight zones of the harbour for a dip, four city beaches and two public pools.

2.

Zürich

The convivial all-rounder.

The cafés are full and if the lack of space for towels at the Letten lido is anything to go by, the city is bustling and ready to enjoy the summer sun. Zürich is back in full swing and the population is ticking up. The city's pull is also evident in the packed pavement cafés, the competition for apartments and the low unemployment rate (2 per cent).

It is also doing its best to tempt people to linger. Parliament recently decided to allow restaurants and bars to permanently occupy the public spaces that they temporarily took over during the pandemic. Bravo. Along with plans to make 30km/h the maximum speed and add more bike lanes, Zürich is moving ahead in cutting emissions and making the city a more pleasant place to be (though in true Swiss fashion, these things will take time).

With the return of events such as Street Parade and the Sechseläuten festival – in which a snowman-like figure is filled with explosives and burned – and restrictions shelved, hoteliers are seeing a bump in guests. Overnight stays are rebounding, rising by more than 200 per cent from January to March 2022 compared to the same period last year.

Overall, Zürich continues to offer great food, drink, culture and retail. To make sure that it stays on top, it might have to reckon with the cost of living, which remains resolutely high, and graffiti is a problem that needs to be scrubbed out fast. — DBA

Adopt: Electric car charging points. One station per 41 vehicles isn't enough.

Drop: The bureaucracy.

Population: 436,332 (city), 1,553,423 (metropolitan area).

Social housing: 56,958 flats or 25 per cent of the total stock.

Number of museums: 64 (35 are free).

Public transport investment: CHF1bn (€972m) a year.

Public parks: 72.

Hospitals: 16 (city), 29 (canton).

3.

Lisbon

The taste of life's sunny side.

The Portuguese capital knows how to welcome newcomers: there's nice weather, the airport serves an ever-increasing number of international destinations and there's a sense of community that's attracting people, businesses and opportunities.

Couple that with comparatively low levels of pollution, as well as mayor Carlos Moedas's efforts to re-green the city, and its growth is beginning to look rather sustainable too. The city plans to slash its carbon emissions by 60 per cent by 2030 and a third of the mayoral budget has been dedicated to making this lofty rhetoric a reality.

It has been a good year for businesses. As tourism numbers creep back up towards pre-pandemic levels, spending has increased and helped the city's many independent shops and restaurants. There has also been a boom in entrepreneurship. There was a 39 per cent increase in new businesses in the year to April 2022.

Despite Lisbon's good looks, lustre and charm, there are challenges and housing is the most pressing. A new law limiting what types of building can be rented as short-term lets will help residents, while there's also a programme to make use of the estimated 48,000 homes that are now empty.

Talent continues to be tempted by being able to go from desk to beach in less than 30 minutes. The city's rise has been impressive, especially after the recent financial crisis. The next challenge? Making sure that the rising tide raises all boats. — CCR

Adopt: Underground investment. The metro is dirty and sluggish.

Drop: Cash. People carry cards now.

Population: 544,851 (city), 2,871,133 (metropolitan area).

Average monthly cost of renting a one-bedroom flat: €900.

Companies started in year to April 2022: 1,866.

Cup of coffee costs on average: About €0.80 for an espresso, €2.30 for a flat white.

Average commute: 20 minutes.

4.

Helsinki

The flourishing outdoor city.

Helsinki is a city that somehow balances functionality and fun – two words that almost never belong in the same sentence. It's among the safest capitals in the world, where the city's proactive public-housing policy has managed to avoid the segregation that troubles its Nordic neighbours. As well as free healthcare and education to university level, there's a vibrant start-up scene, thanks to a city hall that helps with office space and advice on financing. This generates an equality of opportunity that pushes many people to try something new, though more could be done to help high-street and home-grown businesses.

Surrounded by the sea and hundreds of islands, and criss-crossed with verdant parks and forests, Helsinki is an outdoor city where nature and fresh air are never far away. In the summer months, its residents flock to the outdoor pools, seaside saunas and squares filled with restaurants to frolic in the sun. In the winter months, you can ski in the city itself and you'll find children building snowmen and riding sledges in parks. Music festivals such as Flow and art museums, including Amos Rex, attract visitors from around the world and the plans for a new architecture museum are promising.

The city administration is transparent and approachable and allocates almost €10m a year to citizen-led initiatives, from a simple bench to new parks and swimming jetties. Come to see the success for yourself. — PBU

Adopt: Pedestrian areas – more traffic could be shifted out of the city centre.

Drop: Building suburban malls.

Population: 656,920 (city), 1,524,489 (metropolitan area).

Average ambulance response: Seven minutes and 47 seconds.

Monthly rent of a one-bed flat: €749.

Social housing: 19 per cent of stock.

Number of museums: 60.

Average commute time: 15 minutes.

Bike lanes: More than 1,500km.

Stockholm
The Swedish sweet spot.

Tokyo
The ever-surprising megacity.

True belonging
Brussels

Stockholm has struggled with integration outside its pretty and polished city centre but over the past decade its outlook has become much more international. There's more to do but you can feel that the city is alive and thriving, from café terraces to museums and the leafy Djurgården. There have been plenty of openings, thanks to the city's lenient take on lockdowns.

Fortunately, measures have been taken to cut the number of pesky electric scooters and longer-term infrastructure upgrades in areas such as Slussen in Södermalm are continuing. There is also great public healthcare and a top-notch free education system, alongside enlightened policies regarding time off when it comes to having (then raising) children.

The population is ticking up and city authorities are doing their best to keep up the supply of housing stock to meet demand, even if it seems as though those apartments can't be built fast enough. So what's the draw for newcomers? First, there's Stockholm's natural beauty: picture thousands of sailboats headed from Lake Mälaren out to the Baltic Sea, the pristine islands that make up the archipelago surrounding Stockholm, the city's beaches and forests both in the centre of town as well as its easily-reachable outskirts.

And then there are Stockholm's progressive policies and a tradition of putting equality at the top of the agenda. That makes it a (nearly) perfect place to put down roots. — LL

The pandemic shifted the discussion around work-life balance here more significantly than years of legislation. Working from home wasn't a serious proposition for many in Tokyo but the pausing of the commuter treadmill prompted a rethink of office life.

As a more relaxed Tokyo opens up to visitors and hits its stride again, good restaurants are as busy as ever and queues form for whatever brand that young shoppers deem worthy of their money. But the pandemic has altered the rhythm of the city in subtle ways. While retail is as immaculate as ever and Ginza cocktail bars just as precise, dinners now start and end earlier. Hospitality soldiered on in the absence of overseas tourists (and, for long stretches, domestic travel too). Some places didn't make it, but other hotels opened and more are planned.

A city the scale of Tokyo has its own life with or without tourists and development is at its usual relentless pace. There is no lack of ambition: Tokyu Corporation's complex reconfiguration of Shibuya continues, Mori Building is working on its giant Toranomon-Azabudai Project, opening next year, and Mitsubishi Jisho Sekkei is building the enormous Torch Tower near Tokyo Station. At 390 metres, the soaring skyscraper will be the tallest in Japan by 2027.

Meanwhile, dog walkers were cheered by the belated reopening of Yoyogi Park, which was closed for an extended period. Outdoor spaces have never been more cherished. — FW

Home to a significant number of international organisations, Brussels has many foreign-born residents. But despite making up about a third of the city's population, non-Belgian residents can't vote in regional elections, which decide on everything from public transport to security. "Without this right there is a huge democratic deficit," says Pascal Smet, secretary of state for the Brussels-Capital region.

Smet and his team have been working to change this and recently unveiled the results of a yearlong project. The initiative, called "Live here. Speak, hear", encourages international residents to present their concerns over how the city is governed. These have now been turned into a manifesto that will be presented to the Brussels regional parliament later this year. According to Smet, these demands aren't dissimilar to those of other *bruxellois*. "The international inhabitants live in the same city and the same reality," he says. "They want a peaceful, clean city with fewer cars and accessible housing."

"Giving all Brusselers the right to vote is a priority," says Smet. "We're working to change the legislation."

This will be no mean feat, as national implementation would require approval from Wallonia and Flanders. Another option is to apply for changes specific to the Brussels-Capital region on the grounds of its international character. "Brussels is not a city of 'love at first sight'," says Smet. "It's a city that seduces over time." The hope is that by giving foreign-born residents more of a democratic stake, Brussels will become less of a transitory place and more of a long-term home. — CFC

Adopt: A better cycling scheme, sooner.

Drop: Quibbling and delays over new and much-needed developments.

Population: 978,770 (city), 1,679,000 (metropolitan area).

New homes: 140,000 by 2030.

E-scooters allowed on city streets: 12,000 (down from 23,000).

Restaurants opened in the past year: About 30.

Independent bookshops: 15, plus 20 secondhand or antiquarian bookshops.

Adopt: Vacant lots as green spaces. Kitaya Park opened last year and transformed its small corner of Shibuya.

Drop: Electric scooters – at least until the bike lanes work.

Population: 9,660,461 (city), 13,972,039 (metropolitan area).

Number of cinemas: 65 (295 screens).

Public bike-share scheme? Yes. It is available across 21 of 23 districts and was used more than 12 million times last year.

Average commute time: 47 minutes.

Monthly travel card: ¥17,300 (€127).

7.

POSITION LAST YEAR **06**

Vienna

The well-connected capital.

Vienna had a rotten pandemic. It didn't help itself with hair-trigger lockdowns that felt harsh and out of step with the rest of Europe. That said, Austria supported the health of its citizens and its businesses admirably. As such, most of its independent restaurants, shops and hotels survived to trade another day.

As the sun returns, there's plenty to see and do from a world-leading line-up of 100 museums, places to swim, eat and drink – and some new overnighters too. Openings include Hotel Gilbert by Austrian architecture firm BWM, Hotel Motto (an offshoot of the restaurant of the same name) and a new Rosewood property.

About one in four houses is still owned by the municipality, making Vienna one of Europe's biggest landlords and living here affordable. Costs are rising but from a low base.

The city has added to housing in the central 2nd district and created the new U5 subway line; plus, its cycling network of more than 1,650km is growing constantly. Vienna is an easy city to saunter around and between the U-Bahn and trams, the average length of a city commute is an enviable 26 minutes. Getting fresh air is easy too, with immaculate green spaces, such as the Volksgarten and Stadtpark, and the chance to splash out in the Alte Donau or take a short drive to the forested Wienerwald. Meanwhile ÖBB's investment in overnight rail is quietly adding to the allure of this already well-connected city. — AKO

Adopt: A kinder, less bureaucratic stance to refugees fleeing Ukraine.

Drop: Limited Sunday opening hours. It's an easy economic win.

Population: 1,920,949 (city), 3,700,000 (metropolitan area).

Average monthly cost of renting a one-bedroom flat: €873.

Crime rate at its lowest for: 20 years.

Number of international destinations from main airport: 217.

Number of trees: About 500,000.

Gift of giving
Istanbul

Like history, inflation in Turkey's biggest city is cyclical. Peer at a curio-seller's stall and you'll find TL1m notes, throwbacks to the mid-1990s, when it ran at more than 100 per cent.

The rate is heading skywards again, hitting 70 per cent in May. Inflation in Turkey is one of the highest in the G20. The effects are acute in Istanbul, where rents in popular neighbourhoods have spiralled beyond the budget of most who earn in the local currency. Imported products are seeing price hikes; the cost of Turkish produce is increasing too due to soaring fuel prices.

Istanbul's municipal council, run by the opposition Republican People's Party (CHP), has come up with a scheme to aid the city's poorest: *askida fatura* ("bills on the hanger"). People who need help upload their bills on a website, where benefactors can pay them. More than TL50m (€2.8m) have been paid in the two years since its launch.

Askida fatura is inspired by two Turkish traditions: the practice of overpaying at bakeries so that hard-up customers can take a loaf for free and political parties' tactic of winning votes with welfare. President Recep Tayyip Erdogan's Justice and Development Party (AKP) has a long history of handing alms to the poor to win support. Before 2019's local elections the government set up subsidised vegetable markets but closed them the day after the ballots.

The CHP, traditionally the party of the elite, is now taking up the informal welfare cause. "It has grown huge in a short time and boosted solidarity in the city," says Ekrem Imamoglu, Istanbul's mayor. "Our next goal is to make this permanent and take it to other cities." — HLS

8.

Sydney

The Harbour City awaiting rebirth.

Lord mayor Clover Moore continues to reign over Sydney, which was closed for business for three and a half months in 2021 and has suffered a galling 160-plus days of rain so far this year, thanks to La Niña. That said, the year-round sun, energy and a thriving cultural scene still make the Harbour City an attractive place to live. But it's not without its problems. Inadequate public transport to the suburbs has left residents reliant on cars, resulting in gridlock. Major road projects are under way, including a series of tunnels stretching 19km that will link the west and northwestern suburbs to the CBD; this is expected to reduce travel times by 40 minutes on major routes and help drivers avoid 52 sets of traffic lights.

Housing is an issue and many social housing complexes have been sold or repurposed. The brutalist Sirius Building and Victorian terraced housing by the Sydney Harbour Bridge have been flogged to developers or private buyers. Rents have rocketed and property values have shot up by more than 33 per cent in the past year. The average price of a three-bedroom house is AU$1.6m (€1m) and the weekly rent for a one-bedroom flat in the CBD is in the region of AU$2,500 (€1,666). Some 50,000 families are on the waiting list for social housing in New South Wales.

The retail landscape wasn't helped by the 107-day citywide lockdown in mid-2021 and the high streets of many inner-city suburbs now have plenty of "For lease" signs. But could this be an opportunity? — CR

Adopt: Better drainage. Ferocious, monsoon-like conditions have taken the city by surprise.

Drop: The idea that residents should be confined to car travel. It will take time but better public transport is needed.

Population: 5,360,000 (metropolitan area).

Chain test: 24 Starbucks branches in Greater Sydney.

Average length of commute: 46 minutes.

Getting moving: By 2024, Sydney will have 32 metro stations.

9.

Vancouver
The west-coast wonder.

Most Canadian cities dragged their heels when it came to opening up but authorities in British Columbia were comparatively nimble. As a result, life in Vancouver resumed more swiftly than elsewhere. Pressures remain, particularly for more affordable housing. Residents also had an uncomfortable first-hand experience of the effects of climate change during last summer's record-breaking heatwave. That said, there's confidence in the city, whose population growth is among the fastest in the country.

The next few years promise plenty too. A landmark expansion of the Millennium Line underground railway, which will improve connections with some of Vancouver's outer suburbs, is on schedule to be up and running by 2025. Meanwhile, consultations on an international high-speed Cascadia rail route between Vancouver, Seattle and Portland continue.

In culture, a major expansion of the Vancouver Art Gallery, designed by the Swiss firm Herzog & de Meuron, will break ground next year and open in 2028. The city is also expected to host matches in the forthcoming Fifa World Cup, staged jointly by the US, Canada and Mexico. Vancouver's quality of life remains anchored in its proximity to nature, from the North Shore Mountains to the dramatic Pacific coastline. Recent efforts to make access to and between the city's over 250 public parks and its vast cycling network better are a move in the right direction. — TLE

Adopt: Swifter construction of affordable housing units that were pledged in 2020.

Drop: Restrictions on the consumption of alcohol within the city's parks.

Population: 662,248 (city), 2,630,000 (metropolitan area).

New houses approved for building last year: 28,724.

Restaurants opened last year: 37.

Swimming: Nine beaches and five outdoor public pools that open seasonally.

Number of restaurants opened in the past year: 37.

Burning money
Buenos Aires

Since Buenos Aires emerged from one of the longest lockdowns anywhere in the world, it seems as though a new restaurant or bar is opening every other week. Yet amid the clinking of glasses there's a lingering question: if the economy is in free fall, how do people have the money to spend?

The answer: inflation. Prices were rising at pace long before the war in Ukraine sparked global supply disruptions. Last year inflation topped 50 per cent and some fear that it could hit 70 per cent in a few months – at the time of writing, Argentina is outpacing Venezuela in the region's inflation tables. So there is an incentive to spend what is in your wallet as soon as you get it: money that sits in the bank will lose value.

Take La Biela bar. Since October a glass of house red served on the same terrace by the same waiter has gone up by almost 40 per cent. This translates well beyond nightlife. Buying staples in bulk can feel like saving money. Taking on loans and paying in instalments is also encouraged, since interest rates are running below inflation. Any pesos left over are automatically exchanged into the more trustworthy US dollars – but in limited amounts due to tight government restrictions, so pesos keep circulating and the wine keeps flowing.

One politician who is successfully tapping into the mood of the nation is Javier Milei, an economist and congressman for the capital. Radical proposals to abolish the central bank and dollarise the economy speak directly to exhausted voters worn out by the complexities of buying basic groceries. Milei has his eye on a place in the 2023 presidential race and Buenos Aires appears to have eyes on him. — LE

10.

Taipei
The hidden Asian gem.

Taipei is a subtropical oasis teeming with stunning hiking trails and walkable city streets. It is known for its tantalising food stalls that are open 24 hours a day, with vendors slinging out cheap bowls of rice and noodles for early commuters or night owls.

With a low crime rate and a world-class healthcare system, the city is also surprisingly affordable, given its perks. The average monthly cost of renting a one-bedroom flat is about €750 and most neighbourhoods have their own feel, charm and wet market.

Taipei's public transport system is also an urban designer's dream. There are more than 1,000 bike-share stations, which amount to about one station every 150 metres. Buses and trains are rarely late and the metro system continues to expand and grow, thanks to steady and far-sighted investment. Speaking of which, OMA's Taipei Performing Arts Center is finally opening too.

Nature nestles in rather nicely with the buildings. There are wild ferns hanging from the sides of many balconies and tens of thousands of trees in the city have QR codes attached, which passers-by can scan to look up their size and species. Just north of downtown Taipei is the lush Yangmingshan National Park, which is dotted with hot springs.

While borders are still closed, the government has announced its plan to slowly open up to visitors later this year. For now, residents are enjoying having the city to themselves. — CWE

Adopt: A right of way for people crossing the street. Despite improvements, it is still not always safe.

Drop: The antiquated banking system needs an upgrade. It should be easier to use for both locals and blow-ins.

Population: 2,646,000 (city), 6,700,000 (metropolitan area, including Taipei and New Taipei).

Newspapers: Four national newspapers and a local paper.

Number of museums: 46.

Waste recycled: 55 per cent.

Deeper roots
Helsinki

Citizens form a stronger bond with a city when they feel connected to both the built and natural environment. That's why urban planners have coined the term "place-making" to describe a more neighbourhood-focused approach to building better cities. Major initiatives often neglect simple things, like a well-placed park bench.

Helsinki-based Parkly manufactures durable wooden units that can be used as benches, street libraries or tree-planters, among many other things. "We want to offer people the tools to shape their neighbourhoods in a quick, experimental way," Päivi Raivio, the company's co-founder, tells MONOCLE. Raivio is a designer by training and her Swiss co-founder, Daniel Bumann, is a set designer. This has shaped the way that they view urban spaces. "They're like stages that are shaped by the people in them," says Raivio.

Helsinki's municipal government has used Parkly's furniture to shape some of the city's most visited public areas. Unlike those in central and southern Europe, Nordic cities such as Helsinki haven't always fostered outdoor socialising. The city has plenty of nature but it is often in strictly delineated places, like parks. "We want people to be able to plant an urban garden in their city block, instead of having to walk to a park,", says Raivio.

Helsinki has also invested in other initiatives to help residents to shape their environment. Community-organised events turn the city into an open-air restaurant, while the budgeting tool Omastadi encourages people to launch small urban planning projects, for which the city has allocated a budget of almost €10m. — PBU

Three cities on the up
Africa

Freetown
Sierra Leone
When Yvonne Aki-Sawyerr was elected mayor of Sierra Leone's capital in 2018, the former finance professional put environmental concerns at the top of her agenda. She has since appointed a chief heat officer, the first such post in Africa and one of the few globally along with Athens and Miami. Other initiatives from the visionary mayor include a huge tree-planting project and efforts to encourage sustainable tourism, as well as to tackle the legacy of Sierra Leone's civil war.

Dakar
Senegal
The Senegalese capital is home to Dak'Art, the continent's oldest art biennial, as well as new initiatives such as Black Rock. Founded by Nigerian-American artist Kehinde Wiley in 2019, the multidisciplinary residency brings together international artists, film-makers and writers to examine "what Africa means today". Residents can seek inspiration from within Black Rock's seafront compound, designed by Senegalese architect Abib Djenne and set amid the black volcanic rocks that give the programme its name.

Rabat
Morocco
In a capital city dotted with minarets, Rabat's As-Sounna mosque stands out. One of the largest in Morocco, it's a prime example of the country's "green mosque" programme. Launched in 2016, it aims to make thousands of state-owned mosques more sustainable. After As-Sounna was fitted with solar panels, its energy costs fell by more than 80 per cent. Greenpeace has named it one of the world's most environmentally friendly mosques. — MFI

II.

Munich
The dynamic alfresco city.

Munich has long enjoyed the idea of being "Italy's northernmost city". Its mix of sunshine, joviality and open-air attractions, ranging from beer gardens and Olympic sports grounds to a pristine Alpine river, all make for a well-run Bavarian version of *la dolce vita*.

The city's love of alfresco life was boosted during the pandemic restrictions. Munich allowed bars and restaurants to temporarily set up tables on pavements and car parks – a popular development that has become a permanent feature. Today, hundreds of restaurants and cafés make use of extra seating outdoors.

Similarly flexible solutions were found for a decommissioned concrete factory and a public pool that require renovation and have temporarily been transformed into colourful locations for basketball and beach-volleyball tournaments, flea markets, concerts and merrymaking.

Munich even mustered a reply to Hamburg's Elbphilharmonie. While that concert hall took more than 10 years and about €850m to build, Munich turned a former industrial site into a venue and cultural centre in 18 months, all for just €43m. Originally envisioned as a temporary replacement for Munich's main classical music venue while it is under renovation, the Isarphilharmonie concert hall has been so enthusiastically embraced that it is expected to stick around. And it has given a welcome boost to discussions about future urban development. — JSC

Adopt: The city should boost solar-panel installation on residential, industrial and public buildings – especially its own.

Drop: Instead of spending €1bn on a tunnel connecting BMW's research centre to the motorway, the city should expand infrastructure for green modes of transport.

Population: 1,574,110 (city), 1,923,795 (Munich district).

Sports clubs: 673.

Homes expected to be served by new geothermal power station: 80,000.

Public outdoor pools: Seven.

I2.

Seoul
The resilient all-night capital.

After 566 days, Seoul lifted its outdoor mask mandate in May but many still don them. Though businesses are taking stock and tourism has yet to return, most restaurants, cafés and museums are bustling. Seoul is looking more like its old self. Curfews were eliminated in April, which means that clubs, bars and karaoke spots are fun once more. It's easy to find 24/7 restaurants and shops; public transport is cheap and accessible; and taxis roam the streets all night.

It's hard to say how the city will fare in the near future. Seoul has mostly kept infection numbers low since coronavirus emerged but the Omicron variant created a surge that has never felt fully under control.

Life in Seoul comes with long working hours, with people putting in 200 more hours a year on average than toilers elsewhere in the OECD. On weekends many flock to nearby mountains and streams, including the Cheonggyecheon restoration project, where fish swim in the shadow of skyscrapers. Seoul is adding more greenery: the newly renovated Gwanghwamun Square will soon reopen, while a former US military base will be transformed into a big park in the next few years.

President Yoon Suk-yeol has vowed to provide more assistance to citizens by easing finance rules and expanding housing projects to address the property crisis. Despite the hardships, the city has remained resilient, blooming this spring with verve and grit. — HK

Adopt: There are nearly 1,000km of bicycle lanes but more won't hurt.

Drop: Seoul's government is lukewarm on LGBTQ rights. The conservative mayor doesn't support the cause.

Population: 9,736,027 (city), 25,925,799 (metropolitan area).

Main airport serves: 129 destinations in 48 countries.

Hours of sunshine a year: 2,428.

Number of houses the mayor is pledging to add a year: 38,000.

State education free until: 18.

Berlin
The reliably buzzing wonderland.

Amsterdam
The city of contradictions.

Madrid
The fearless high-flier.

Franziska Giffey is not only Berlin's first female mayor but also the first East German to hold the top municipality since the fall of the wall. Berliners are keen to see what she and her Green-Left coalition will do beyond guiding the city past the pandemic and the effects of the war in Ukraine. Berlin received as many as 10,000 refugees a day in the early weeks of the invasion. Despite the influx, things have gone more smoothly than past refugee crises.

Berlin is breathing easier: poring over coronavirus statistics feels passé when clubs are open, workplaces are buzzing and masks are mostly off (except on public transport). Tourists are back, arriving in Berlin's newish Brandenburg airport and filling the hotels and restaurants that made it through the lean years. In the arts, two major museums (Haus der Kulturen der Welt and Gropius Bau) will have new directors starting next year. A new art museum by architects Herzog & de Meuron is under construction too.

Tesla has opened its Gigafactory near Berlin. The former site of Tegel airport is amid an ambitious revamp which will create 5,000 new homes, a university campus and space for 1,000 businesses, all aiming for net-zero energy use – sustainability is now one of the city's top aims. Much is changing and one of Giffey's challenges is to look after the city's long-term interests. For now, Berliners are soaking up the sun. — KAB

Amsterdam shouldn't work as well as it does. Much of it is below sea level and its cycling success continues despite the combined dangers of loose cobbles, tram tracks and steep-sided canals – not to mention stoned tourists who don't look where they're going.

Thank heavens that Amsterdamers are an easy-going and circumspect crowd, eh? There's a rejig of cycle lanes under way, as well as efforts to calm the traffic and some much-needed canal maintenance, but more affordable housing is needed. Attempts to improve connections with the Noord area, across the Ij river, would help by reducing the commute for many and provide space for the city to grow.

Amsterdam is also at last dealing with the seedy stag-dos that once blighted its streets. The plan is to confine its legal but licentious activities to select parts of the city centre. This and the pandemic-related hiatus on visitors have helped neighbourhood restaurants and shops to thrive.

In terms of business, Amsterdam is an attractive place. While a trickle of UK businesses moved here after Brexit, the city needs to do more to sell itself as a place of opportunity. You only need to wander around the 17th-century canals amid the wonky gabled houses and spot smiling neighbours clinking glasses on their stoop at 16.00 to know that you're not in nose-to-the-grindstone London or Paris territory. The city also has a global gateway through Schiphol and swift rail links. Getting away for the weekend has never been easier. — JAF

Perhaps it's all the sunshine – 2,691 hours a year, almost double that of London – but Madrid's future is looking rather bright. Its touchy-feely side was shelved during the pandemic but kissing, hugging and hand-holding have slowly returned and helped the city become its welcoming self again.

The Spanish capital has been dubbed many things – cheerful, resilient, even raucous – but it has never felt this fearless. New openings are bolstering the confident mood, from opulent new hotels to department stores and theatres. Buoyed by some of Europe's least restrictive lockdown measures, the restaurant sector got a head start on hospitality and groups headed by celebrated chefs have taken seats at the table.

Construction has also started on Europe's biggest housing development to date, Madrid Nuevo Norte, set to provide more than 10,500 new homes (and much-needed social housing) in a district the size of 470 football pitches. The central area around Sol is finally getting a facelift, spurred by the Canalejas retail and hotel development. The Plaza de España took its time to open but the project is a game changer – and it will be even better once those weedy trees grow tall and links are forged to adjacent parks, plazas and the river. That said, the archaic small-business licensing regime is a barrier to entrepreneurs. For a city so bullish about the future, those with bold ideas shouldn't be afraid to flap their wings. — LA

Adopt: Car-free zones in favour of more cycling and permanently lower costs for public transport (the new monthly €9 train pass is a start).

Drop: Red tape. From immigration to driver's licences, the bottlenecks slow down or halt good ideas from becoming reality.

Population: 3,645,000 (city), 6,004,857 (metropolitan area).

Proportion who are renters: 86 per cent.

Number of museums: 170.

Cost of monthly travel card: €107.

Bikes stolen a year: 30,000.

Adopt: A campaign to tempt talent and new businesses to the city from abroad.

Drop: The stoners and stag-dos.

Population: 862,987 (city), 2,480,000 (metropolitan area).

Average number of working hours a week: 34.

Restaurants opened in the past year: 25.

International destinations served by the airport: 327.

Hours of sunshine a year: 1,662.

Adopt: More city-centre greenery. Let shops have pots.

Drop: The annual public-art show 'Las Meninas'. It cheapens the streetscape.

Population: 3,286,662 (city), 6,714,000 (metropolitan area).

Cost of a month travel card: €54.60.

Number of newspapers: 19.

Number of museums: 44.

Number of public parks: 40 that are more than 33 million sq m.

Number of trees: 248,000.

16.

Auckland
The liberated metropolis.

New Zealand's largest city has been in a deep freeze for two years of lockdowns and restrictions but it's finally getting back to business. The borders are reopening, which is handy because tourism was the country's biggest revenue generator before the pandemic. Many of Auckland's retail and hospitality businesses have survived the thaw, helped by government grants, wage subsidies and targeted help. While agriculture and technology have been useful and haven't suffered much from Auckland's isolation, attracting people back for work and play needs to be the city's top priority.

There's more foot traffic in the Beaumont Quarter, with its alfresco restaurants and fun public spaces. By the harbour, the NZ$1bn (€610m) Commercial Bay redevelopment, which opened after the country's first lockdown, is attracting crowds at last. With busy shopfronts and plenty of greenery, it reflects Auckland's forward-thinking policy of combining businesses and public space.

House prices remain quite high but dropped to a median price of NZ$1,141,000 (€690,000) in April. Thousands of new builds are springing up on the city's fringes, supported by road and infrastructure projects. To unclog motorways, it's full steam ahead on the NZ$4.4bn (€2.6bn) underground City Rail Link.

Meanwhile, Auckland's culture scene has re-emerged with plays, gigs, exhibitions and festivals. Visitors are very welcome, by the way. — SLA

Adopt: A congestion tax for drivers entering central Auckland at peak times.

Drop: Allowing cars into the CBD on and around Queen Street and instead create an appealing and useful pedestrianised area where people will enjoy spending time.

Population: 417,910 (city), 1,720,000 (metropolitan area).

Houses built in 2021: 20,500.

Trees in the city: 440,000.

Number of destinations served by Auckland airport: 57 in 21 countries.

17.

Paris
The global cultural centre.

Paris is back on form and the terraces, parks and banks of the Seine are buzzing with people – often reuniting over a bottle of wine. The French capital is still *the* place to be for culture, whether you're interested in fashion, retail, craft, theatre, TV or exhibitions. An evening of world-class dance or a life-drawing class is only ever a Métro ride away, as are countless independent bookshops and more than 400 cinema screens. For those who prefer to drink and dine outside, there are thousands of *terrasses* at which to sit and watch the world go by. And when it comes to places to stay, new openings abound, from Cheval Blanc and Soho House to Château Voltaire and Hôtel Madame Rêve.

In addition to being fairly walkable, Paris has emerged from the pandemic as a more bike-friendly place. The authorities recently unveiled rather vaguely worded plans to make it "100 per cent cyclable". In practical terms, that means adding a further 180km of bike lanes by 2026, bringing the total to about 1,200 km.

On the horizon are the 2024 Olympics, the biggest event ever organised in France. In addition to bringing in the world's best athletes, the Games will leave a mark on the urban landscape, from an expansion of the Métro to a green facelift for the Champs-Élysées. Apartments in Paris are relatively small and expensive but with so much going on outside and the sun shining, many are more than happy to compromise. — ABC

Adopt: More green spaces. The Champs-Élysées is a good start but there are communities and areas that need it more.

Drop: Cars in the city centre.

Population: 2,161,000 (city), 11,142,000 (metropolitan area).

Commuters who cycle to work: 5 per cent.

Number of destinations that Charles de Gaulle airport serves: 272 in 113 countries.

Number of hospitals: 19, with a ratio of almost 400 physicians per 100,000 people.

18.

Barcelona
The coveted coastal paradise.

Barcelona arguably became *too* attractive to tourists, new businesses and blow-ins before the pandemic. Back then it was pulling in some 12 million visitors a year, which was overwhelming the population of about 1.6 million, creating transport snarl-ups and pricing long-term residents out of desirable neighbourhoods.

Getting back to normal is therefore bittersweet. The influx of cash is welcome but the silver lining of the past two years was that Barcelonans reclaimed their streets and liked it. All eyes are now on mayor Ada Colau to see if the activist-turned-politician can balance the city's tourist pull with the pleasure of living in a calmer Catalan capital. She has already introduced some of the world's tightest Airbnb restrictions and plans to invest €16m to buy empty commercial spaces and fill them with shops and businesses catering to residents.

Colau is also focusing on tactical urbanism, intended to yield practical ways of using public space and getting people around. The best example is her *superille* (superblock) initiative: restricting traffic and pedestrianising swaths of city streets and furnishing them with tables, chairs and playground equipment. While this looks good on paper, you'll often hear Barcelonans complaining that it has concentrated traffic in different areas. So it's lucky that Colau has doubled the city's bike network during her time as mayor. It's never been easier to pedal down to the beach for a sunset *cervesa*. — HU

Adopt: A contactless payment system on public transport would convince more people to use it.

Drop: Spain's *autónomo* (freelance) tax makes it difficult to be self-employed.

Population: 1,621,000 (city), 5,658,472 (metropolitan area).

Number of new restaurants opened in the past year: 104

Chain test: 18 branches of Starbucks.

Electric-car charging points: More than 500.

Beaches: 4.5km within the city.

Melbourne
The growing hub of creativity.

Kyoto
The old city with a bright future.

Milan
The city on the cusp of greatness.

No conversation about the Victorian capital can skirt the lockdowns that kept Melburnians isolated longer than any other city in the world. It also led to widespread business failures and to thousands leaving the city. But Melbourne is building back and its residents are looking to the attributes that made the city globally desirable before this dark chapter.

Melbourne remains progressive, artistic and cerebral; it values creativity and independence and is the place that took the fine coffee of its migrant Italian population and elevated it to an art form worthy of global export. There's good reason why coffee chains never dominated here. The city also offers world-class culture, an exciting food scene, great architecture, sport and space to roam.

But the real indicators of its quality of life are in its communities and facilities. Here you'll find that excellent parks, schools, hospitals and public transport make it a drawcard for migrants moving to Australia. But there's the rub: Melbourne is now the country's fastest-growing city and if the rate stays steady it will overtake Sydney's population by 2030. As such people are increasingly being forced to live in the outer suburbs, which currently lack much of what draws people to live in Melbourne in the first place.

Without swift development, the city could suffer the same fate as other desirable cities worldwide: a population cleaved into haves and have-nots, divided by their postcode. — AB

In the past two years, Kyoto seems to have hurtled back decades – in an appealing way. Border closures have affected everyone in Japan but not all places felt the pinch equally. Tokyo, with a population nearly seven times that of the ancient capital, remained busy and economically self-sustaining, despite a lack of tourists. Kyoto felt abandoned at times. Before the pandemic tourism was growing at an extraordinary pace; the number of places to stay nearly quadrupled between 2014 and 2019 and hospitality businesses were geared up to welcome some 53 million domestic and foreign tourists a year before those numbers tumbled, thanks to lockdowns.

Tourism has long been crucial to the city but the heavy foot traffic was already proving unsustainable for residents' quality of life. The battalions of taxis that once clogged traffic are gone for now and so too are the illegally parked bicycles and crowds that once beset this small city. Kyoto now has a chance to rethink its future. Its charm has always been its slower pace of life and connection to the Kamogawa river, a centre of civic and social life that many have rediscovered. The mountains in the distance offer a sense of the nature that can be enjoyed.

Meanwhile, cultural events such as the Kyotographie photography festival have reminded people that Kyoto is about more than old temples. The city should use this moment to find a healthier balance between economy and quality of life. — JT

Milan yearns to be considered one of Europe's great cities and it's improving at a fast clip. A star turn in June's flagship furniture fair bolstered the Lombard capital's cosmopolitan credentials, while showing off its retail scene and places to eat and drink.

Beyond the fleeting annual fashion and design exhibits, there's also a flurry of construction under way on municipal parks, as well as giant public-private initiatives ahead of the 2026 Winter Olympics. The metro is being extended and the new M4 line should ease connections to the already convenient Linate airport (the less said about the mega-hub of Malpensa, the better).

Mayor Beppe Sala was re-elected last year partly on a mandate to improve bike lanes and is looking at so-called "corridors", with some separate from traffic. It's a nice idea but cobbles, tram tracks and traffic can make cycling feel like an extreme sport here. Milanese are attached to their cars but new high-speed train stations and one of Europe's largest limited-traffic zones (for which the final cameras were installed in April) might help. Air quality, among the worst in western Europe, will be much improved if the scheme is successful.

Getting around is improving but getting away is easy too. You're never far from the Alps, lakes or seaside. Both international and provincial, Milan is thinking bigger than any other Italian city. It is on its way to greatness but it's not quite there yet. — EJS

Adopt: An ambitious plan to connect the suburbs to the city centre and each other.

Drop: The obsession with construction in the central business district. Focusing beyond it will have long-term benefits.

Population: 169,860 (city), 5,096,300 (metropolitan area).

Number of cinemas: 60 (413 screens).

Amount invested in infrastructure in 2022: AU$3.5bn (€2.3bn).

Number of libraries: 53.

Average ambulance response time: About 12 minutes.

Adopt: A proactive way to keep people from leaving – the population is falling.

Drop: Total reliance on tourism. A rich cultural city needs more.

Population: 1,444,649 (city), 2,546,189 (metropolitan area).

Unemployment: 2.5 per cent (prefecture).

Number of museums: About 200.

Independent bookshops: About 130.

Chain test: 38 branches of Starbucks.

Average ambulance response time: Seven minutes and 18 seconds.

Adopt: More measures to address air pollution and calm traffic.

Drop: The outdoor smoking ban – or enforce it. The response is muddled.

Population: 1,386,285 (city), 3,241,813 (metropolitan area).

Average hours of work a week: 38.8.

National newspapers: 13.

Number of design schools: 15.

International destinations served by city airports: 161.

Bike lanes: 300km.

22.

Fukuoka

The balanced Japanese city.

Self-isolation has made Fukuoka's charms shine more brightly. The city of over 1.6 million in southern Japan is a better place than most to seek an ideal mix of work and fun. Ohori Park is a draw for running or respite amid the trees, while for volleyball, stand-up paddle-boarding and windsurfing, there's Momochi Beach, just 20 minutes by bike from the city centre.

The food scene is among the best in Japan and, in terms of shops, there are plenty of independent fashion boutiques, furniture stores, quirky little bookshops and more to balance the international names. Most have survived the pandemic in good health.

Hakata station, Fukuoka's transport hub, connects the city with everywhere on and beyond Kyushu island, with a network of local lines and bullet trains. The international airport is five minutes away by metro from Hakata, which makes a business lunch in Tokyo (about two hours away by plane) a realistic option.

The cost of living is much lower than in the capital, which hasn't gone unnoticed by graduates and blow-ins. Fukuoka has hosted more new businesses than any other Japanese city for the past three years. It's also Japan's fastest-growing city. What the numbers can't fully explain is the sense of pride that comes from living here. Locals tend to be warm and friendly, community-minded and very open to newcomers – never a bad thing if you're starting a business or putting down roots. — JT

Adopt: More greenery. It has suffered as the city centre has expanded.

Drop: The ambition to compete with bigger cities. Fukuoka's strength is that it's not like them.

Population: 1,620,000.

Unemployment: 2.6 per cent (prefecture).

Bike-share scheme consists of: 2,600 bicycles used for an average of 320,000 monthly rides.

Hours of sunshine a year: 2,043.

Beaches: Nine in close proximity.

23.

POSITION IN 2019 **24**

24.

POSITION IN 2019 **25**

25.

POSITION LAST YEAR **19**

Oslo
The compact green giant.

Singapore
The outward-looking city-state.

Brisbane
The quiet high-achiever.

No Norwegian city had a longer lockdown than Oslo but it has made up for lost time. Some 70 new bars and restaurants have opened in the past 12 months and the city now has a growing street-food scene offering affordable, high-quality alternatives to the nice-but-expensive restaurants on offer.

Oslo remains one of Europe's fastest-growing cities and now an ambitious regeneration project of abandoned industrial port areas is nearly complete after 20 years. The resulting "Fjord City", a near-10km stretch of new urban spaces, has transformed the south-facing waterfront. Cultural giants including the Munch Museum and the new National Museum, the largest art exhibition space in the Nordics, are jostling for room among floating saunas, city beaches, about 9,000 new homes and 52 hectares of parks and urban spaces.

Next to the fjord, Oslo's other main asset is the forest, which can be reached by underground train in 15 minutes. It offers thousands of kilometres of paths for trekking in summer and cross-country skiing in winter, as well as organised activities such as zip-lining, skiing and horse riding.

The city has never felt greener, with a near-total electrification of public transport, while six in 10 private cars are now electric. A new carbon capture and storage system is also being developed to make Oslo's waste incinerator plant, which provides heating to a large portion of the city's houses, almost carbon neutral. — LB

Singapore was at the forefront of Asia's post-pandemic reopening. Today nightlife is back with unrestricted hours and people are thronging shopping centres, parks and riverside bars. Joo Chiat Road has blossomed into an independent retail and restaurant hub, flocked with natural wine bars, Japanese bakeries and fashion labels, signalling how government support has helped businesses to thrive. Food here remains affordable and top quality and the beaches, pools and sunshine are a draw, even if the advantages of the city's connectivity are somewhat wasted while swaths of Asia remain closed to travel.

As part of the Singapore Green Plan 2030, which includes targets for electric vehicles and sustainable agriculture, the government has increased the city's walking and bicycling network to 500km of paths, with a total of 1,300km expected by the end of the decade. The 24km Rail Corridor reopened last year and offers families and weekend walkers a nature trail that takes city slickers past restored bridges, forests and troupes of surprisingly placid macaques.

Singapore's expat population shrank as lockdowns and visa uncertainties sent foreigners packing. Many have returned and new arrivals seem eager to take their place. Singapore should be a shoo-in to capitalise on Hong Kong's talent exodus but stringent visa requirements are stopping the city-state from seizing the opportunity with both hands. — NXE

Australia's third city is subtropical Brisbane, a short flight north of Sydney in the state of Queensland. Brisbane is sunny with an ideal combination of easy-going Aussie lifestyle and plentiful job opportunities, industry and space, as well as relatively affordable housing compared to bigger cities – though more could be done in terms of social housing. Brisbane has few pressing problems but this year we found one: it is rather flood-prone. Earlier in 2022, large parts of the city suburbs were subject to torrential rain.

City authorities have swung into action, recognising the need for changes to planning laws and preventative measures to stop such crises from occuring in future. It's a practical recognition that issues involving climate-related weather anomalies are only likely to get worse.

Sydney and Melbourne have long bickered about which is the better or more exciting city – but Brisbane is the quiet achiever of Australia's eastern seaboard and scores high in our quality of life indicators. It's safe, has good schools, hospitals and transport connections, as well as a growing arts and culture scene. It's sunny for two thirds of the year and often above 20C even in winter. It has an enviable proximity to beaches and national parks, and has its own burgeoning restaurant and retail scene that has survived the pandemic largely intact. It would be splitting hairs to find elements of the city that don't meet the needs of those in search of a better quality of life. — AB

Adopt: A system for tidying the thousands of rentable electric scooters often abandoned on pavements and in parks.

Drop: The number of cruise ships docking in front of Oslo's Akershus Fortress. Cutting them would lop off 10 per cent of all harbour emissions too.

Population: 699,827 (city), 1,546,706 (metropolitan area).

Unemployment: 3.7 per cent.

Amount invested in public transport last year: €400m.

Newspapers: Eight (national), six (city).

Adopt: A faster system for dealing with the arrival of eager future residents.

Drop: Capital punishment and the stone-age stance on sexuality. Both are at odds with the city-state's otherwise fairly progressive inclinations.

Population: 5,685,800.

Proportion of nationals living in public housing: 80 per cent.

Homes built last year: 14,500.

Chain test: 130 branches of Starbucks.

Airport serves: 400 cities in more than 100 countries and territories.

Adopt: A better and more tasteful approach to new buildings. Ugly towers abound.

Drop: The strictness of rules and fines. Let a little common sense prevail.

Population: 2,582,000 (metropolitan area).

Number of trees: 454,000 (across the city and suburbs).

Public tennis courts: 61.

Capacity of Brisbane Live Arena, an entertainment venue to be built by 2024: 17,000.

NBA

ON THE ROAD

1

HEADS UP!

Balancing act
Basketball specialists are on hand to pass on their expertise – and show off their skills.

PLAY BY PLAY

Leading the way
NBA events give youngsters access to first-class coaching, just like the pros.

HIGHER LEARNING

GAME ON

LEADER BOARD

The National Basketball Association (NBA) is far more than a professional sports league. Today it's known internationally as an advocate for diversity, inclusion and camaraderie, a cultural juggernaut that proves that sport can enhance the way we live. Alongside the game itself, the association has taken its values of community-building, openness, innovation and integrity far and wide. To celebrate its achievements, Monocle is embarking on a series of editorial showcases with the NBA, highlighting its latest initiatives as well as the sport at its heart.

GAME CHANGERS

The NBA will offer its action-packed brand of sport to the United Arab Emirates (UAE) in a multi-year tie-up with Abu Dhabi, which centres around annual mega-matches at the Etihad Arena, the Middle East's largest indoor entertainment venue. In May the NBA announced that it will bring 2021 champions the Milwaukee Bucks and fellow Eastern Conference giants the Atlanta Hawks to the UAE's sunny capital in October. A huge coup for the region, the move will not only bolster an appreciation of basketball in the UAE but offer residents an opportunity to absorb the NBA's positive brand values.

Beyond the high-profile games, the NBA is operating at a grass-roots level and establishing a junior league, drawing in children from a diverse range of backgrounds. Teaching them about teamwork, determination, diversity and inclusion on the court, this programme, which has already been a success in other nations, is a fun, effective way for children to learn to better themselves through basketball.

Joining forces

DCT Abu Dhabi director-general, HE Saleh Mohamed Al Geziry (on left) and NBA Europe and Middle East managing director, Ralph Rivera

TIP OFF
The NBA and Abu Dhabi's Department of Culture and Tourism (DCT) announced the team's participating in the 2022 games at an event at Dubai's recent Arabian Travel Market. In attendance were a team of street ball entertainers and Atlanta's mascot, Harry the Hawk.

TEAM SPIRIT
The pre-season NBA match-ups on 6 and 8 October at The Etihad Arena will give Abu Dhabi's visitors and residents opportunities to witness some of the world's best basketball players in action. Both the Hawks and the Bucks have rosters packed with stars; Milwaukee's Giannis Antetokounmpo and Atlanta's Trae Young, who led the NBA this year in both points scored and assists made, will be among the key draws.

KIDS ARE ALRIGHT
Earlier this year, the NBA and Abu Dhabi's DCT launched the first Jr. NBA Abu Dhabi League, which gives 450 boys and girls between the ages of 11 and 14 the chance to develop skills with mentoring from pros. The initiative, with events featuring appearances by former NBA superstars, is expected to expand further in the region.

GLOBAL REACH
The NBA's move into Abu Dhabi is just one of many initiatives that it has launched to foster basketball culture in cities around the world. The brand also enjoys strong organic growth internationally due to the accessibility of the sport and the NBA's cultural allure. The result? About a quarter of NBA pros have international backgrounds and the sport is enjoyed in almost every corner of the world.

The NBA has worked hard for its global success. Its leadership is well aware that less than 1 per cent of NBA fans will actually watch a game at an arena. To the majority of fans who won't, the NBA promotes itself through both a comprehensive broadcasting and communications strategy, and a determined push to encourage people of all backgrounds, all over the globe, to play the game.

For decades the NBA has operated camps and academies in various countries, collaborated with international leagues and pioneered community-focused initiatives in developing nations. For example, the success of the NBA's Basketball Without Borders programme in Africa, which provided education and training to young people, led to the establishment of the professional Basketball Africa League in 2020.

HOOP DREAMS

HIGH FLIERS

The NBA and Abu Dhabi DCT's Jr. NBA Abu Dhabi League saw hundreds of boys and girls take to the court to put into practice the tricks of the trade picked up from professional mentors, including four-time NBA champion Tony Parker (*pictured*). From shooting technique to the virtues of playing as a team, the initiative teaches skills that can be used in all walks of life.

Pursuits of happiness
Global

Whether it's walking, drawing or playing tennis (badly), six writers and artists share their thoughts on the things that bring them joy.

ILLUSTRATOR
Motiejus Vaura

1 Quick on the draw
Culture

WRITER
Shantell Martin (as told to Sonia Zhuravlyova)

Known for her stream-of-consciousness line-drawings, US-based British artist Shantell Martin shares the power and pure joy of creating.

I encourage everyone to pick up a pen and just draw. You don't have to be an artist. That mechanism of connecting your head to your heart to your hand is so powerful. There's a reason that we all draw as children. We're given this gift that allows us to calibrate ourselves to the world. But along the way, perhaps by design or just through bad luck, it is trained out of us by society.

I never knew that being an artist was a career option so I studied graphic design because at least I would be in the creative space. When I graduated I went to Japan. I wanted to be in a place that was completely unfamiliar. I found a job teaching English and didn't draw for a while; I pushed it away but it came back to me.

A friend who organised avant garde concerts asked whether I would like do some of my drawing on an overhead projector when one of the bands was playing. That experience changed my life because it was the first time that I found peace within myself. While drawing live, I switched off and it gave me complete focus in the moment. Initially I froze but then I just started drawing. Then, 45 minutes later, I lifted my head and saw that the show had finished. I looked down and there was this magical drawing. "Wow," I thought. "That's me. I did that."

After that it was about finding technical clarity, wanting that line to be as crisp and perfect as possible. In Japan there is a craft-based culture focused on attaining mastery over a lifetime, which I absorbed. Drawing for a live audience was about being present and creating an experience. That gave me a foundation of who I am as an artist and accelerated my career.

We all have a style within us, a creative fingerprint, and I've been able to extract that through the process of live drawing. You could say that it's a kind of performance. What's wonderful about it is that it doesn't give you *time* to be anyone else. You can only be yourself. So it's the most honest way to find your style – you don't consider what someone else might do.

For every new work or show, I think about what I want to say. I'm always asking questions. I want to put a wish, hope or an intention out with my work. For example, for my latest show at Subliminal Projects in Los Angeles, I spent weeks just thinking and writing a 27-point manifesto about the future of art, then created a show around that.

I also use words. But words are made up of lines too; it's just that we give them more power or they come with more baggage. I'm a very proud dyslexic. As an artist I have creative freedom to make all of these lines and also the freedom to create words as I hear them. I see this as a superpower, a way of seeing things from a different perspective. But words have a power over us. I use them to pull people into the drawing because I rarely use colour.

When I create a show or an installation, although the scale might be big there's nothing in there that you couldn't do yourself. All of the tools and the media that I've used are accessible. I love showing that a simple line can be so powerful that you can use it to create installations that are larger than life.

Creativity is finding yourself in environments and situations where you can forget about time. When that happens you put yourself in the moment. You can have honest actions and reactions. It's the freedom to know that you can create when you want, where you want, how you want, without any judgement, assumptions or pressure. It's also about the experience of making a mark and seeing what it looks like. And when I say "mark", that doesn't have to mean a physical mark. It could be cooking, dancing or moving your body – whatever sort of creative expression that works for you. So do it. Make your mark. — Ⓜ

About the writer: British visual artist Martin grew up in southeast London and attended Camberwell College of Arts and Central Saint Martins. Today she divides her time between New York and Los Angeles, where she has worked on everything from live drawing installations to designing and choreographing a ballet.

Walking the walk
Travel

WRITER
Annabel Streets

Author Annabel Streets explores what makes cities a pleasure to perambulate and how to get the most out of your stroll.

Most people decide to visit a city based on what they might see and do there. Not me. Because of my personal and professional interest in seeing things on two legs I seek out walkable cities. In my decades of pounding the pavements in hundreds of cities around the world, something struck me: the ones that properly revive me are those around which I can easily and pleasurably walk.

Strangely, these aren't always the places that are lauded in studies or rankings of the world's most walkable cities. So I put one foot in front of the other to find out a little more. Like many of us I have a sedentary job so a break means getting moving – no lying by a pool for me. I also want the chance to see, hear, smell and taste new things. A walkable city should provide a sense of escape and novelty while you're on foot. I want to stroll from market to museum to monument, while eyeing up beguiling buildings and flamboyant fashionistas along the way. Herein lies the problem: many cities deemed walkable aren't *pleasurably* walkable.

Paris, Venice and Athens, for example, regularly top the league of Europe's most easily strollable cities. Their attractions are in close proximity and their pavements are generous in size. Yet these are among the most polluted places in Europe. Time spent inhaling exhaust emissions (*vaporetto* fumes in Venice), accompanied by the screech of motorbikes, does little for our health or mood. A study published last year described air pollution as a bigger killer than Aids, HIV, tuberculosis and malaria combined, not to mention being more deleterious to public health than smoking or war. The last time I visited Paris, which was once my favourite city, I felt as though I was inhaling diesel and vowed never to return.

But if you must hit the bucket list of big-city locations, don't despair because I have a few tips. Air pollution and traffic noise fall at certain times of the day and in certain weather conditions. The best time to walk larger, polluted cities is in the rain, which disperses harmful emissions,

muffles noise and reduces the crowds – just remember to take an umbrella. Wind is similarly effective at cleaning the air, so breezy days are good for a city ramble. Try to walk when traffic is at its least busy: avoid rush hour or opt for early mornings or evenings. Even better, take an old-fashioned map and plot out routes that avoid arterial roads or download one of the newer mapping apps, such as Go Jauntly, which can plot green routes that are less polluted and frequently more interesting. If you still can't avoid traffic-clogged routes, walk at the furthest edge of the pavement and breath through your nose – our nasal cavities contain a remarkable air-filtration system.

Instead of big, blockbuster cities, I now prefer to walk in smaller, quieter cities with cleaner air. So I'd rank Salamanca over Barcelona, Toulouse over Paris, Tallinn over Kraków, for example. But my real favourites are the handful of cities that have banned traffic altogether from their centres, such as Dubrovnik and Ghent. I have a hunch that

"I want to stroll from market to museum to monument, while eyeing up beguiling buildings and flamboyant fashionistas along the way. Herein lies the problem: many cities deemed walkable aren't *pleasurably* walkable"

we'll see many more of these in the coming decade. I also like larger cities with extensive pedestrianised areas, such as Munich, Stockholm and Oslo. Nordic cities have among the cleanest urban air.

Alongside uncrowded pavements and traffic-free zones, a joyfully walkable city also needs plenty of green, open spaces, which is one of the reasons why London routinely appears in the top five of the world's most walkable cities. But it's not just bounteous greenery that makes a city enjoyable for pedestrians. Cities with plentiful water, be it a coast, canals or a river, often overflow with walking opportunities. Some of my favourite places have miles of beautifully reclaimed river frontage designed solely for walkers: think Brisbane and Bordeaux.

Good public transport is perhaps paradoxically vital for a properly walkable city as it enables pedestrians to take short cuts or carry home their shopping. It also allows those living or staying outside the city to visit without their wheels. Even the old-fashioned idea of a network of trams, which produces significantly less air pollution than cars, is coming back into fashion. As I write, I'm just back from a working visit to Sydney, where the original tram system was ripped out in the 1960s to make way for cars but is now being reinstalled. On this trip I used the tram when I wanted to discover walking routes that were often further afield. A study carried out during the pandemic found that walkers who sought out diverse routes reported feeling happier than those who trundled along the same well-walked paths. A change of scenery is often all it takes to shift our perspective and our mood. — Ⓜ

> **About the writer:** Streets is the author of *52 Ways to Walk*, published by Bloomsbury, and *Windswept: Why Women Walk* (under the name Annabel Abbs), published by Two Roads.

③ Great expectation
Science

WRITER
David Robson

Author David Robson holds forth on the psychology of expectation and how small changes in the way we think can help create a brighter future.

Whether you want to lose weight, get stacked, write a novel or learn to play a musical instrument, almost all positive life changes ultimately come down to willpower. Do you have the self-control and focus to stick to your goals? Will you avoid the temptations that will lead you astray?

You might know some rather irritating people who can truthfully answer this with a resounding "yes". These are the folks who seem to be able to effortlessly achieve whatever they turn their mind to. For others, the temptations of junk food, phone-scrolling or trash TV seem too great and so their goals fall by the wayside. These decisions aren't trivial either: scientists estimate that up to 40 per cent of premature deaths can be attributed to lifestyle decisions stemming from low self-control (a fatty feast here, another drink or cigarette there).

It might be comforting to assume that these differences are hardwired into our brains. Some people just have better will-power than others. Research, however, suggests another alternative: that our willpower is shaped by our beliefs, which in turn are learned from people around us. Our ideas can become a self-fulfilling prophecy. They determine how easily we lose mental focus or give in to temptation. And by changing their ideas, anyone can improve their self-control.

These findings build on emerging evidence that "expectation effects" can transform our lives. The most famous is the placebo response, in which our belief in a medicine's effectiveness can actually increase its benefits.

So are you ready for an experiment? First let's establish how you frame challenges. Do you feel that as challenging situations accumulate, it gets more and more difficult to resist the temptations? Do you feel the need to refuel with snacks or TV or a treat after something strenuous? Do you need time to recover your mental energy after strenuous mental activity? If so, you have what psychologists, including Veronika Job at the University of Vienna, Austria, call a "limited" theory of willpower.

By contrast, people with a "non-limited" theory of willpower take another view. They might feel energised by strenuous mental activity and seek out new challenges (rather than chocolates) as a result. When they resist temptation they feel strengthened to withstand new ones. They are also more likely to believe that mental exertion helps build cerebral stamina so they can continue hard tasks for longer. These are the effortlessly purposeful people.

In laboratory studies, people with a limited willpower mindset tended to be more easily distracted after tasks requiring deep

> "For many people, a single setback can be taken as evidence that their willpower is weak. As a result, people abandon goals and give in wholeheartedly to vices, a phenomenon pleasingly known in psychological literature as the 'what-the-hell effect'."

concentration. Those with the non-limited willpower mindset remained focused for far longer. Indeed, in many situations, their willpower actually increased over time, like a muscle toned by repeated use. Their mental stamina becomes self-perpetuating.

The long-term consequences of these findings are profound. Whether they devote themselves to study, eating healthily or exercising, people with a non-limited mindset tend to be far better at sticking to their goals. Intriguingly, Job found that these differences are especially visible at times of stress, precisely when people are most likely to abandon their goals.

Our mindsets tend to be shaped by the people around us as well as our upbringing. One cross-cultural study by Krishna Savani at the Nanyang Technological University in Singapore found that, based on their performance in laboratory tests on focus and self-control, people in India are more likely to endorse the non-limited viewpoints than people in the US. Indian respondents tended to welcome challenges to their willpower and gave in less often than Americans.

Fortunately, and wherever we come from, our mindsets can be changed. Even reading about non-limited willpower was enough to shift some participants' beliefs. This very essay might have already given you a head start (you're welcome). Evidence also shows that finding a role model and reminding yourself of their iron will can galvanise your determination.

But we also need to rethink our attitudes to failure. For many, a single setback can be taken as evidence that their willpower is weak and they are doomed to repeat the stumble. As a result, we abandon our goals and give in wholeheartedly to vices, a phenomenon pleasingly known in psychological literature as the "what-the-hell effect". We need to avoid this all-or-nothing way of thinking and focus on the overall progress leading up to that point.

The past three years have yielded plenty of stress that was beyond our control but the latest neuroscience shows that we all have the power to change our habits for the better. The question is, what are you expecting? — Ⓜ

About the writer: Robson is a science writer and the author of *The Expectation Effect: How Your Mindset Can Change Your World*, published by Canongate in the UK and by Henry Holt in the US.

④ The big retreat
Leisure

WRITER
Petri Burtsoff

There is no better way to de-stress than to take yourself away from the distractions of daily life. Here's what the Finns do.

Long before "mindfulness", "going offline" and "switching off" became part of our language, the Finns had a simple antidote to the stress of city life. They leave and head to simple cottages in the countryside. In a country of five million people, there are more than 500,000 such cottages, almost all of them in the woods, beside a lake or by the seaside. Finns retreat to their cottages en masse during the summer holidays, often spending weeks living a simpler life, some voluntarily foregoing even the basic luxuries of electricity or running water.

The Finns aren't alone in retreating somewhere for the summer break either. Italians flock to the sea during the *ferragosto* holiday in mid-August and many inhabitants of the cooler corners of northern and western Europe make for the Med. Many Parisians are rarely seen in Paris in July and August. But, in my humble and highly partisan opinion, it doesn't compare to the benefits of disconnecting the Finnish way.

Research shows that recovering from work stress takes time and it only happens when your mind and body are removed from the cause of stress. The recovery can be hastened when you move to a place that's disconnected from work and where you can occupy your mind with something else (I suggest mushroom picking and skinny dipping).

Finnish cottage holidays aren't at all sedentary. Potatoes, onions, tomatoes and herbs need to be planted, tended and harvested. That wood for the lakeside sauna won't chop itself. Come to think of it, that picnic table could do with a quick sanding down and varnishing and woe betide the holidaymaker who falls behind on maintaining his or her fishing boat after the ravages of winter.

This might sound stressful to some readers but rest assured, when there's no one breathing down your neck, no deadlines to meet and no client to please, chores become leisurely pastimes that help you shift your focus. And that's really the key. When your brain focuses on a new activity you'll quickly feel a sense of disconnect from common concerns such as a bulging inbox.

But this isn't a self-help book, more a piece of shared wisdom. In my opinion there are no quick fixes to help you achieve meaningful and effective rest. That said, Finns have learned that disconnecting properly takes time – the idea of a measly week or two off every year, as is the standard in Japan or the US, sounds rather disagreeable to our ears. Summer houses prove that disconnecting is possible – even in the age of email – and it does not even have to mean switching your phone off.

After a few days of rusticity, surrounded by nature and living a simpler life, you'll find yourself forgetting where you left it. Or, with a little luck, the battery will die and you'll find yourself without the electricity to charge it. — Ⓜ

About the writer: MONOCLE's Helsinki correspondent Burtsoff has contributed countless reports to the magazine and Monocle 24 radio. After embedding with Nato's Cold Response forces in northern Norway recently we decided that he'd earnt a break.

Advantage set
Sport

WRITER
Michael Booth

Monocle's Copenhagen correspondent excels at many things but his lamentable tennis skills are something from which he draws both comfort and amusement. Even, that is, if he was beaten to the baseline by a 12-year-old girl.

One of my best friends is a life coach. I was visiting her in her life-coachy home in a converted bakery in the north of England recently when she asked me, "Michael, what makes you happy?" I suspect she was hoping for something like "seeing my family flourish", or "pushing beyond my comfort zone" or "my volunteer work". My response, however, was to focus on me. I've always thought that "comfort" is the best of all the zones and I don't do any volunteer work. So I found myself answering, "Hitting a tennis ball."

Not much for a life coach to work with there: an uncomplicated, almost brainless pursuit, something a labrador retriever might choose. But, for me, hitting a tennis ball is far from simple because I am completely shit at it. Whether playing in the garden as a child, loping around the municipal courts as a teenager or on the rare occasion when I've had chance to pick up a racket as an adult, my game has been lamentable.

But recently I began talking about joining the local club and playing again. There was scepticism from some members of my family because of my perceived decrepitude and lack of fitness but, for some reason, my wife had faith and for my 50th birthday she booked a week of intensive training at a club in Mallorca as a gift.

We were a mixed group of men and women, ranging from our early twenties to properly elderly. On the first morning, the scowling, leather-skinned Spanish ex-pros charged with

"Even someone of almost wilful physical ineptitude can shrug off the shackles of lifelong rubbishness and find joy in hitting a ball"

our instruction told us to warm up by jogging around the court so they might also assess our fitness and place us in the various ability groups.

It turns out I excel at gently shuffle-jogging around a tennis court because I was put in a group of men in their early thirties, all of whom had that lean, mean look of club tournament players. I knew even before we started that I would be hopelessly out of my depth but a tiny voice in my head told me to go with the flow. What if I wasn't actually that pitiful after all?

We were told to start knocking the ball to one another. And I was as atrocious as I'd ever been. It took the instructor less than 20 seconds to realise his error and direct me to a far court, where I was told to start hitting with a Spanish man, Olivier, who I later discovered was 72. (He was good but I destroyed him with the drop shots.)

At one point during my third day my instructor, visibly agitated with my slow progress, invited a 12-year-old girl onto the court to demonstrate where I was going wrong with my backhand. She was amazing. A champion in her age group, apparently. He didn't do it to humiliate me; it was just an effective way to show me a great backhand. Still, a 12-year-old girl.

But you know what? I absolutely loved my Balearic boot camp. I loved the potential energy of that ball in my hand, the eternal hope in defiance of all the evidence that I wouldn't shank it to the moon or once again plop it straight into the net. I loved the gratifying "thwock" when it hit the sweet spot. And is there anything more exhilarating than executing a proper top-spin backhand, concluding with your arms spread, head turned to the left as the ball describes a sleek parabola into the opposite corner?

I managed it for the first time ever on the third day. Slowly, I was becoming slightly less rubbish. The instructors introduced tiny adjustments to my swing, my positioning, my grip, which had a transformative effect. I found that it was possible to change, to improve.

This was a revelation to me. If you are prepared to open yourself to new ideas, to sacrifice some dignity and learn from 12-year-old girls, even someone of almost wilful physical ineptitude can shrug off the shackles of lifelong rubbishness and find joy in something as simple as hitting a tennis ball. Turns out it wasn't a life coach I needed. — Ⓜ

About the writer: Booth is an award-winning, best-selling author of seven non-fiction books. He is MONOCLE's Denmark correspondent, and contributes to numerous newspapers and magazines.

6 Just for the joy of it
Keyif

WRITER
Hannah Lucinda Smith

What can Istanbul's cats and that eccentric gentleman with his feet in the Bosphorus teach us about taking time to enjoy urban life? Hannah Lucinda Smith decodes the ancient Ottoman art of 'keyif'.

When was the last time you did something simply for the joy of it? Not to learn anything new, nor develop a skill, not for the likes on social media but just for the delectation of the moment and pursuit of sublime sensations washing over you? I would wager it has been a while. If so, you need to get acquainted with the concept of *keyif*.

The word translates from Turkish as "pleasure", but in practice it is much more than that. *Keyif* can be found in the feeling of the sea lapping around your toes as you smoke your hookah pipe, having dragged your deck chair and plastic table out to paddling depth. It can be found in an hours-long breakfast that meanders through courses of cheeses, eggs, jams and honey and keeps you full until dinner. It is there in the delight of rocking in a hammock, watching the clouds and listening to the cicadas. For a pastime to count as *keyif* it must involve minimum effort, maximum gratification and achieve nothing more than a pleasing state of mind.

Here in Istanbul, the Bosphorus is the main source of *keyif*. Sometimes it is enough to simply watch the waves

> "At some point, leisure became a commodity, a product to be sold rather than a lack of anything dull or pressing to do. We have managed to turn our time off work into yet more work"

from the deck of a passenger ferry on a sunny day or from the window of a top floor apartment in a storm. If the weather is clement, find a spot on one of the city's corniches, park a camping chair and simply stare out into the water. Find one of Istanbul's public beaches and dive in if you're feeling more daring or, if you're lucky enough to have one, take your fishing boat out and simply bob around for a few hours to enjoy solitude in the middle of a city of more than 15 million.

Walking aimlessly, hands clasped behind your back and brow knitted in contemplation, was a traditional Turkish way to find *keyif* but these days many of Istanbul's young men prefer to drive around in cars garlanded with Turkish

flags and alloys, pumping music through boom boxes at window-rattling levels. *Keyif* for them, maybe, but not for the rest of us. As a rule, though, this pursuit should be conducted at low speed and low volume. Nature, food, chatter and idleness: these are the key ingredients of *keyif*.

It is a shame that such a concept has come to be seen as alien, or even sacrilegious. At some point, leisure became a commodity, a product to be sold, rather than a lack of anything dull or pressing to do. And if something is to be sold, then it must have a value: it has to promise to improve you in some way. Sports to make you live longer, travel to broaden your mind, creative hobbies to make you more interesting and marketable; we have managed to turn our

time off work into yet more work. Pleasingly, *keyif* offers none of this. It will not give you a killer body, nor things to brag about to your friends. There is nothing to make you fitter, better, faster or stronger. And that's OK too.

Another rule for recognising the concept is that if something calls itself *keyif*, then it is probably not. In

Turkey, you'll find countless restaurants and cafés of this name, and most of them will be stressful and over-priced. The concept is far too nebulous to be utilised like that. Even Turks can't fully explain it, nor very often tell you whether an experience can be classed as *keyif* or not. Only you can decide that and only in the moment that it is happening. It might be found as you sip from a cheap flute of tea on a plastic stool in a pavement café or as you observe the beautiful people going about their day in an upmarket neighbourhood. There is no set price range for *keyif*.

Neither is it something that can be captured and shared. Your *keyif* location is probably photogenic but the spell will be broken as soon as you even consider taking a picture. If you are thinking of the future, of how your photograph will turn out and how much attention it might garner, then what you are experiencing is no longer *keyif*. You have allowed the banality of your ego to sneak in and break your connection with the moment. Stop. Switch your phone off along with your brain and try turning yourself into a sensory receptacle – a human being – rather than a content creator.

For inspiration look to the street cats, Istanbul's real masters of *keyif*. Note the expressions on their faces as they stretch out in the sun, snoozing as everyone else hurries around them. Watch how they ascend to ecstasy as a passerby stops to tickle their ears. Then see how they immediately disappear as soon as someone whips a camera phone out. Cats do not care about life hacking. They are not bothered about how many times their photo is liked and shared (although that will probably be more than any photos of you). They don't even care about being liked in real life. Their existence is dedicated almost entirely to the pursuit of sensory pleasure and the joy of lazing.

Holidays are the perfect time to explore the concept of *keyif*. If going to a beauty spot and posing for endless photos or doing extreme sports really pleases your soul, then congratulations: you have found your path to *keyif*. But before you start, take a moment to ask yourself where the pleasure really lies.

Is it in the moment of doing those things or is it in the anticipation of what benefits they will bring you? If it's the latter, then you might need to keep searching. Because most of us, whether or not we would ever admit it, are happiest when we are doing not very much at all. — Ⓜ

About the writer: Smith is a journalist who has lived in Turkey for the past decade, reporting on everything from conflicts and coups to culture and street cats. She is also the author of *Erdogan Rising*, a biography of the Turkish president, and co-author of *Zarifa*, a memoir of Afghan women's rights activist Zarifa Ghafari.

7 Passage of time
History

WRITER
Joseph Pearson

Historian and author Joseph Pearson traces the history of the European summer holiday from Roman roads to Romantic rogues and today's knights in silicon armour on smartphones.

The summer holiday is a recent invention. More often in human history, voyagers have travelled long and far to find new shores and bounded along beaches in search of riches rather than for the sheer sunny joy of it. Well, mostly.

The closest antecedent of the modern beach break can be found among the ancient Roman holidaymakers – and it was the success of their cities that helped. With some 400,000km of road, a common gold currency to trade in and relative peace for 200 years, this enormous, prosperous empire allowed – perhaps for the first time – an untrammelled mobility for the purposes of hedonism for people of (almost) all classes.

This might mean nipping down to your beach villa on the Gulf of Naples to hobnob with the Caesars at Baiae, Campania. Those wealthy enough to head farther afield for a Greek beach vacation – say a tour of the Homeric lands – or an Egyptian Nile cruise would have been gone for much longer and paid much more than the package travellers of today. In fact, the "father of the guidebook", the early geographer Pausanias, developed and honed his skills in the 2nd century AD. That said, the fruit of his work, the first-ever tourist guide (to Greece, in Greek) was notorious even in its time for its misleading directions and digressions – sure proof of both the fact that the Ancients had much to learn about the art of tourism and that getting a guidebook right is hard work.

"Lord Byron's shacking up with a Venetian mistress, complete with pet fox and two monkeys, is just one example of the Romantic-era idea of the package holiday"

The fall of Rome in the 5th century AD led to the deterioration of the roads that had so reliably borne holidaymakers to their escapes. The summer holiday, in its Roman format, was put on ice for a millennium and a half. During the Middle Ages and the Renaissance, only the truly dedicated crossed the continent and swimming trunks and a towel were the last thing on these intrepid ramblers' minds. Purposeful voyages were undertaken by journeymen and artisans, religious pilgrims and, naturally, knights rescuing fair maidens. Some travelled to improve their health. Michel de Montaigne, for example, turned to horseback riding to forget his bouts of potentially fatal kidney stones, travelling as far as Italy in search of curative waters. That said, in a rather modern spirit of the holiday, Montaigne drank rather more wine than water. His 1580s travel journal memorably warns that his favourite tipple was "rather undrinkable in Florence and diluted in Rome". All roads, it seems, return here.

The most epic continental journey was the Grand Tour of the 17th to 19th centuries – a sprawling itinerary taking one to three years and not simply confined to a single summer. Wealthy young men were chaperoned through the Swiss lakes down to the crumbling ruins of Ancient Rome. The trip was, ostensibly, educational – an opportunity to dally with aristocrats, brush up on languages and "come of age". Lord Byron's shacking up with a Venetian mistress, complete with a pet fox and two monkeys, is just one example of the Romantic-era idea of the package holiday.

If the Romans both invented, then killed, the summer holiday, it took an enterprising British Baptist, teetotaller and cabinet-maker called Thomas Cook, to resuscitate something like it in 1841. His idea to herd 500 people to a railway excursion from Leicester to Loughborough (for a shilling each on the newly opened Midlands Counties Railway) inadvertently invented the world's first package tour. This was just the beginning. By 1855, Thomas Cook & Son offered a tour to Europe and, by 1872, the first round-the-world all-inclusive.

The British Industrial Revolution and the attendant railroads and steamships opened up transport in a way unknown since Roman times. Adventurers zipped overseas for novel, if not dangerous, purposes: swimming between continents (after Byron in the Dardanelles) or climbing the Matterhorn (the Londoner Edward Whymper). The first Alpine Club in the UK dates from 1857, just as Swiss railway engineers conquered the vertiginous mountain passes. French writer Marcel Proust, an insomniac, read the train timetables to put himself to sleep. Travel was in the collective consciousness. By 1906, with the opening of the Simplon tunnel, Paris to Venice on the Orient Express took less than a day. Swish.

Even as late as the 1970s, the countries boasting the most summer travellers were those that had industrialised first and grown wealthy from it (up to 80 per cent of Northern Europeans went on summer holiday, while only 25 per cent of Italians did). Meanwhile, from the 1970s, the rise of affordable air travel took over from the railroads, a path leading to the unimaginably cheap flights today.

The summer holiday is therefore a rather recent reinvention thanks to Cook and the railways. But could it also disappear, just as suddenly as with the destruction of the Roman Empire? Surging fuel prices and responses to the climate crisis could both be causes. And holidays could once again become less common and, sadly, less pleasurable, for another reason: now that our devices follow us everywhere, people are abandoning our cubicles to become remote workers. The machines they service and the work they do are no longer bolted to the factory floor. Rather, laptops and phones fit into our carry-on baggage. These knights in silicon armour stay away for longer – and for work. Ironically enough, the rise of the digital nomad, on a warming planet, could make us rethink the value of those long but purposeful journeys perfected in the Middle Ages. — Ⓜ

About the writer: Canada-born Pearson is a Berlin-based author and historian. His latest book, *My Grandfather's Knife*, is published by Harper Collins and The History Press. He also writes for the BBC, *Newsweek*, and the *New England Review*.

making places
iconic

Configure your
individual piece
of USM online!
usm.com

Meeting in the middle
Miami

Long the first stop for migrants coming into the US, Miami is now bursting at the seams with New Yorkers heading south for the city's sunshine, music and burgeoning technology scene.

WRITER
Christopher Lord

PHOTOGRAPHY
Alfonso Duran

1

What hits you first is the noise. Stepping out of a taxi in Wynwood on a Sunday evening (a Sunday!) your hair seems to flutter with the ruckus of bars competing to make their Cumbia music the loudest and the stretch monster trucks cruising by. Miami has always had a reputation as a party town, a place of ubiquitous hot pink where the 1980s never completely ended. Over the past two years, however, thousands of people have relocated to the city – in the year to July 2021, 260,000 more people arrived in Florida than left – and that has ratcheted the decibels up a notch.

Long a first port-of-call for people coming to the US from Latin America and the Caribbean, Miami's recent population surge has been led by Americans, many of them New Yorkers seeking a sunnier spot on the East Coast. Partly, it's because Florida never really shut down: Governor Ron DeSantis defiantly kept the state open for business throughout the pandemic. But what's happening in Miami is more than just a Zoom boom.

Isabella Acker, originally from Atlanta, runs a creative agency in Little Haiti and last year turned her office into a tiny recording studio, hosting impromptu candlelit performances by musicians from around the world, pairing them with Miami-based artists. "Now we have all these recordings we've collected and we're planning to turn them into physical records," says Acker, who launched her label, Tigre Den Recordings, in March. She compares the musical boom to when early underground Salsa recordings were pressed in 1960s New York. "Everyone thinks of Gloria Estefan but the real sound of Miami is Afro-Cuban funk. What we've found is that global music fuses so well with that. If you can make people dance in Miami, you're all set."

Crypto is also upping the city's tempo. The word is everywhere: on billboards, on the side

of gleaming new skyscrapers. Even the home stadium of the basketball team, Miami Heat, has been renamed FXT Arena after a cryptocurrency exchange. The mayor, Francis X Suarez, has said that he wants to refashion the city's "fun in the sun image" into a technology town and crypto hub. He even backed the creation of a "MiamiCoin", although the value has tanked in the past few months.

With crypto, Suarez tied his city's wagon to a skittish horse but it has had the desired effect: Florida added 2,715 new technology businesses last year, more than any other US state. "When Silicon Valley really was Silicon Valley, you wanted to be in the room and so you moved to Palo Alto," says Pablo Quiroga, who moved from Las Vegas in November. "Miami is that place now." His company Star Atlas has built a virtual universe where everything can be bought and sold on a blockchain; he talks dizzyingly about the millions of dollars of investment his company has attracted. Being in Miami kicked that into overdrive.

"I grew up in Orlando and Miami was always just a place for partying," he says. "I only came here initially for a bitcoin conference but I could taste the opportunity in the air: capital,

"I could taste the opportunity in the air: capital, technology, culture"

1. Miami's beaches are about 32km long
2. Cranes are a fixture on the city's skyline
3. Art deco dining at Krüs Kitchen

technology, culture." Quiroga says that it's the city's tropical beauty that brings him back to earth. "In crypto, everything moves in seconds, so it's healthy to step away and reconnect with nature," he says. "I live in Coconut Grove and every day I run up Old Cutler Road, beneath the banyan trees that line the street. In Miami the ocean is always a step away." He can't resist a techie metaphor: "It's nature on-demand."

Coconut Grove bears some of the construction-related marks of the new technology money that's washed into Biscayne Bay over the past couple of years but it's still a peaceful neighbourhood of cafés and strollable pavements shaded by palm fronds. Josh Hackler's Krüs Kitchen on Main is a new restaurant and mini-market selling products from Miami start-up producers – sesame butters, hand-milled granola and chocolate bars packed with toasted coconut. "I feel like the city has gone from being a teenage party animal and is now rolling into its mid twenties," says Hackler, who came to Miami in 2018. He sees the artisanal products on his shelves as a sign of how entrepreneurial the city has become. Hackler runs Krüs with

Pili Hackler and Colombian chef Sebastián Vargas in an art deco building where light pours in through a wall of glass blocks. Californians and Australians who have moved to the city are bolstering a healthy trade. Diners come for Vargas's signature coconut rice – a taste of home – and line-caught fish from the Jupiter inlet. "I don't necessarily look at this as a boomtime," says Hackler. "I just think more people are realising how interesting Miami actually is."

Sensing opportunity, Argentinian architects Leonardo Militello and Fernando Hitzig opened a satellite office in 2021. Their studio in Buenos Aires has earned awards for bar and restaurant designs, and in Miami they say there's a surfeit of work to be won.

"It's a place where people need to have fun," says Militello, noting that there's a shared culture, which can open doors with some developers. "We always say that Miami is not in the American south but is the north of Latin America; we understand each other in a way that only Latin Americans can."

Miami's image is not exactly changing, it's just that the city is revealing itself to more people. The arrival of Art Basel in 2002 was a watershed moment and today there's a rich gallery scene. Small, ambitious spaces are popping up in Jupiter; the artist studio complex Oolite Arts is planning a vast $30m (€28m) headquarters; and there's a new museum called Superblue dedicated to immersive installations. In 2010, Craig Robins founded the Design District, a high-end retail quarter with an enviable public sculpture collection.

When we meet, he's doing a re-hang in his own offices, debating whether a Cy Twombly or a young Miami artist should take pride of place in the foyer. "We've seen a much higher migration to the city in a short time and that has created a critical mass of business and technology coming from around America that has catapulted Miami into another category," says Robins. He's excited about all the new energy but adds that housing, schools and infrastructure will need to catch up. Indeed, rents are soaring: a recent survey by property site Realtor found that Miami rents will eat up 60 per cent of the typical household income.

Mitch Kaplan opened Books & Books 40 years ago. He grew up in South Beach when it was a rundown part of town, and remembers sailing catamarans to Fisher Island, which

today has the highest per capita income in the US. "If you look at the old postcards of the bathing beauties in South Beach, we're always about pumping ourselves up," says Kaplan, adding that the place has oscillated between boom and bust for much of his life. "But this idea of style over substance, I've discovered, is a myth. There are very solid people living here, I see them every day coming to the bookshop."

At the Coral Gables branch of Books & Books, Kaplan and his son Jonah are preparing the reading room for an evening talk by Douglas Stuart, a recent Booker Prize winner. "What troubles me is that the sizzle always gets all the attention when it comes to Miami," says Mitch, pointing to the confluence of literary luminaries from around the world who made their names in the city and now line his shelves. "You have an amazing community that's right here." — Ⓜ

1

2

City in the sun
The powder blue suits and pink velour tracksuits never entirely went away but life in Miami goes far beyond its reputation as an 1980s throwback. It's embedded in Latin American economies, has a rich art and dining scene, and there is money moving to the city every day. True, it has become far too expensive for its own good but people are willing to pay for a sun-drenched spot on a New York time zone.

3

4

5

BOOKS & BOOKS

6

Active Lifestyle in Vibrant Cities

Quality of Food means Quality of Life

People and Planet First

Fast, Flexible and Fossil Free

denmark.dk

Liveable Cities and Captivating Architecture

TIME & STYLE

Peter
Zumthor
collection

Time & Style

Milan
Via Eugenio Balzan, 4, Largo Claudio Treves, 2
Via San Marco, 13, 20121 Milan, Italy

Amsterdam
Marnixstraat 148, 1016 TE Amsterdam
the Netherlands

Tokyo
Tokyo Midtown Galleria 3F
9-7-4 Akasaka, Minato-ku, Tokyo 107-0052 Japan

Hokkaido – Factory
4-13-2 Kitamachi, Higashikawa-cho
Kamikawa-gun, Hokkaido 071-1426 Japan

www.timeandstyle.com

All Time & Style furniture and tableware are handcrafted in Japan

② AFFAIRS: Fantasy cities

Cities, slicker
Global

Neglected industrial parts of cities, from Rome to Istanbul, are in the throes of thrilling regeneration.

ILLUSTRATOR
Mikael Moune

Eternal life
Campo Urbano, Rome

Is it possible to create a truly mixed-use urban district that provides quality housing, offices, a hotel, an energy centre and plenty of retail, all on a difficult brownfield site near the centre of one of the world's most notoriously development-averse cities? Yes, according to the architects, developers, designers and other stakeholders that have put together the Campo Urbano proposal for a scruffy industrial site around Rome's Tuscolana railway station. C40, a respected global network of mayors, seems to agree.

"The Campo Urbano team were good on everything, across the board," says C40's director of urban planning and design, Hélène Chartier. So good, in fact, that in 2021 the

"Tuscolano has many of the ingredients to be a great neighbourhood"

project won C40's Reinventing Cities competition, an initiative to stimulate sustainable urban development.

So could Rome finally be waking up to its potential? Perhaps the most fundamental aspect of the Campo Urbano project is its site. Like countless other places in Rome, Tuscolano has many of the ingredients to be a great neighbourhood. It's close to both the centre and thriving outer hotspots, such as Pigneto, and has all the pleasant trappings of urban life in Italy. Indeed most streets here still teem with small shops, pizzerias and people. It is also (unusually for Rome) well served by rail and metro links. However, as lead architect Tommaso Franzolini says, walking past graffiti and a potholed carpark in front of the station, "It just feels like a bit of a no-man's-land." Franzolini is a member of London-based architecture and interior design studio Arney Fender Katsalidis which, together with Rome-based developers Fresia RE, lead the Campo Urbano consortium.

The problems that cause this kind of urban blight are many and solutions tend to be inherently complex, especially in Rome, where municipal mismanagement has let the city crumble for decades (*see Issue 124*). However, Franzolini and his impressively interdisciplinary team are aiming to bring together the public and private sectors.

Campo Urbano will be "a landmark decarbonised urban development for Rome", says Franzolini, making an undeniably credible pitch. "Most importantly it will be a catalyst to do things differently."

Embedded in C40's competition rules is the need to have the broadest possible group of stakeholders from the beginning. Franzolini and Fresia RE have gathered designers, developers and experts in the fields of sustainability, engineering and mobility, as well as future residents, to create an economic proposal that is both deliverable and desirable.

The land for the new and repurposed buildings, and parkland for recreation and biomass-energy production, will soon be purchased from Sistemi Urbani, the property arm of FSI, Italy's state-owned railway company, which possesses a vast and often unused portfolio of urban assets. This aspect of the proposal makes it particularly important on a national level. Just about every Italian city, large or small, contains masses of unused former railway land.

Urban regeneration – like London buses – can be slow to arrive. Then, as if from nowhere, it all comes along at once. With added incentive in the form of generous environmentally beneficial new construction and retrofit tax incentives, mainly funded by Next Generation EU, the bloc's pandemic recovery fund, the sector is feeling flush. "We have so many Italian projects being submitted," says Chartier at C40's offices in Paris. "Italy is going crazy for this kind of development." Indeed, of the 12 cities involved in the Reinventing Cities competition, a list that includes Montréal, Houston and São Paulo, four are in Italy – Bologna, Milan, Naples and Rome. That's more than any other country.

By using the tools that are part of the Reinventing Cities application process, Franzolini and the Campo Urbano team have created a proposal that certainly ticks many boxes. Moreover, unlike many regeneration projects in the Eternal City, where red tape often leads construction to stall or be cancelled, this new neighbourhood will benefit from C40's strict delivery monitoring system, meaning that a prize winner must be built as specified in the pitch.

When it opens, Campo Urbano will be one of the best-served, best-connected and greenest places (literally and metaphorically) to live and work in Italy. "Rome is ready," says Franzolini, as he looks out at a neighbourhood that is ripe for development. sweeping his arms outwards, towards the future. — DMP

Building better
With San Francisco, Rome and Istanbul all turning fantasy into reality, here are three other cities planning to make dreams come true.

Tokyo: The area around Tokyo's Shibuya station, a cultural and transport hub, is set to be transformed with several new mixed-use skyscrapers currently under construction, and a pedestrian walkway with smart shops and plenty of greenery.

Sydney: Travel to Australia's largest metropolis will be revolutionised when the long-awaited Western Sydney International Airport opens in 2026. The state government is planning on making the area around it a regional industrial hub called Aerotropolis.

Berlin: An industrial wasteland north of the city's central station is being turned into a new neighbourhood, dubbed Europacity. When complete, it will be home to thousands of homes, a new school and plenty of green spaces.

"This will be a new Rome landmark, and a catalyst to do things differently"

Power to the people
Gasworks, Istanbul

Last July a 19th-century Ottoman-era gasworks in the Hasanpasa neighbourhood in Istanbul's Kadikoy district was reborn as Müze Gazhane, a massive museum and community space. The city's switch to natural gas had left the plant, at one time the main supplier of electricity on the Asian side of Istanbul, sitting empty since its closure in 1993. It was set to be torn down and replaced with yet another shopping mall until a residents' group, the Gasworks Environment Volunteers, paired up with Istanbul Technical University to reclaim it. After a 20-year battle, restorations began in 2015 and today the former industrial site powers the city's imagination – if not its generators.

Sprawled across 32,000 sq m, the complex is bursting with modern Turkish delights. The circular buildings at the rear end of the compound have been adapted into stages for concerts and theatre, while another one hosts the Cartoon and Comics Museum. The former furnace tower hovers over the venue like an eagle's nest and contains an observation deck on its upper level. There are two libraries (one of which is open 24 hours a day), a study hall, bookshop and workshop, which is available to use free of charge.

"Kadikoy has a very young population and there aren't many public areas to go to," says

Sinan Caglar, who runs the space on behalf of the Istanbul municipal authority. "The avenue we are based on goes straight down to Sali Pazari district, which is filled with schools. Bogazici University dormitories are right across from us. This has become a lively area where young people can socialise, learn and study."

Elsewhere, a former warehouse has been converted into an art gallery, one of six such spaces dedicated to different disciplines. Currently on display is an exhibition, curated by Marcus Graf, of 85 Turkish painters from the municipality's collection. In September it will be used as one of the main venues for the Istanbul Biennial, the first such location on the Asian side of the city.

In front of the warehouse and adjacent to the main entrance in the piazza stands artist Kemal Tufan's statue, Soaring Towards the Blue, next to a former steel wagon. The cobalt-blue sculpture is one of seven in the vicinity, all commissioned by the municipality and all made from scraps of metal and rubbish found scattered across the shipyard in Halic.

As well as its sizeable cultural footprint, promoting climate awareness is also an important part of Müze Gazhane's role. The former gasworks boasts Turkey's first museum dedicated to climate change, a laboratory and an energy museum where visitors can learn about energy production through various interactive machines and modules. Fittingly, most of the

"This is a former industrial site that powers the city's imagination – if not its generators"

new materials used in its construction were either recycled or salvaged.

After Turkey ratified the Paris Agreement in October, Istanbul's mayor, Ekrem Imamoglu, presented the city's customised climate-action plan at the Gasworks Museum. The following day, demonstrations in support of Cop26 took place there. Environmental organisations such as Roots and Shoots Turkey, the Yuva Association and IKSV Alt Kat are using it for their workshops, conferences and events.

"Our intention is that this space becomes a hub for those working with climate change," says Caglar. "At this stage, it is a public service to promote climate literacy. Last year's sea snot that clogged up the Marmara sea shows how Istanbul is directly affected by climate change," adds Caglar, who is interrupted by the barking of a golden-haired street dog named Bal ("honey" in Turkish). "She has been here since 2015, it is her ground first," he says good-naturedly.

He points out the location of a soon-to-be-built children's playground that will be made from upcycled city waste. "This project is the outcome of one of our workshops, where the local community identified what was missing and decided what they required from the space." It is a testament to the venue's main mission, which is to empower people by bringing them together to learn about many things: music, theatre, the environment but, perhaps most of all, one another. — ADC

Elevated living
Presidio, San Francisco

Children scamper around a wild maze while their parents relax on a sturdy driftwood bench. When a chill settles in, the family retreats to a roaring campfire before meeting a park ranger to study local rocks and plants. Is this Yosemite? Or Big Sur?

This is, in fact, the heart of San Francisco, the Presidio Tunnel Tops, a new 5.7 hectare park designed by New York-based practice James Corner Field Operations (JCFO) that replaces an unloved highway. It's a model for how to turn yesterday's infrastructure into tomorrow's urban oasis.

"In a world of increasing density and not adding to sprawl, inevitably we're going to start building more parks like this one," says Michael Boland, chief park officer of the Presidio Trust, which looks after the area.

The Golden Gate Bridge opened to much fanfare in 1937. Less heralded was the 2.6km viaduct that funnelled cars to and from the bridge. Why did officials build an elevated section of an otherwise surface-level road connecting their new landmark to downtown? They were just following orders. The southern foot of the bridge sits in the Presidio area of San Francisco, then an active military base.

"The motivation was to get people through without touching the ground," says Boland. Over 150 years the army transformed the grounds from windswept dunes to a verdant base. Since opening to the public, it has transformed into a paradise of trails and beaches. But Doyle Drive, as the highway was known, lingered as an eyesore and road hazard after an earthquake damaged its structural integrity in 1989.

> "In a world of increasing density, it's inevitable we'll build more parks like this one"

It took 20 years to tunnel a new road underneath at a cost of $1.1bn (€1bn). Doyle Drive finally came down in 2012. It took another 10 years to make something bloom in the viaduct's absence. From July, when Presidio Tunnel Tops opens, San Franciscans – and the 25 million annual visitors to the city – can enjoy the fruits of this 30-year labour. The park allows for unimpeded pedestrian access from the Presidio's stately grounds down to bayfront Crissy Field, a former army airfield restored as marshland and a grassy park in 2001. The Tunnel Tops also offers visitors panoramic views from the height of the former viaduct, more than 12 metres above the waterfront. That vista guided the firm's design philosophy.

"We were really restrained about the design so as not to detract from that view," says the project's lead landscape architect, Richard Kennedy. "We weren't looking to create big earthworks or sculptural forms that would occlude the scene."

Benches use wide planks rather than wooden slats. The pathways are made from exposed aggregate concrete in warm, sandy tan to resemble trails. A campfire circle recreates the quintessential national park experience. The new Presidio Steps connect the upper and lower sections, offering a terraced lawn and seating area before plunging into the park's most creative feature: a play area where children can climb on a series of logs and boulders. The playground, not part of the original brief, was envisioned through the project's public-engagement process and intended to make San Francisco more child-friendly.

By carving a new marquee park out of the wreckage of a derelict piece of infrastructure, San Francisco is showing that there's light at the end of the tunnels. — GRS

BETTER NEVER STOPS

CASTORE.COM

TIMO TRUNKS

SWIM LIKE NO OTHER

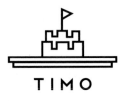

TIMO

1

2

② BUSINESS: Languages

Talking point
Global

Learning a language opens up the world but studying in a classroom can feel dull. Why not throw aperitivos and K-pop ballads into the mix? We immerse ourselves in schools with a novel approach to the business of teaching.

The travel industry boosts the economy of desirable places but all too often it can produce sterile experiences that hermetically seal tourists off from their destination. Fortunately, there's a gentler world of business that teaches people languages away from screens and deepens encounters. We spread the word about the courses that bring drawing, dancing and aperitivos into the conversation. — ⓜ

1.
Community spirit
Il Sasso, Montepulciano

Montepulciano's Piazza Grande is home to a palazzo designed by architects sent to the hillside town by the Medici family. Across the square, though, is the town's relatively unremarkable-looking cathedral. The church's backers spent so much money on its ornate interior that they had none left for the outside. Like the church's builders, the students of Tuscany's Il Sasso language school have arrived at the conclusion that it's what's inside that matters most. They're prioritising learning over gilding their façades on a beach.

Previous page
1. Il Sasso students practising Italian
2. Montepulciano's cathedral

This page
1. View to learn
2. Sunshine and syntax
3. Activities include discussing recipes
4. Students at CESA

Rebecca Mason made the bold move of quitting her technology marketing job and moving to Italy to improve her language skills. "I realised that I had this amazing job and I had everything going for me back in Sydney but is that all there is?" she says. After a long pandemic, Mason, 30, wanted to reset. "I thought, I can't just keep climbing the corporate ladder, taking that next promotion and that next pay packet," she adds. "Now I'm at a language level where I can get by awkwardly; it's in the immersion that the magic happens."

Founded in 1983, Il Sasso initially catered to German and Austrian tourists, although most of the students that MONOCLE meets are from the Anglosphere. The school charges €779 per person for a four-week group class and takes in about 500 students a year, rarely exceeding 45 at any given time. Private classes are also on offer, however, and not just for the business leaders, ambassadors and one Hungarian ex-president who have all studied here before.

Some classes take place in the cool, high-ceilinged classrooms but owner-director Silvia Celli prides herself on Il Sasso's place in the Montepulciano community. Classes regularly involve visits to farmers' markets where students take it in turns to play the role of tour guide around town. "We do not have a vending machine here because we want you to spend as much time as possible outside talking," says Celli. "That way you feel part of something bigger."

Celli found herself here during her previous career in publishing, when looking for a rural place to work on revising the Italian dictionary. "I wanted to write in a beautiful setting," she says as a breeze disturbs the wind chimes in her office. "A friend of mine was working at the school and asked whether I could help." Unlike many of its competitors, Il Sasso survived the pandemic with a temporary pivot to online lessons.

Now that in-person classes are back, there are a number of reasons why people enrol. Husband and wife Michael Roesslein, 41 and Mira Danysh, 34, relocated permanently from California's Bay Area after the stress of being a nurse during the pandemic aggravated Mira's autoimmune disorder. "We wanted to assimilate as quickly as possible," says Roesslein. "For the first two weeks, though, I was too scared to try to buy anything at the market. But my teacher took me to order stuff and then I felt confident enough."

Most students are here temporarily, though. American constitutional law student Ned, 29, wants to access Machiavelli untranslated and Judi, 25, from Leipzig, is here to supplement her local internship. Jet-lagged 64-year-old Bruce Johnson has just flown in from Calgary but started his years-long love affair with Italian in his former career as a fashion buyer. "The experience of meeting people from all over the world is enriching in itself but my hope is to start thinking about winding down work; my three weeks here are my mini-sabbatical," he says.

The programme, which includes perfecting one's coffee order at the local café and colloquial Italian practice sessions over aperitivos, would be sumptuous enough in any context but when muddled with Montepulciano's setting – vineyards and cypress trees carpet the rolling Tuscan hills that stretch out below the town – it's hard to think of a more intoxicating place to watch the sun slowly melt the ice in your Aperol spritz. — DHO
ilsasso.com

"We do not have a vending machine here because we want you to spend as much time as possible outside talking. That way you feel part of something bigger"

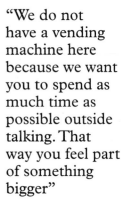

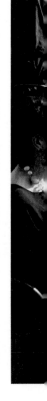

1

PHOTOGRAPHERS: *James Mollison, Dan Wilton*

2

3

4

2.
French connections
CESA, Aix-en-Provence

Most people learn to tell their passé composé from their imparfait in a classroom near home but a lucky few get to study verb tenses in the south of France. At the CESA school in Aix-en-Provence, students come from far and wide to hone their language skills – and have a glass of Provençal rosé while they're at it.

Founded in 1972, CESA's Aix-en-Provence branch began as a language centre geared towards Swedish students looking to learn French in the region. But as the school broadened its services to include more people, it soon became clear they would need to widen their remit too. These days, CESA combines traditional language classes in the classroom with a number of hands-on activities, including wine tastings, hiking, yoga, pétanque and drawing. The twist? Every conversation, from reading a map to discussing mourvèdre grape varieties, must happen in French. "We see the activities as a complement to learning the language," says the school's director Anna Díaz. "They present students with the opportunity to meet other people and become more familiar with the culture."

Díaz, who is originally from Stockholm, is no stranger to the art of language learning. She agrees that for her school, choosing to offer a more holistic approach was a smart decision; as post-pandemic travel ramps up again, spots on language programmes like CESA's have become increasingly sought-after. "We're not the cheapest school but the people who come here come looking for quality," says Díaz. "We have small groups in classes; the city is beautiful. Lots of people like that small-town charm." It's easy to see the appeal. Nestled in a sunny villa overlooking the mountains, the building has a rustic appeal. "Back in the day, women used to come down here and wash their clothes in the river," says Díaz.

When MONOCLE visits CESA, a group of young Swedish students is gathering outside for a break. "They're here to study for their exams," says Díaz. "But people come here for many reasons." Claudia Rodriguez, a Colombian massage therapist based in Mexico City, says that she wanted to learn French for her clients, who are often francophone. "Plus, she's here for love," says her classmate, Leonardo Cavalcanti, a professor at the University of Brasília. Rodriguez's partner is French and she has always wanted to speak his first language.

For most of the staff, being able to interact with different types of people is the best part of the job. "I once taught the CEO of a huge Brazilian company basic French," says Mathilde Couderc, a new hire who, at the time, was just out of university.

Later that day, a group of students gathers around the foot of the Sainte-Victoire mountain for today's activity. Here, no English is allowed and, as the students chat and hike up a hill, it's clear that they are following the rules. It isn't always easy, though. Jennifer Edson, a New York-based creative director, is still figuring out what makes the language tick. But while she has found the learning curve difficult, the experience has been immensely rewarding. Being in Provence is, of course, half the fun. "I'm in heaven," she says.

Learning a new language can be a daunting experience. But, like Edson, many have found out that jumping off the deep end often yields the best results. As more businesses realise that people are willing to spend their money on experiences, language-learning schools have the opportunity to increase their marketability – that is if, like CESA, they play their cards right. "Things have started picking up in the spring and we're headed towards a busy summer," says Díaz. "Hopefully a good winter too." — CAG
is-aix.com

1

2

3

4

1. Note to self
2. Outside the box
3. Practising vocabulary
4. Did you hear that?
5. Tour guide setting ground rules
6. Cézanne's trail
7. Hiking in the Provençal hills
8. Rolling Korea student
9. Learning with music

3.
K-pop performances optional
Rolling Korea, Seoul

During Korean class, Lisa Scholer, a pink-haired 23-year-old from Luxembourg, sings a K-pop ballad. She's at the Rolling Korea language school, which integrates K-pop vocals and dance into its Korean classes, in Seoul's hip Seogyo-dong neighbourhood. "Everything comes back to its place," Lisa sings, following the Korean lyrics from musician Taeyeon's "11:11." The teacher observes her closely, commenting on breathing, rhythm and pronunciation, while accompanying on the keyboard.

"We don't just teach regular grammar; we combine education with entertainment," says Lee Junmi, co-founder of Rolling Korea and a BTS fan. Lisa, whose Korean is intermediate, double majored in Japanese and Korean Studies at university in Germany. "I didn't know a lot about Korea until I looked more into the language and culture; then I really started getting interested, because it's so different from what I'm used to."

At Rolling Korea's weekly dance class, the teacher speaks mostly in Korean, "which helps a lot," says Lisa. It's her third time participating in the school, each time spending a month or two here. Today the school offers Korean language packages – with or without the K-pop options – costing anywhere from less than $1,000 (€933) to more than $3,000 (€2,800) a month. Most students come from North America and Europe but before the pandemic it was Japan.

Pre-pandemic, the institute averaged 100 students per month; it's now around 50. Lee is no stranger to hard times; when she and her husband founded the school in 2012, they only had two students: a Japanese couple in their sixties with family roots in Korea. "The first time I came to Rolling Korea," says Lisa, "I was the only student here because nobody got a visa during the pandemic." She says she likes the school as there's less pressure and more fun. "It feels like a second home." — HK
rollingkorea.com

PHOTOGRAPHER: Julie Mayfeng

Objects for Home and Life

HANDPICKED OBJECTS SOURCED FROM INDEPENDENT
BRANDS FROM ACROSS THE GLOBE — SCAN THE CODE
OR VISIT — **HOLD.SHOP**

1

② BUSINESS: Chiringuitos

Changing tides
Spain

A staple of the Spanish coastline is in the balance. We meet the people behind Formentera's chiringuitos.

WRITER
Liam Aldous

PHOTOGRAPHY
Nathalie Mohadjer

2

3

"They tried to take me down but I outsmarted them," says José Luís Pelayo, grinning defiantly. A beer in hand, Pelayo is accompanied by his teenage son, who is neatly folding cutlery into serviettes after a busy lunch service at Restaurante Pelayo. We're sitting around a plastic outdoor table by the beach as the low-hanging sun bounces blinding light off the waters of Formentera's Migjorn beach. At the bar, a woman with a bad Spanish accent struggles to order paella. It's a familiar scene of the Spanish early summer: sanguine, unhurried, far-removed from the pace of city life. But all is not as it seems in Spain's beachside-restaurant trade.

"This is a weird time for our tranquil little island," says Pelayo, as the waves crash nearby. A recent (and hastily announced) government decision to re-tender operating licences for the island's chiringuitos and smaller *kioscos* has

put business here on hold. These seasonal, no-frills eateries are staples of the Spanish coast and, despite their size, still do a mean trade. In Formentera, nervous chatter abounds about what many see as a hostile takeover of their shoreline. Legal challenges were launched and protests erupted. As decades-old family-run eating spots draw battle lines in the sand, the structures of several of the yet-to-open beach huts sit unopened like washed-up hulls of forgotten boats. Beachgoers have been left confused, adrift and hungry for answers.

Formentera's charm has always been the simple life. Here, like much of Spain, a chiringuito is somewhere to switch off, tuck in to some fresh, lightly seared seafood and let the sound of the ocean calm the mind. Now, even these secluded sands are feeling the force of private equity and property speculation lapping at the legs of the plastic chairs. A typical "government concession" for operating a small *kiosco* can currently cost the owners about €20,000 a year. But talk of "professionalising operations" has seen some rates jump to an eye-watering €173,500. Locals are dubious about the motives but also worried about losing their affordable places to eat.

1

"We're the only one still open," says Pelayo, with just a hint of glee. Pelayo will be able to extend the 43 years he has spent darting between the multi-coloured chairs of his ramshackle restaurant thanks to the decision his father made 50 years ago to purchase the land outright. That ownership has complicated any potential backroom deals to uproot his family's livelihood. The Pelayo family have watched fashion moguls, football club owners and hedge-fund directors snap up nearby properties. Their giant Sunday paella feeds up to 400 people on Sundays – for €16.50 a head. Keeping such customs alive is as much about standing up for the everyman as defending the island's simpler way of life.

Under Cala Saona's tall juniper pines, waiter Miguel brings one of Formentera's best-known dishes – a giant tray of lobster, fried potatoes and eggs – out to a table of still-dripping swimmers. "Restaurante Chacala started with just a grill on the rocks in 1969 but we made some improvements," he says, gesturing to the roof and fitted-out kitchen; it's a monument to the way many popular beach businesses here have evolved. Miguel is

2

Previous page
1. Grilled fish sitting
   at El Bigotes
2. El Bigotes in
   Cala Mestella
3. Post-lunch sea-gazing
   at Restaurante Pelayo

This page
1. Cala Mestella's
   stone pier
2. Dog days at Cala Molí
3. Es Xarcu in Ibiza

also concerned about the inflationary squeeze of "bigger fortunes, soaring prices and fewer places opening."

Politics and finance have always been table fodder, though. This summer, as conversations about uneasy futures flavour many meals, signs of the gradual creep of commercialisation sit in plain sight. A serviette dispenser sponsored by Coca-Cola here; chairs branded by a beer company there; coffee cups stamped with the insignia of an importer for your post-meal espresso. At many beach restaurants such as the Formentera family-owned Chacala, big companies have found a way to secure seats at a table.

Passing the baton between the old guard and new has always presented opportunities too. Such transitions are a natural part of the tide of change. For restaurant Es Còdol Foradat, the former owners had grown tired

after 25 years of continuous service in the sand dunes and sold their leasing rights to Catalan chef Nandu Jubany. The food here is now more refined – and pricier – than before but it's still acceptable to stroll in barefoot with a *pareo* wrapped around your waist. Here, under the swaying rattan lampshades, the over-branded plastic is replaced by bespoke ceramics and hand-woven chairs: the upshot of more expensive paella (meals can cost up to €150 a head) but it's also a visual tribute to the simplicity of seaside restaurants.

The neighbouring island of Ibiza is no stranger to the spectre of popularity. An abridged version of the island's success story goes a bit like this: some free-thinking icono-clasts found paradise. A new-age mythology about hedonistic life-on-the-fringe became a magnet for the masses. First bemused,

3

1

1. El Silencio's stylish
   sun-protectors
2. Host at El Silencio
3. One of the venue's
   busy chefs

then opportunistic, local farmers got rich, then greedy – and richer still. Paradise now comes with a price-tag and lots of stakeholders seeking a slice of the profits. While this has presented new opportunities to many, some smaller businesses have been priced out and faltered.

Some stubborn strongholds still quietly fend off the commercial currents. In the stony alcove of Cala Mestella, El Bigotes started as a fisherman's shack where Juan Ferrer prepared Bullit de Peix, an Ibicenco fish-and-rice stew, for friends. With smoke billowing from under the roof, the maître-d' clutches a vast reservations book to confirm that arrivals are in the right place. There are two daily sittings: wood-fire grilled seafood at midday (€17) and the coveted fish stew served at 14.00 (€22). Reservations for the latter need to be made nearly two months in advance. This said,

"A lot of people don't realise the work that goes into setting up a place like this"

prices have remained low. Loyal patrons are also lured by the continuity (a novelty here). The family's traditional *llaüt* fishing boat is anchored at arm's length from the restaurant and the old chairs are as sturdy as ever. The unspoilt views of the cove do the rest.

Down south, behind the dunes of Ses Salinas beach, Quim Coll is readying the reopening of Mar y Sal, a once-dilapidated beach bar and eight-room hostel purchased by a group of Barcelona-based restaurateurs. "We don't want to open another expensive, exclusive place," says Coll, the kitchen director. "The bar used to be open 24 hours a day, catering to all types, so veteran customers shouldn't be left out in the cold." After 57 years of service, this changing of the guard shouldn't rock the boat.

Now in its second season, the Ibiza restaurant El Silencio has qualms about tending to the wealthy blow-ins at the expense of locals and it has done something about it. The Paris-based hospitality proprietors split their venue in two: catering to the bold and beautiful on one sand-floored side and offering another, more affordable menu around the pool. "A lot of people don't realise the work that goes

2

3

into setting up a place like this," says Antoine Caton, head of operations, about their seasonal operation, which involves bringing in sand and water as well as bringing in guests.

Elsewhere, Caridad Cabañero has been running Es Xarcu with husband Mariano Torres for 40 years. She knows long-time customers' table preferences by heart and Torres's mobile phone rings hot with requests for the restaurant's tender to come and pick them up from their boats. "It's the love of people that motivates me every day," says Cabañero, brushing off talk about profits or the economics of the restaurant business. "Although this year rising fuel prices have put the pinch on our fisherman: some aren't even taking their boats out."

Back on the mainland, it's a few ticks before 11.00 on the Costa Brava's Platja Canadell and the sea mist hasn't deterred a sprinkling of morning sun-chasers. Children skim stones into the small waves. A mother and son battle over a game of *padel* while a furrowed señor surveys the beach, his expression flapping between indifference and inquisition.

Under the orange awning of seaside restaurant Tragamar, waitress Julieta is too focused on the here and now to talk about the future; she's chalking up today's *peix salvatge* (wild fish) specials, which are cooked in salt, grilled or baked to the customers' liking. Inside, manager Marc is trying to stem the flow of people who see the 180-cover restaurant – the only establishment on the lower beach – more like a facility than fancy eatery. "The trick is patience, knowing how to lay down the law, and being *simpatico*," he says. Half a dozen people have already poked their heads through the door asking for takeaway drinks or a quick trip to the bathroom. Marc, understandably, would be more interested in getting them to fork out for the grilled squid garnished with *sobrasada*.

Not far away, on the postcard-perfect beach of Tamariu, Carlos Herrera is standing in front of Es Dofí ("the dolphin" in Catalan), anticipating the midday rush of customers. "We don't take reservations," he says. "Our first-come-first-served rule gives everyone a chance to get the best table." He and his brothers, Ilario and Alfonso, took over their father's 50-year-old restaurant several years ago. "Even if the

queen came, she'd have to wait her turn," he says in jest. Carlos greets many customers by name, some with hugs, aware of everyone around him. As people feast on plates of *sonsos* (tiny fried fish) and sip on *tissana* (sangria with cava), Es Dofí has a spontaneous, unfussy feel, despite being run like a tight ship.

Nextdoor, a gentleman in a low-slung deckchair gestures MONOCLE over. "This house was built by Spain's best architect," he says. He's not wrong. The four-storey town house was designed by modernist Josep Antoni Coderch and the sunlounger-slumped, Barcelona-based publisher Antoni Paricio has been visiting here in style most summers since 1976.

Whisking us up for a tour to the rooftop, Paricio points to the shore where fishermen once operated makeshift restaurants on the sand. "Change always comes; things get bigger," he says, pointing to the row of evolved esplanade restaurants. "But sometimes we don't really need so much." As the waves slide in and out, his poignant words could be about the sea or about life itself. "But create something with integrity," he says. "Then you can resist the stronger tides." — Ⓜ

1. Es Xarcu serves seafood among the palm fronds
2. Clams at Es Xarcu
3. Youngsters catching some rays on Tamariu beach
4. Veteran customer at Es Xarcu
5. Chalking up the specials at Tragamar

"We don't take reservations. Our first-come-first-served rule gives everyone a chance to get the best table. Even if the queen came, she'd have to wait her turn"

1

2

3

4

5

5

V-ZUG IN PARIS
HAUTE CUISINE

After London, Paris. At the new V-Zug flagship in the French capital, kitchen appliances designed with Swiss precision blend with Parisian flair. We get a sneak peek of the well-appointed showroom in the company of Gabriel Castelló Pinyon, who designed and oversaw the execution of the project.

Gabriel Castelló Pinyon

Head of brand displays international, V-Zug

How did you root the venue in its Parisian setting?
I wanted to give visitors the feeling of walking through an old French apartment, consisting of a kitchen, dining area and lounge, among other rooms. I see Paris as a romantic city with cosy cafés and dim lighting wherever you go. Fashion has a strong creative influence in Paris, which, with the likes of Yves Saint Laurent and Sonia Rykiel in the 1980s, was marked by chic, dark colours. This is where the inspiration for the black ceilings and the all-black show kitchen comes from.

Why do physical spaces still matter?
Having showrooms allows us to open the door to the V-Zug lifestyle. It has only been 10 years since we started selling our products internationally and we already have a presence in top locations – first in London, now in Paris. You're never just buying a V-Zug appliance; you're buying an experience that needs to be lived in the physical realm. That's why our flagships resemble real lived-in spaces equipped not only with beautifully designed appliances but also with sophisticated furniture.

How have you curated the interiors?
We work with European companies that are driven by the same values as V-Zug. In the Paris showroom we have Swiss design classics including Vitra chairs and Peter Zumthor light fittings next to cutlery by Italy's Sambonet, textiles by Denmark's Kvadrat and side tables by Spain's Viccarbe. I like that the Vitra chairs are designed by France's Bouroullec brothers; there's a nice French-Swiss link here, which is particularly fitting for the first France showroom of a Swiss brand like us.

1

1. — Gabriel Castellò Pinyon 2. — Kitchen in V-Zug Studio Paris 3. — Customers can see products such as the WineCooler in action 4. — Staff are on hand to help you take control 5. — Come on in 6. — The showroom was designed by V-Zug's in-house team

2

3

4

5

Sixth sense

V-Zug's Paris home is located in the elegant 6th arrondissement, opposite Le Bon Marché department store and design emporium The Conran Shop. V-Zug's dedicated in-house brand display team has designed a premium environment in which visitors can witness the appliances in a wide array of settings, including an event kitchen where renowned local chefs will be showing the products in action.

6

Read all about it
Kuala Lumpur

There's a bookshop boom in Malaysia aided by unconventional business models and pandemic-changed reading habits.

WRITER
Naomi Xu Elegant

PHOTOGRAPHY
Paulius Staniunas

When former journalists Fong Min Hun and Elaine Lau opened Lit Books in Kuala Lumpur in 2017, they fielded "a lot of scepticism" about the prospect of running a bricks-and-mortar bookshop. Critics speculated that it was a sunset industry, and that people were only interested in e-books now.

"But no," says Lau. "People still read physical books." And so the husband-and-wife team rented a shop with high ceilings and ample sunlight. The cashier desk doubles as a counter where guests can sit with tea or coffee and flip through a novel. Bookshelves have wheels so that they can be easily moved aside for a jazz performance, author reading or literary quiz.

Malaysia boasts one of the world's highest literacy rates but a 2016 report found that among Malaysians who read regularly, just 3 per cent picked up a book, most preferring to read a newspaper. It's why the pre-pandemic book industry here was suffering from closures and shrinking revenue. Two years of lockdowns also hurt retail and forced booksellers online. But when people were stuck at home, they began to read more: according to the National Library of Malaysia, demand for digital reading material doubled in 2020 compared to 2019. Lit Books, meanwhile, recorded monthly sales increases of up to 60 per cent in 2020.

Now KL is experiencing a resurgence of bricks-and-mortar bookshops. Independent sellers are betting that the pandemic-era pick-up in reading will sustain and translate into in-store sales. They are finding ways to boost physical retail, from befriending customers and stocking niche paperbacks to opening cafés and curating the shelves of boutique hotels.

In 2020, Malaysian book retailer MPH closed scores of shops and shifted to

2

"It's not all about making money. It's about enriching your own thinking, your life, and your mind through knowledge."

e-commerce. Malaysian chain Bookxcess faced a similar crisis. "We were literally going to go bust," says Bookxcess co-founder Andrew Yap. Most sales came from the international Big Bad Wolf fairs that Bookxcess runs, which sell remaindered books at steep discounts. The pandemic rendered the fairs impossible and Yap went online, which kept the business afloat. But the moment he could, he doubled down on bricks-and-mortar. The stores are designed to lure customers in. Each has a different, eclectic design: one is housed in an old cinema complex; another has an ice-cream bar; and many are in malls, a popular weekend destination guaranteed to bring foot traffic. Bookxcess has gone from eight shops before the pandemic to 19 in July 2022.

It's not just chains that are bouncing back. Independent seller Monsoon Books opened in 2021 in Petaling Jaya and caters to Malaysia's Chinese-speaking population — around two-thirds of its books are in Chinese. The selection is diverse and tends toward the highbrow; readers can purchase a treatise on Beethoven's piano sonatas or the latest issue of Malaysian indie magazine *Process*.

"People come to our shop and say, 'Wow, I never expected to see these kinds of books in a Malaysian bookshop'," says store manager Gan Han Lin. Gan left his job as a schoolteacher to run Monsoon. He hired a local designer to build shelves and a clean, cosy interior. Visitors can relax and read inside or

ROOM TO READ

3   4

buy a drink at the café downstairs to enjoy on the plant-filled balcony.

"We want to establish a little bit of a niche market," says Ng Kok Heong, a retired timber salesman who invested in Monsoon as a passion project. "If you go into the big chain bookshops you'll see that most of the shelf is all books about wealth management and how to make money. We don't want to sell those books. It's not about simply making money; it's about enriching your own thinking, your life and your mind through knowledge."

Nazir Harith Fadzilah amassed a huge collection of books as an engineering student in Melbourne and wanted to bring his favourites back to Malaysia. In 2006 he opened independent bookshop Tintabudi in KL and began selling from his personal library alongside publishers he discovered at book festivals. Nazir has expanded Tintabudi's business model, publishing a local author's poetry collection and collaborating with the Kloé Hotel to curate their "room to read", one of five culture-themed suites on offer at the venue. Some Kloé guests have become Tintabudi patrons.

Nazir has seen interest in printed books grow in the years since he opened Tintabudi, especially among younger readers. "There is a movement [away] from the internet and back to books," says Nazir. "It's an exciting progression." For independent bookshops, customer relationships are the cornerstone of their business, a trump card over chains and the best part of the job. The vast majority of Lit Books' sales are from repeat customers and shelves are lined with a mixture of owners' picks and regulars' favourites. Much of what they sell is available in bigger shops but people seek them out because they feel a connection to the business.

"We meet every single person," says Elaine Lau. "We do spend a lot of time just talking and it doesn't always convert to sales but the relationship is set and people appreciate that. We have people who didn't buy something the first time but they're back here now to purchase today." — Ⓜ

1. Kloé Hotel founder Ng Ping Ho
2. Writer's desk
3. Monsoon Books in Petaling Jaya

Book bargains

In 1992, American author Kathi Kamen Goldmark founded a rock band called the Rock Bottom Remainders. It grew into a literary supergroup of sorts, with Stephen King, Barbara Kingsolver, Amy Tan and other writers as members. The name is a tongue-in-cheek reference to remaindered books, which are books deemed unsellable after languishing on shelves for too long. Bookshops return the unsold volumes to the publisher and many are pulped and recycled or discarded. Some publishing companies, however, sell the books at vastly reduced prices to shops such as Bookxcess, which can then offer customers 90 per cent discounts and still make money. Such cheap books can rattle the market and some governments have instituted laws to prevent the practice. In France, for instance, it's illegal to sell new books with any more than a 5 per cent discount on the cover price. France's parliament passed that law in 1981 to protect independent booksellers from chains that could afford to sell with bigger discounts; other European countries have similar fixed-book-price laws. For customers, lower prices can mean more accessible reading material. But buyers should beware, as rock-bottom prices aren't always a signal that a book is remaindered: some cheap books in online marketplaces have been illegally photocopied and distributed. E-books have also made book piracy even easier.

The 'Big D' is a Texan gem that has for too long flown under the radar; as thousands of people relocate to the city, they're finding there's more to this place than tall hats – and even taller buildings. Let's take a closer look.

Better business
We visit the innovative companies and young entrepreneurs putting down roots in this budding metropolis.

High art
Meet the architects, designers and other creatives who are revamping the city's cultural scene.

On the menu
Get acquainted with the best places to drink, dine, shop and stay for locals and visitors alike.

Urban renewal
From green oases to revamped high-rises, discover the initiatives turning the tide on this Texan town.

The Monocle Guide to Dallas

Catbird — Rooftop Bar & Terrace

49th Floor Penthouse

Monarch — 49th Floor Restaurant

Urban upswing
Taking off

Dallas has sprawled in all directions but much of the action still comes from the city centre: from the Arts District and newly-built parklands to the neighbourhoods that are being brought back to life as new residents move in. Here's a guide to the historic downtown and its immediate surroundings.

There's a particular kind of southern heat that greets you as you step out of the airport in Dallas. It's a warm welcome that comes in over the wide, flat prairies that extend to the Texas horizon and – as we've discovered – the world is increasingly keen on catching that breeze.

Dallas, together with its neighbour Fort Worth, was the fastest-growing metropolitan area in the US last year. People are coming for the plentiful jobs as global companies relocate their headquarters to a city that's affordable but also has ample space to grow. With this shift has come a new cache of places to eat and art galleries to peruse that are reinvigorating overlooked neighbourhoods and kindling fresh energy in a city steeped in American history.

While many American cities have watched their downtowns wither over the past decade, Dallas is turning the tide by enticing people to live and work in its urban core. "The Big D" is again assuming its famously broad stature among Texas's metropolises, and while the place has sometimes struggled to shake off an image of being a buttoned-down trading town, we'll show you how it's ironed out a few kinks, attracted top-class chefs and built an impressive design district. There's still much to be done, of course.

Despite the association with tycoon JR Ewing, Dallas never had any oil of its own and without natural resources, you'll often hear it said, there's a special ingenuity to the Dallas character. Locals are proud that their 'hood is on the up, so don't be surprised if you hear a little *yee-haw* now and then. — Ⓜ

Getting here
Dallas-Fort Worth International Airport (DFW) was the world's second-busiest airport last year, with some 62.5 million passengers passing through. As the home base for American Airlines, DFW has non-stop daily flights to Paris and the Gulf States, and is adding a number of new routes – not least to the Nordic nations. Dallas Love Field airport is a prized gateway for Southwest Airlines that regularly bags an impressive share of awards for its service – it has a new runway in the works too.

Dallas Love Field
It's a 20-minute dash to this regional airport, which is perfect for connections across the US

Trammell Crow Park
The Trinity river weaves through this vast green belt. Keep an eye out for the marble cows.

35E

Dallas in numbers
1.3 million
City of Dallas population
(9th largest in the US)

230
Days of sunshine per year

$62,000
Median household income
(Dallas County)

9
Pulitzer prizes for *The Dallas Morning News*

64
Number of touchdowns by the Dallas Cowboys in 2021
(1st in NFL)

Getting around
01 Alto is a Texas ride-hailing app, offering a service that's a cut above

02 The DART light rail gets you downtown from the international airport in 50 minutes

03 The tangle of freeways at the city's entrance is nicknamed the High Five; avoid at 17.00

30

Bishop Arts District
Walkable streets of quaint bungalows with verdant garden bars and craft markets.

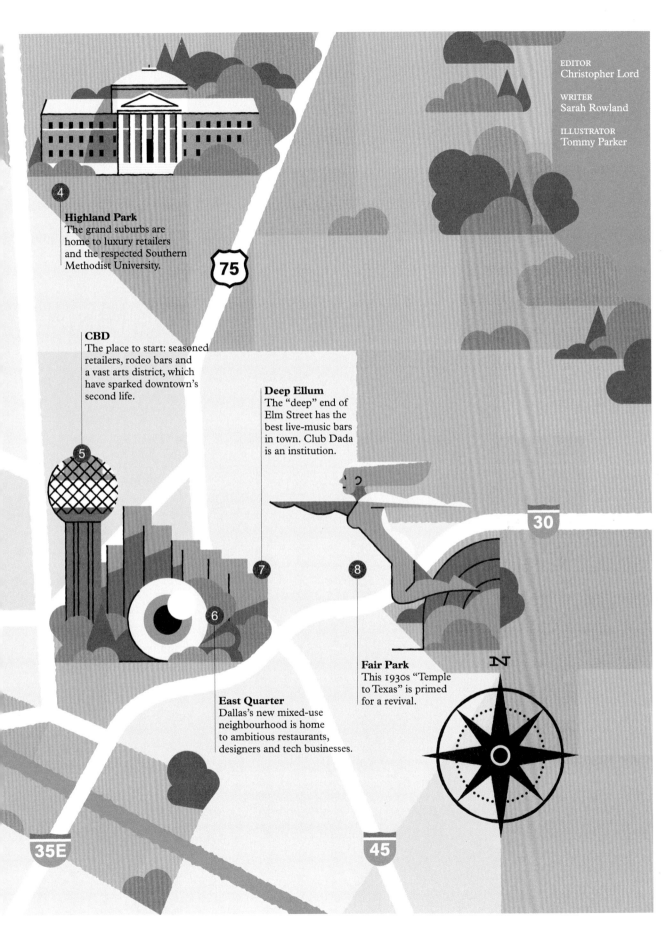

EDITOR
Christopher Lord

WRITER
Sarah Rowland

ILLUSTRATOR
Tommy Parker

Highland Park
The grand suburbs are home to luxury retailers and the respected Southern Methodist University.

CBD
The place to start: seasoned retailers, rodeo bars and a vast arts district, which have sparked downtown's second life.

Deep Ellum
The "deep" end of Elm Street has the best live-music bars in town. Club Dada is an institution.

East Quarter
Dallas's new mixed-use neighbourhood is home to ambitious restaurants, designers and tech businesses.

Fair Park
This 1930s "Temple to Texas" is primed for a revival.

TAKE IN DALLAS ART

Dallas Museum of Art
Dallas Arts District, Downtown

With new exhibits rotating throughout the year and unique collections by world-famous artists, the Dallas Museum of Art inspires visitors of all ages. And, if you'd like to feed more than your imagination, you can simply walk across the street to the food trucks at Klyde Warren Park and sample any number of diverse cuisines. Whatever your all is, you'll find it here.

To plan your trip, go to VisitDallas.com

VISIT**DALLAS** & FIND YOUR ALL

Changing tides
City on the up

Dallas has gone from a deserted downtown to a place where people want to be – but it didn't happen overnight. Here we look at how this urban turnaround was made.

Q&A
Driving force

Mayor of Dallas
Eric Johnson

Mayor Eric Johnson, who was elected in 2019, is a Democrat in a Republican state. On his watch, a reform of the police has been enacted that has seen violent crime fall.

Is this a liberal or a conservative city?
It's not an overtly political town. We're pro-business and want people to be the best versions of themselves. There are no natural resources that would have warranted there being a city here, so it's a place built on ingenuity and the wish to make something of nothing. That spirit defines Dallas.

How has the city changed in your lifetime?
The private sector is helping address Dallas's historical inequities. This is a southern city and it's had an arc in terms of race relations. Tremendous progress has been made.

A lot of people are moving to Dallas. How do you manage that growth?
Affordability is becoming a challenge. We're trying to grow incomes by developing the workforce through education. We're building in the city centre and creating green spaces. But the house with a white picket fence is still achievable here.

Fixer uppers
Renewed fortunes

Dallas was, for much of the 20th century, a nexus for Texas's oil magnates. But after the 1980s recession many of the banks left and it became a drive-in, drive-out city. "You could roll up the sidewalks at 17.30, they were so empty," says Jennifer Scripps, CEO of Downtown Dallas Inc. The non-profit organisation is recognised for its neighbourhood renewal work and focus on improving safety – in the early 1990s, there were 200 people living in downtown Dallas while today 15,000 people call the city centre home.

Shawn Todd, founder of Todd Interests, led investors to acquire The National in 2019. The building had sat vacant for almost a decade when Todd set about restoring its pinstriped marble façade. In 2020 he opened a hotel and residences within it. Today it's the centrepiece for downtown's change of fortune, and the Todds are rejuvenating the historic East Quarter. "There's something about lasting architecture that gives you a sense of place," says Todd. "You're seeing people move because there's a way of life they wouldn't get elsewhere."

Down under

Dallas's summers can be punishingly hot and, from the 1960s, the city started constructing temperature-controlled underground tunnels to connect the main buildings. Naturally, this emptied the streets above. Most tunnels have now been blocked off but you can still get a peek at this urban experiment beneath the Bank of America Plaza.

Reconnecting the city
Going green

The defining feature of the city's landscape is the web of freeways that surrounds downtown. The network was built through many lower-income areas, cutting them off from the urban core. But that dominance is slowly being unpicked: Klyde Warren Park, which opened a decade ago, sits atop one of these vast freeways sending cars underground and connecting the Arts District with Uptown. It's part of a growing collection of verdant oases that weaves through the city centre. "Dallas has built 23 acres of parks inside the freeway loop in 20 years," says Robert Decherd, chairman of Parks For Downtown Dallas, which transforms disused plots into green spaces. The foundation's work includes Carpenter Park, which opened in May 2022. Meanwhile, the Kay Bailey Hutchison Convention Center is set to undergo a $2bn (€1.875bn) expansion. The project will create a new entertainment district to straddle the interstate and reconnect neighbourhoods in the less affluent south of the city with downtown.

> "Dallas has built 23 acres of parks inside the freeway loop in 20 years"

Preserving the past
Urban revival

In the rush to modernise, many US cities lose sight of what's on their doorstep: in 1936, Fair Park in south Dallas played host to the Texas Centennial Exposition, an event marking one hundred years of the Lone Star state's independence from Mexico. Today, the area's esplanade and "Texanic" monuments represent one of the largest collections of art deco structures in the US. Now the city is trying to do more with Fair Park's extraordinary architecture and a public referendum in November could see it gain a $300m (€281m) investment.

Getting around
Making tracks

Dallas is a city where the car is king. However, a shakeup of the Dallas Area Rapid Transit (DART) – the longest light-rail network in the US, which extends from downtown to the suburbs – is underway: there's talk of a new subway system while urban planners want to link the historic trolleybus network with the streetcars that ply Oak Cliff. After much delay, the proposal for a high-speed rail route that would connect Dallas to Houston in 90 minutes is gathering steam – but teasing Texans out of their trucks will still be a challenge.

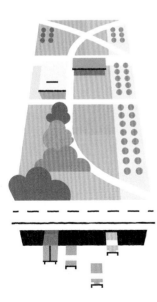

Back in business
Crowd pleasers

As Dallas city centre has revved back to life, it has caught the attention of big businesses looking for a new home (low tax and state incentives also help). The telecommunications giant AT&T relocated in 2008 and last year opened its vast Discovery District campus downtown. The company's new base spans four blocks and includes a video wall that has transformed the area into a public square. Digital artwork is shown as well as Dallas Cowboys games, regularly drawing a crowd of deckchairs. It proves that if you build it, they will come.

New kids in town
Open for business

Thousands of Americans have decamped to the Lone Star state over the past two years: Dallas-Fort Worth's population grew by more than 97,000 residents between 2020 and 2021. Meet the city's latest arrivals.

Dialexa
Tech on the horizon

Dallas may not be a tech hub like Austin *yet*, says Scott Harper, who co-founded Dialexa in 2010 alongside Mark Haidar, but over the last two years the pair have more than doubled their coders and designers to 250 people. Most are based at the company's head office in East Quarter. Recent projects include a tool for monitoring eye health and software for Dallas-based Parkhub, a startup that has bagged $100m (€93m) in investments. "Dallas has already got a lot of talent and is attracting more," says Harper. *dialexa.com*

The businesses Dallas needs
Calling all entrepreneurs

1. **Room to grow**
With the beloved Belmont Hotel's doors shuttered, there's a gap in the market for an evocative boutique replacement.

2. **Not the average corn dog**
A healthy street-food concept serving the new parks downtown.

3. **Breaking news**
City kiosks: finding a newspaper or magazine can be a challenge. It's time for change.

4. **Novel approach**
Dallas is calling out for a central bookshop that specialises in international titles.

5. **Local sole**
Residents should walk the walk with a shoe brand that shows off Made in Dallas.

Tangram
Smart move

As Dallas's population expands, so does the infrastructure: new schools and offices are currently being built around the city. Enter Tangram. The Californian business – which designs furniture fit-outs for work and learning environments – opened a Dallas office in 2021. "We needed to be where the butts on seats are," says Tangram's vice president of sales Amber Jones. The company's southern operation is its first base outside California, but being three hours from either coast helps the firm serve customers across the US. "Dallas made a lot of sense for us."
tangraminteriors.com

Galderma
Smooth operator

Galderma has a long history of smoothing wrinkles in northern Texas. The Swiss skincare brand evolved from a company founded in Dallas in 1961 and has since developed many of its products in Fort Worth labs. In 2022, the firm moved its US headquarters – and 400-strong workforce – to the city's downtown area.

"Dallas has always been a great marketplace for us, so moving here was a bridge to that," says Diane Gomez-Thinnes, head of Galderma US. "There is real energy in the revitalisation of this city."
galderma.com

The Dallas Morning News
Read all about it

The city's much-loved local paper *The Dallas Morning News* was founded in 1885 and has nine Pulitzer prizes under its belt. Recently, the daily has seen a surge of new business as people move to the city: in 2021, the paper saw a 22 per cent rise in digital subscriptions and a bump in print sales.

"When you look at who is moving to Dallas and the census projections for where we're going to be, we have to present that with our coverage. We have to tell these stories and cover the inequities," says executive editor Katrice Hardy, the first black journalist to take the reins of the paper. "Pulitzers are amazing but it's the work behind these awards that benefits the community."
dallasmorningnews.com

Neighborhood Services
Branching out

Chef Nick Badovinus has built an empire of restaurants across Dallas over the last 20 years and is now taking Neighborhood Services, the brand he built locally, into Arizona and Kentucky. One of his outposts, National Anthem (*pictured*) in East Quarter, serves classic all-American plates with a few flourishes in a restored 1920s gas station. In short, he has found his niche in the city. "Dallas is a place where all the current food fashions are represented but that's not necessarily the reason why people are going out. Service still matters here, there's a real spirit of hospitality."

Originally from Seattle, Badovinus says he finds the Dallas food scene less reserved and more eager to support new ventures. "This is a city that roots for its own."
nationalanthemdtx.com

Who's new in town?
Office migration

Toyota has moved its US headquarters to Plano, a city in north Texas, while Californian infrastructure giant AECOM is repositioning its global base to Dallas. Jacobs Engineering, another West Coast firm, made the move six years ago. But a major influx is coming from investment bank Goldman Sachs, with almost 4,000 employees relocating to the area. Oliver Cooke works for a recruiter that has helped 100 workers move to the state over the past year: "Dallas is in the middle of the country and, when it comes to real estate, it's much more affordable than New York or California."

Lucchese Bootmaker
Best foot forward

There are few items as Texan as the cowboy boot and, despite being designed for cattle-driving ranchers at the end of the American civil war, these sturdy shoes have endured as business attire. In Dallas, you're as likely to see them donned with a well-cut suit as a pair of Wranglers. The 130-year-old Lucchese Bootmaker has helped keep the style one step ahead. "They've remained a staple in Texas," says Stephanie Saunders of Lucchese's Dallas shop. "The cowboy hat has become more of a companion for the rodeo or a day on the ranch."
lucchese.com

Southern style
On the ground

There's more to Dallas than cowboy hats and big belts. Here are the collections, curators and creatives to know in a city where vast swathes of downtown are dedicated to art and design.

Dallas Design District
One-stop shop

Once a collection of dusty 1950s warehouses on the banks of the Trinity River, the Dallas Design District is now one of the country's great shopping clusters. Home to more than 500 showrooms and galleries: Moroccan rugs and lighting shops sit alongside specialists in reclaimed lumber and surfacing. Neighbourhood mainstay Sputnik Modern has been seeking out mid-century furniture for over 20 years: "Shop owners want to keep the area's authenticity, while also building something new," says founder Chris Thurman, whose Mies van der Rohe Barcelona stools caught our eye. The area is also home to the Dallas Decorative Center, a leafy, secluded collection of retailers that was built in 1954. Stop at Scott + Cooner for hidden gems by Poliform, Cassina and Moooi and finish up with a hearty Italian dinner at modern outpost, Carbone's.
dallasdesigndistrict.com

Mirror architecture
Time to reflect

No one has shaped the Dallas skyline as much as IM Pei, the late Chinese-American architect who conceived five major buildings in the city. In fact, urban planners took Pei's adage that "Architecture is the mirror of life" to heart: the skyline is awash with mirror-clad high-rises. Built in the 1970s by various designers, these glitzy skyscrapers reflect the flashiness of the era's banking boom – not least the Campbell Centre, its façade finished with a fine gold sheen. While this style of architecture is often dismissed as opaque and corporate, others see value in this school of American brutalism. "These buildings are meant to look sculptured and futuristic but were actually economical," says architectural historian Daniel Paul. "They keep out the light and the heat but you also get something quite glitzy."

Swoon the Studio
Open house

Swoon the Studio made its name while working on branding projects for the likes of Dallas Museum of Art and department store Neiman Marcus, but it has since completed interior design ventures in its signature understated style. Swoon's co-founders Samantha Sano and Joslyn Taylor recently finished work on Charleston boutique hotel, Emeline: "We wanted to work with clients that we connect with aesthetically or philosophically," says Taylor. "There's a real openness to new ideas here."
swoonthestudio.com

Swoon's recommendations

Carrie White and Matthew Gilley
Specialists in ceramics and installations for interiors.

Brooks Thomas Studio
British-made textiles, wall coverings and furniture.
brooks-thomas.com

Conduit Gallery
Exhibits homegrown talent.
conduitgallery.com

Q&A
Creative spirit

Executive director
Carolina Alvarez-Mathies

The recently-appointed director of Dallas Contemporary, Carolina Alvarez-Mathies has a grand vision for the art museum. Originally from El Salvador, she's pushing to make this purveyor of daring exhibitions a linchpin of the city's creative community.

What is your vision for Dallas Contemporary?
It is our mission to present the most compelling art of this era, from both a local and international perspective. I want to establish new platforms for innovation within Dallas's art scene itself and reimagine the role this institution plays.

How will the museum change with you at the helm?
I've been asking myself how we can build a stronger community of creatives here in Dallas. We also want to look at more programming that crosses disciplines as well as find ways to engage a broader audience. We're doing our first-ever summer series this year, with day and evening events from pop-ups by local makers through to a partnership with Dallas-based label Dolfin Records, which will curate a set of performances.

Tell us about the art scene.
The level of commitment from patrons here is unparalleled. Whatever the institution – the ballet, the opera or a contemporary museum like ours – Texans are continually supportive and open. Dallas is fast becoming competitive as a major arts city in the US.
dallascontemporary.org

Ghost signs
Bricking it

Many of the hand-painted business signs that adorned the city streets in the early-20th century are still going strong today. Sean Starr, a modern-day sign painter working in Dallas, says these "ghost signs" are a record of the area's successive boom eras from the turn of the century through to the 1950s. The colourful brickwork at the restored East Quarter Residences in downtown Dallas is particularly striking. The bricks were originally shipped to the area as cheap materials following the Great Chicago Fire in 1871, which laid waste to much of the Illinois city. The mix of hues still visible on the bricks today is from the various hand-painted signs that would have once adorned them.

Nasher Sculpture Center
On home turf

Dallas mall moguls Raymond and Patsy Nasher were the owners of an extraordinary collection of postwar and contemporary sculpture. What began as a fascination with pre-Columbian art from Latin America developed when the couple acquired pieces by Jean Arp and Henry Moore – by the time the Nasher Sculpture Center was launched in 2003 in the city's Arts District, the pair had amassed more than 300 masterpieces. "As their collection grew, they started to envision a way to showcase their beloved pieces to the public," says curator Jed Morse. "Lucky for us, it remained right here in Dallas." Works by Pablo Picasso and Barbara Hepworth can be seen alongside American masters Alexander Calder, Donald Judd and Richard Serra.
nashersculpturecenter.org

Modern Electric Sound Recorders
Texans in town

Dating back to the 1960s, the Modern Electric Sound Recorders has been carefully restored over the past decade by owner Jeffrey Saenz. Today, vintage touches hark back to the great West Coast studios, such as Sunset Sound. "Dallas is a music hub and we've seen the city draw notable artists away from their homes in New York, Nashville and LA to record here," says Saenz. The studio has seen homegrown talent such as Leon Bridges and The Texas Gentlemen lay down tracks at its microphones.
modernelectricsound.com

Plug into Dallas's rich live-music scene at these stops.

1.
The Factory in Deep Ellum
Don't be fooled by the modest exterior, this downtown venue plays host to the greats.
thefactoryindeepellum.com

2.
Granada Theatre
This art deco icon is a firm stop for touring bands – its storied stage has welcomed the likes of Adele and Dolly Parton.
granadatheater.com

3.
Club Dada
Club Dada and its neon facade has been drawing in a loyal late-night crowd since 1986.
dadadallas.com

Local flavour
At your service

Southern hospitality done well is about personability and attention to detail – and Dallas has a crop of well-appointed hotels that's honed the craft for years. It's also a city that makes a point of mixing a good martini – or margarita – come sundown. Here's our edit of where to eat, drink, shop and stay.

The Monocle Guide to Dallas

The Joule
Bank on it

The Joule hotel is credited with sparking a revival of downtown Dallas. This 1920s former bank underwent an extensive renovation and the smart lobby is filled with the art collection of owner Timothy Headington.
thejouledallas.com

Other places to rest your head:

1.
The Mansion on Turtle Creek
Rosewood hotel in a grand dame mansion.

2.
Sova
An affordable stay inspired by Japanese-hotels

3.
Hall Arts
Situated in the heart of the Arts District.

Thompson Dallas
Crowning glory

The Thompson's suites offer the perfect perspective on the city. Located in The National, an iconic 51-storey building, much of the hotel's interior takes its cues from the original 1960s design, conceived by architect George Dahl: brass clad walls and teak wood are emblematic of an earlier golden age. This theme continues into the lobby which is decked out with ceramics and artworks collected on international travels by Caroline Todd, whose firm Todd Interiors worked on the fitout. The hotel's showpiece, however, can be found on the 49th floor: the Monarch restaurant dishes up some of the best views in town. Helmed by Michelin-starred chef Danny Grant, the Monarch's wood-fired fare has made this the go-to destination for the well-heeled.
hyatt.com
monarchrestaurants.com

Department stores
Retail therapy

Department stores are intrinsic to the city's history – they are, after all, where Texans go to shop. Founded in Dallas, Neiman Marcus is an icon of mid-century luxury and its white terracotta-fronted flagship has stood on Main Street since 1914. "We're as much rooted in the city's DNA as Dallas is rooted in ours," says Belgian CEO Geoffroy van Raemdonck, who is returning the business to its luxury-first origins. The multibrand womenswear boutique Forty Five Ten taps into the same legacy and is a firm fixture in downtown Dallas.

The Adolphus
French fancy

Modelled on a beaux arts castle, The Adolphus hotel was built in 1912 by the German founder of the Anheuser-Busch brewery empire. This European flavour has been continued through the outpost's redesign, which was completed in 2016. Make sure to visit The French Room, the popular onsite restaurant which serves classic French cuisine, as well as Commerce Goods + Supply, a shop stocked by local retail specialist Makeready which sells JW Marshall wide-brimmed hats and travel essentials.
adolphus.com

Highland Park
Suburban splendour

The grand mansions of Highland Park show the extraordinary wealth that once accumulated in Dallas's suburbs. Southern Methodist University is the local landmark while Highland Park Village, which opened in 1931, is believed to be America's first shopping centre. Today, there is a steady bustle about the area's cafés and luxury retailers.

Shop
Hadleigh's offers bespoke tailoring for men and women – its handmade slippers are a local favourite. "Everything is designed in-house, from our packaging to every last button," says co-founder Ed Shaikh. *hadleighs.com*

Dine
Stop at Sadelle's for all-day brunch with New York-inspired dishes that's popular post-shop. *sadelles.com*

Bishop Arts District
On the make

The low-slung brick shopfronts and wide-porched bungalows of the Bishop Arts District are a respite from the bustling city centre. This walkable area has been extensively restored over the past decade and it is a haven for craft shops and cocktail bars.

Shop
Concept store Marcel Market offers an exclusive selection of French brands curated by its Parisian owners while nearby Poets Bookshop, run by local wordsmith Marco Cavazos, is also worth a browse. *marcel-market.com* *poetsbookshop.com*

Dine
Sleek all-day café Written By The Seasons opened in 2022. It has a quarterly menu that prides itself on its north Texas produce. *writtenbytheseasons.com*

Dining destinations
All you can eat

1.
Muchacho Tex Mex
Dallas invented the frozen margarita: the first machine is at the Smithsonian Institution. Try a modern take here. *laharanch.com*

2.
Terry Black's Barbecue
They take barbecue seriously in Dallas – the mayor suggests Terry Black's in Deep Ellum. *terryblacksbbq.com*

3.
Rex's Seafood & Market
Oysters at the farmers' market is a Friday tradition. *rexsseafood.com*

Knox-Henderson
Top of the shops

This crossroads (dubbed as Dallas's future retail hub) is welcoming major brands and independent retailers who want to sit between downtown and the affluent suburbs.

Shop
Founded in Austin, Stag stocks a Texas-inspired menswear edit with shirts ready for the prairies by Beams Plus, Universal Works and Faherty. Shoppers will also spy a wide-brimmed hat or two here, and eyewear by California's Garrett Leight. *stagprovisions.com*

Dine
Clifton Club is a new cocktail bar on the fringe of Knox-Henderson run by South African Greg Katz. "Dallas was missing a place to go for pre-dinner drinks," says Katz, who also runs Beverley's Bistro & Bar nextdoor.

Katy Trail
The green miles

Before the Highline opened in New York, there was the Katy Trail in Dallas: in 2000, a stretch of abandoned Union Pacific Railroad was turned into a greenbelt stretching from Uptown to Highland Park. The path is an artery for joggers and cyclists, and acts as a respite from its concrete surrounds. Pop-up art installations have become regular features and the track now hosts an annual 5K race. As the local saying goes: "Trains don't run here anymore, Dallas does." Thankfully, there's the Katy Trail Ice House on the route, where cold Texan drafts are served in the garden.

DOWNTOWN DALLAS NOW

Downtown Dallas is moving in a distinct direction, where progressive influence and cultural inspiration define an evolution of industry. Strengthened by top educational institutions and renowned innovation initiatives, this community fosters a diverse set of minds to create one of the most dynamic destinations for any business. Plan your visit and discover how Downtown Dallas does business differently.

downtowndallasnow.com

DOWNTOWN DALLAS INC

② BUSINESS: Urban farming

Strawberry yields
New Jersey

In a warehouse outside Jersey City, a Japanese-flavoured start-up is growing berries so coveted that people happily pay $50 for a bowlful. Is this vertical farming's first luxury brand?

WRITER
Tom Vanderbilt

PHOTOGRAPHY
Levi Mandel

1. Oishii's strawberries,
   the only fruit it grows

The offices of Oishii, located in a former Anheuser-Busch distribution facility on the industrial outskirts of Jersey City, just across the Hudson River from New York, resemble those of any other hi-tech start-up. There are whiteboards decorated with the fevered scratchings of nascent corporate strategies, an automated control centre where data points scroll across screens, a robot patrolling a brightly lit clean-room environment and twenty-somethings grazing on healthy snacks. Oishii produces, for the moment at least, precisely one thing: strawberries.

The product in question sits eight to a pack on a conference-room table, where Hiroki Koga, Oishii's Japanese-born CEO and co-founder, offers a lesson in how to eat them properly. "The sweetness in strawberries is concentrated toward the bottom," he says. "So if you start eating there, it gets less and

1. Robot patrolling
   the strawberry farm

less sweet." Eating from the side, he says, offers the proper sensory balance. The fruit should also be at room temperature. Oishii's berries appear uniform and absent of any visible flaw. By American standards, though, they're slightly strange. Instead of the usual bright red, they are almost roseate and their surface, rather than being flecked by visible seeds, is pockmarked by recessed holes.

Eating them reveals more striking differences. The strawberries are remarkably sweet and aromatic, rivalling, if not exceeding, that rare specimen procured from a summer farmers' market in that fleeting window of ideal ripeness. "These typically contain two to three times the sweetness of what's available here traditionally," says Koga. This isn't just taste perception but empirical fact, per the fruit's Brix score, its value on a scale of sweetness obtained by refractometer measurement. The sweet taste is made more jarring by the berry's pale hue. "We wanted to prove to everyone that it's not how it looks," says Koga. "Everything in the US is engineered to be red."

This is a Japanese berry, a varietal that, like some secret algorithm, can't be disclosed but is typically grown in the country's northern alps. The ones on Koga's table were produced a few dozen feet away from where they sit, in a setting with climatic parameters that have been tuned to a location 11,000 km away. "These berries still think they're in Japan," says Koga. Next to them are the raw materials of Oishii's process: a small shoot grown via in-vitro fertilisation and suspended in a clear nutrient-rich gel; and a larger plant resting in a proprietary growing medium.

Oishii, which means "delicious" in Japanese, is a rare success story in the world of vertical farming for two reasons. First, Oishii cracked indoor pollination. "Bees were known to not operate well in an indoor farm environment," says Koga. "We figured out how to make them believe that they're in nature." (The method is also proprietary.) Pollination by hand is possible, Koga notes, but not efficient at scale. Second, Oishii was able to create a product for which people are willing to pay $50 (€47) for a tray of eight. That's not unusual in Japan, where high-end purveyors such as Sembikiya elevate fruit to the status of luxury goods.

In the US, where strawberries are sold by the kilogram, it was a novel proposition. Oishii treated it that way, slowly introducing its berries via collaborations with restaurants, including Manhattan's three-Michelin-starred Chef's Table, where a single berry, unadorned, comprised the dessert course. Soon a mix of social-media-driven novelty

and scarcity kicked in: the berry became a viral Veblen good, in demand at least partially because of its price. Word crept out and a waiting list was set up. "We'd give people 24 hours' notice to come to the World Trade Center subway station the next day at 18.00," says Koga. "It was like a drug deal," he adds, laughing.

The global vertical-farming market was a $3bn (€2.8bn) business in 2021, according to researcher Fortune Business Insights. Koga admits that, compared to traditional agriculture, the sector's size represents a "rounding error". But its expansion graph is up and to the right, with varying forecasts of up to 25 per cent annual growth over the next decade. Against a challenging backdrop for traditional agriculture – disrupted supply chains, an increasingly volatile climate, rising fertiliser and labour costs – vertical farming, which offers year-round growing, less water consumption and no reliance on pesticides, looks increasingly attractive. But it depends on technological advancements and requires huge start-up costs. It can also be tricky to execute it at any meaningful size in the urban locations where it's most attractive.

Oishii's strategy is starting to bear fruit. The company, which has secured $55m (€51m) in financing from investors including the Toyota-backed Sparx Group and the Sony Innovation Fund, says that it is profitable on a "per facility" basis, adding that, like many start-ups, it's ploughing funds back into R&D. It has farms in New Jersey and near Los Angeles, an R&D site, 125 employees and plans for domestic and international expansion.

Among Oishii's US competition are two well-funded technology-forward start-ups, Aerofarms and Bowery Farming. Both are within walking distance of Oishii's first facility in Jersey City, New Jersey. In Denmark, Europe's largest vertical farm is churning out 1,000 tonnes of greens and herbs a year – enough to fulfil 5 per cent of Danish consumption. In 2021, Aerofarms broke ground on a 5,000 sq m R&D centre in Abu Dhabi, which hopes to increase domestic food production (the emirate imports 90 per cent of its food). But for all the recent energy, vertical farming took off in earnest several decades ago in Japan, where multinationals such as Panasonic and Sharp entered the arena. They were driven less by a green interest, Koga suggests, than technological prowess. "They just wanted to invent something cool," he says.

In early investor pitches, Koga, along with co-founder Brendan Somerville, a former Marine intelligence officer he met at business school, made two broad points. One – the founding principle of all vertical farms – is the need "to revolutionise agriculture sustainably through vertical

> "We'd give people 24 hours' notice to come to the World Trade Center subway station the next day at 18.00 [to buy strawberries]. It was like a drug deal"

1

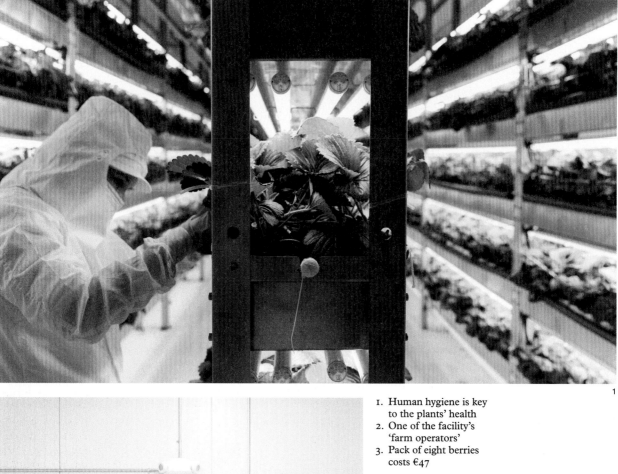

1. Human hygiene is key
   to the plants' health
2. One of the facility's
   'farm operators'
3. Pack of eight berries
   costs €47

2   3

farming," says Koga. The second point? "We don't only want to be a sustainable company; we want to introduce something that is better than what's out there." Koga points to Tesla. "It didn't just introduce any electric vehicle; it had a Roadster, which was faster than a Porsche." People went crazy for it, not because it was more sustainable, "but because it was a superior car". Just as the original Roadster was a six-figure car with an inherently limited audience, a $50 (€47) tray of strawberries is destined to be a niche product. But Oishii has launched a $20 (€18.60) package of the fruit, which will be sold by the taste-setting US retailer Whole Foods. Is this Oishii's Model 3 moment?

Before coming to the US in 2015, Koga had been researching and working with Japan's vertical farming industry as a consultant for Deloitte. The problem he found was that the companies couldn't diversify their products. "There was just no demand for vertical farm leafy greens that had to be sold at a premium," he says. "Shortly after, he enrolled in an MBA course at the University of California, Berkeley while consulting on the side for investors looking at vertical-farm start-ups. What struck him, in the middle of a California drought, was the increasing volatility of agriculture's inputs. "Stable weather conditions, access to water and land, cheap labour – all of these things were getting harder and harder to source," he says. Pesticides were increasingly being regulated and the cost of fertiliser went up. The new breed of start-ups was talking about sustainability but the problem was that they hadn't moved past "commoditised" technology and leafy greens. Despite heavy investment, he says, their greens weren't sufficiently better than those consumers could already access.

There was one product, however, for which Koga thought the juice was worth the squeeze: strawberries. They already come with prestige: they're one of the few fruits or vegetables to have brands attached (in the US, Driscoll's commands nearly a third of the market). But as a crop, they're notoriously difficult; producing them indoors at any scale has tormented any number of companies (French start-up Agricool, which grew strawberries in repurposed shipping containers, recently declared bankruptcy). Unlike short-cycle leafy greens – the butter lettuce or micro rocket sold by competitors including Bowery Farming and Aerofarms – they need to be kept alive longer to turn a profit. This generally requires a lot of chemical intervention – strawberries are at the top of the so-called "dirty dozen" list of fruits and vegetables containing the most pesticides (spinach and apples also rank highly). Then there's pollination. Koga thought that bees held the key to an entire new range

Upward growth
Global farming faces plenty of challenges: supply-chain interruptions; a blockaded Ukraine and a sanctioned Russia (both are major food suppliers); record-high fertiliser prices; and an ongoing La Niña weather event that's cooling the Americas. Vertical farming offers localised distribution andseemingly less resource-intensive farming. It's growing. Deals in the sector in 2021 were worth €900m, double 2019's value, says McAlinden Research Partners. But "in feeding the world in a resource-efficient manner, very often scale is required," says Tracey Allen, agricultural commodities strategist at JP Morgan. "Certainly in very wealthy markets, consumers have the bandwidth to make choices over products," she says. "But choices aren't very widely available to consumers in emerging markets." To make a difference, vertical farmers need to go beyond niche markets.

of indoor agriculture. "If we could figure out how to fly bees and manage disease, that gives us a shortcut to almost every other flowering crop: melons, peppers, aubergines."

To keep its strawberry plants disease-free without pesticide, Oishii relies on an exacting set of hygiene protocols. Moving from room to room requires repeatedly exchanging shoes for sandals and donning hairnets, masks and gloves. Jumpsuit-clad "farm operators" are cleansed by an "air shower" to enter the growing facilities, where no visitors are allowed. Julie Noyce, who manages Oishii's indoor farms, has no agricultural experience: her previous job was at a start-up that robotically produced human handwriting. "Whenever I hire one of our operators, I tell them no one's ever done this before," she says. When MONOCLE visits, only robots and bees move around the production room. "Even people who are skittish of bees really do start to appreciate them as our best co-workers," says Noyce, adding that the clean environment ensures plants' longevity. On an ordinary farm, the cultivars that Oishii uses would last for about a year before dying or developing a disease but "some of the seedlings in our R&D facility have stayed alive for more than two years".

Oishii's farm might depart from the "romantic notion" of agriculture, says Somerville, the company's chief operating officer. But, he argues, consumers increasingly recognise the value of indoor farming. "It's the cleanest strawberry we've ever had," he says. "It has the highest concentration of sugars in the US and it's the freshest. We deliver those things because it's grown in this controlled environment." And rather than being shipped 3,000 miles from California (the origin of more than 90 per cent of American strawberries) it's a 30-minute trip to the country's biggest market.

Having pioneered scalable production of indoor strawberries, Oishii won't be alone for long. Rival Bowery Farming is introducing two indoor strawberries ("Garden" and "Wild"), while San Francisco-based vertical farm start-up Plenty, working with Driscoll's, is said to be moving close to market. Koga is already thinking ahead. He envisions an Oishii-branded section in the supermarket. He's recently been working on melons and tomatoes, and the latter are already at Oishii's R&D farm. For Somerville, a broadening indoor strawberry market means heightened competition but also growing mainstream relevance. "This is an industry that can truly transform how we eat and our ability to feed the world in the future," he says. "We will continue to decrease the cost of production and add new crops. It's really just the beginning." — Ⓜ

MONOCLE
Get set for summer
at Monocle

London | Zürich | Tokyo | Los Angeles
Toronto | Hong Kong | Merano
monocle.com/shop

EASY TROUSERS by *De Bonne Facture*

Different beat
Lisbon

Portugal is a recording mecca for acts from across the Lusophone world. But can it export its stars?

WRITER
Gaia Lutz

PHOTOGRAPHY
Matilde Viegas

It's 22.00 on a Saturday at the sold-out Coliseu dos Recreios and the crowd is waiting anxiously under the domed ceiling of this storied venue in Lisbon. There's excitement in the air as people lean over the balustrades to get a better view of the stage. The auditorium chants in unison: "Dino, Dino, Dino". They're calling for Dino d'Santiago. Despite having been on Portugal's music scene for the past 20 years, the musician became a star here after the 2018 release of his album *Mundu Nôbu* ["New World"]. On this record and two more he has released since, the musician (who grew up in an Algarve fishing village) revisited his roots as a son of the Cape Verdean diaspora, mixing rhythms from the African archipelago with electronic soundscapes and singing in Portuguese and Creole. "Good evening, family," he says effusively, as he walks onto the stage in his shiny black outfit.

Smooth R&B vocals start floating over the galloping rhythm of Cape Verde's high-tempo *funaná*, while hip-hop rhymes are sung over *batuku*, a percussion-led genre that is getting a synth makeover. The crowd goes wild when D'Santiago takes out a *ferrinho*, a traditional elongated metallic instrument played by rubbing a knife on it. Moments of euphoric singing are interspersed with sober storytelling as D'Santiago shares tales of the journey that led him to tonight's glory, as well as historical excerpts recounting the hardships endured by Cape Verde's inhabitants.

Still, the overwhelming sentiment tonight is of hope. "I am here to share my past and dream of the future with you," he says. His track "Nova Lisboa" (New Lisbon) has become an unofficial anthem for a generation eager to turn the page on yesterday's traumas and celebrate the unique mix of cultures that's particular to this city.

D'Santiago might be the latest flagbearer for this movement but the roots of this "new Lisbon" aren't in fact that new. Portugal's colonial past has long created ties between the country, six African nations, Brazil and Timor-Leste – collectively known as the Lusophone world. In the past 50 years, waves

1

of migration from these countries have made Lisbon a place where cultures come together. In music, these influences are now expressed by second-generation artists and foreign-born musicians who come to Lisbon looking to expand their careers after making it big on home soil.

"It's a mark for an African artist to conquer Portugal and to fill arenas here. When they return to their home country their fees can double or triple," says Angolan musician, producer and writer Kalaf Epalanga. As well as being the executive producer behind D'Santiago's latest releases, he shot to fame as a musician in the early 2000s as part of Lisbon-based band Buraka Som Sistema. The group made thumping dance music by mixing Angolan *kuduro* with electronic styles borrowed from São Paulo and New York. One of Portugal's most successful musical exports, the band showed the world a Lisbon different to the home of melancholic *fado* that was lodged in many people's imaginations. Today, Epalanga continues to be involved with the city's cultural scene and championing new acts; he's also working with Angolan singer Toty Sa'Med, who has made the move from Luanda to Lisbon and has become one of the city's most hyped up-and-coming acts.

In the past musicians from Portuguese-speaking Africa have come to Lisbon in search of the industry's infrastructure – studios, labels and venues – as well as a wider market that can push forward their careers. They achieved success here with genres from singalong *kizomba* to avant garde jazz – today, for example, the likes of Calema, two brothers from the island nation of São Tomé and Príncipe, are making strides here with one catchy summer hit after another. But the industry is often quick to dismiss certain some of these dance-floor-ready tunes as fleeting pleasures and fails to capitalise on them.

"Portugal has a lot to gain from these careers," says Epalanga. Keeping this talent in the country would make business sense (it's still a sore point here that Cape Verdean icon Cesária Évora recorded in France after struggling to find recognition in Portugal). Many taste-makers, though, seem to believe that only certain genres should be considered a defining part of Portuguese culture and have been slow to embrace the music coming from Lisbon's rich mix of communities. "One of the

"It could only come from Lisbon, because of the concentration of immigrants, their exposure to European culture and how they interpret African sounds"

biggest Achilles' heels of Portugal's industries is not having the same diversity present as in the streets," says Epalanga.

Musician and label-owner Branko, who used to play with Epalanga in Buraka Som Sistema, agrees. "People say we opened the public's eyes to Lisbon's music of African origin but the city has been consuming this music much before we came along," he says outside Komum, the fashion shop he owns downtown. Before Buraka, a genre such as their up-tempo *batida* stayed in the shadows because it started in the housing estates on the city's periphery where most African communities live. But the band's international success has led many Lisboetas to start embracing this culture as their own.

Today the genre is so beloved that it is taking centre-stage at some of the city's hallmark music events. It's kick-off night at Sónar Lisbon (the first iteration of the famous Barcelona-born festival in Portugal) and producer-cum-DJ Nídia is in the middle of a dizzying set that has the room in a sweaty trance. Her music has won acclaim in clubs from London to Tokyo but it's rooted in her experience of growing up in a multicultural household and neighbourhood on the outskirts of Lisbon. "There were the Portuguese of Portuguese origin, the Guinean, São Toméan and Brazilian – and we'd all be eating together and sharing music," she says, as she cools down backstage.

Previous spread
1. Opening night at Sónar Lisbon

This spread
1. Rua das Pretas
2. Luis Montez
3. Nídia at Sónar festival
4. André, Flur Discos

1

2 3

4

Young producers like her are pushing *batida* into new, exciting directions and many of them are signed with Príncipe Discos. The Lisbon-based label has earned a cult following for focusing on this speaker-rattling genre for more than 10 years. "It's a sound that could only come from Lisbon, because of the concentration of immigrants their exposure to European culture and how they interpret the sounds coming from Africa through those lenses," says label co-founder José Moura. Thanks to their efforts, batida is now a mainstay on dance floors all around Lisbon.

Back at Sónar, Nídia's audience is filled with artsy, cosmopolitan types of all races. Still, Nídia believes that the success of the genre should go hand in hand with people's awareness of its origins – and that cultural events that bring people together from all parts of the city would help. "It's not just about consuming the music; it's knowing the history behind it," she says.

What all of these musicians share is a hope that Lisbon can be seen as more than just a host to different cultures but a fertile ground for new genres and musical developments too. Creating a strategy for this truly multicultural scene would help to attract a 250 million-strong market of Portuguese-speaking listeners around the world. Yet, so far, official institutions haven't jumped at the soft-power chance. "There's no collective organisation working on exporting the idea of Portuguese-expression music as a cohesive block, so that it can gain its own global territory," says Branko.

Some independent players are taking matters into their own hands and organising small Lusophone collectives. Inside a light-filled living room, Brazilian musician Pierre Aderne is gathered with musicians rehearsing for a concert in Porto. Dressed in white linen and equipped with acoustic instruments from guitars to tambourines, the group chit-chats in between samba chords. There's something of a bohemian, 1950s Rio de Janeiro atmosphere in the air – except if you listen closely, neither the songs nor the accents are entirely Brazilian. "We're all drinking from each other's cultures and it's this fusion that I like to call 'Lisbofonia'," says Aderne. Ever since moving to Portugal in 2011 he has been holding informal jam sessions at his house to connect the city's local musicians. These intimate sessions started being attended by distinguished musicians

1. Dino d'Santiago
2. Crowd during Nídia's performance at Sónar
3. Epalanga and Branko

1 2

3

from Brazil, Portugal and Portuguese-speaking Africa; the blend of traditions such as bossa nova, *fado*, *morna* and *funaná* became Rua das Pretas, a band and musical project that's all about showcasing the rich musical expressions of the Lusophone world. "Lisbon is more than [a place uniting] a musical diaspora. This mixture is giving birth to a new musical identity, which puts the Portuguese language above individual flags," says Aderne.

While Brazil has always backed its musical production on the global stage (Lisbon is proficient at twerking, thanks to Rio de Janeiro funk, and samba-infused carnival celebrations get bigger every year), Portugal has struggled to see its own acts make it big abroad. Brazil's behemoth musical output has kept it somewhat uninterested in what's happening across the Atlantic. In Lisbon many still see making it big in Brazil as a crucial step for homegrown music to become a global force.

"The Spanish have been doing this very well, tapping into Latin America and the US; they've structured themselves to do so," says Angolan Luis Montez, sitting in the wood-panelled office of his company Música no Coração. The music-promotion giant organises more than a dozen musical events in Portugal and Angola every year, from niche gatherings of *fado* and jazz musicians to big arena festivals featuring international line-ups. Those events, alongside the handful of radio stations Montez also owns, have played an important role in connecting Portuguese listeners to music from the rest of the Lusophone world. And Montez believes that there's room to grow his audience further; the rhythms from Portuguese-speaking Africa could play an important role in opening doors to Brazilian ears. "Just like the US has been discovering Nigerian music, there's a great potential for Brazil to discover music from Africa by way of Lisbon too," he says.

It's exactly a week from the performance at Coliseu dos Recreios and Dino d'Santiago is having breakfast at O Coqueiro, a Cape Verdean restaurant known for its Sunday *cachupa* stew and live music evenings. We're in Cova da Moura, a disadvantaged neighbourhood that's home to a vibrant Cape Verdean community but still considered by many as a no-go zone. "Lisbon should be studied: it's a city of real 'acculturation'," he says. "It's always been this way but I think it's about time to officially assume this."

Playlist:
Best Lusophone tracks

1. 'Esquinas'
   *Dino d'Santiago
   feat. Slow J*

2. 'Te Amo'
   Calema

3. 'Afeto'
   Mayra Andrade

4. 'BKBN'
   Soraia Ramos

5. 'Não Me Toca'
   Anselmo Ralph

We walk out on the narrow streets, past fruit sellers and the sweet smell of ripe mangoes, past colourful murals of Martin Luther King and Cesária Évora. Acquaintances stop to congratulate him with effusive words in Creole accompanied by kind smiles, fist bumps, hugs and a couple of demands for pictures.

At Kova M, a music studio nearby, D'Santiago sits down to give feedback on tracks recently recorded by teens from the neighbourhood. This studio is a community initiative that has given many young music hopefuls in the area the means to professionalise. "For our music industry to fully take off, we require above all political will; it's about seeing culture as the great aggregator that it is, and investing in it," says D'Santiago. "It's time that this soil becomes a point of union. That's the mission of this new Lisbon." — Ⓜ

Little wonders: Reimagining the bathroom in Denmark, Germany, France, the UK, Switzerland and the Czech Republic

What makes a perfect bathroom? Long dismissed as purely functional, it is now being reconsidered as a space rich in possibilities for aesthetic expression. That's why Geberit launched a contest to truly optimise the compact room.

■ Geberit products can transform a compact bathroom into an elegant yet functional space

Though recognised as one of the world's most innovative sanitaryware manufacturers, with the precision engineering that you would expect of a Swiss company founded in 1874, Geberit isn't resting on its laurels. Building on its reputation for creating high-quality toilets and flushing systems, the brand recently branched out into bathroom cabinets, sinks and lighting solutions. Seeking solutions for the trend for smaller bathrooms, Geberit launched a competition across six European markets inviting the brightest talent in architecture and interior design to reimagine the space. The parameters: to use Geberit products in a bathroom of no more than 6 sq m. We spoke to Martin Baumüller, head of group executive area marketing and brands, and the six entrants whose expertise was put to the test.

6×6 Design Contest

GEBERIT 6×6

Change maker

Bright sparks

The taskmaster

Martin Baumüller, head of group executive area marketing and brands

Where did the idea for the 6x6 design contest originate?
Smaller bathrooms are now more important as living space is getting scarcer and more expensive. We launched this initiative to get inspiration from designers.

What are the challenges involved in designing bathrooms?
The challenge is to optimise a space. At Geberit, we are dedicated to developing solutions that cover these aspects – design and functionality.

What surprised you about the process?
How great designers employed our products and put them into beautiful but highly practical spaces.

Why was the winner victorious?
That entry appealed to a lot of the consumers that took the final vote. The bathroom provides comfort with a choice of Geberit products that maximise space, such as the shower toilet AquaClean Mera or the modular washplace concept. And it features calm, earthy colours with wooden accents, which fits a sustainable bathroom.

Practical magic

Iveta Lajdová, architect, Czech Republic

The bathroom is where we start and end the day. It is a place for hygiene but also for relaxation. When designing a bathroom, it is important to consider both of these aspects. My design works with elements including contrast, industrial character and connection with nature. There are three main parts: a bathtub built into the floor with a view to the outside; a symbol of the moon created by a backlit round mirror above the wash basins; and a toilet with parts hidden by concrete.

■ Dark matter: a functional bathroom that celebrates fine design

All for one, one for all

Eva Ivos, founder, Eva Ivos, France

Client experience has shown me that families are increasingly living together: it's not uncommon to have four generations under one roof. This mainly happens when younger family members take care of the elderly. My approach to the competition was to offer a multifunctional design in which adaptability and durability are the main criteria. Above all, we need to respond to the evolution of users over time. From baby to senior, sportsman to those with reduced mobility, the format and function of the space should suit everyone.

■ A single space that meets the needs of a broad range of users

GEBERIT

Green living

Tilla Goldberg, director brand spaces, Ippolito Fleitz Group, Germany

Geberit is widely known for ingenious technology behind the wall: taking care of water consumption, reducing sound, creating perfect waterflow. The topic of sustainability played a major role in our design and will be one of the most important problems to solve in our society in the future. The user often doesn't know what sophisticated technology is installed in the wall. This can be integrated with the Geberit products in front of the wall to make the life of the users more comfortable.

Style counsel

Andrin Schweizer, founder, Andrin Schweizer Company, Switzerland

The bathroom is the one room in a house that is very technical in its functions but should feel sensual and intimate. I wanted to show that it's not only size that matters in bathroom design but also style. I used a combination of different materials to create a rich and luxurious atmosphere. An opulent and expressive natural stone is combined with a very calm feel. Elements in walnut create storage and divide the space into different areas.

Once in a lifetime

Nimi Attanaque (pictured, on left), partner, Nimtim Architects, UK

We wanted to create a bathroom that would be flexible and adaptable to ensure that it could cater to the various needs and ages of our clients. Our bathroom is designed for interaction and to serve any user, from children who are playing in the bath to adults who might want a quiet sanctuary and the elderly who need additional support. Creating a bathroom that can last a lifetime means choosing materials and products that are simple, resilient and enduring.

■ Green machine: a bathroom that emphasises efficient water use

■ Schweizer's bathroom balances technical brilliance with a sense of luxury

■ An inviting space that's suitable for users at any stage of life

What was your first thought when you received the brief?
It was that you can easily do a 6 sq m bathroom, or even smaller. The tricky part is doing something effective that gives users a positive experience. Early on we decided to choose a strong focus; we didn't want to attempt 10 different things and show off a lot of different possibilities. It needed to be clear and strong, and offer users some sort of calmness.

What was your approach?
There is a Danish word, *ro*, which has gained some traction lately. It means "serenity". It's an ultra-short word and very clear. We wanted to evoke this experience by toning the room down. A major focal point of our design is the idea of what's beyond the room, so we introduced a green space. So that was the approach: to evoke a strong feeling of warmth in the space and allow you to look out at nature.

Why do you enjoy working with Geberit products?
The products are of a very high quality. These are great products that evoke the right feeling: not only do these look right, but they are built right too. That's a strong point for us, related to sustainability. We appreciate items that have strong design and can be used for years without dating, or worse, breaking.

Nurturing nature

Carsten Wraae Jensen, partner, Bjerg Arkitektur, Denmark

■ Danish practice Bjerg Arkitektur's design, which makes innovative use of the space beyond the bathroom itself

Serenity now

Follow your art
Marseille

Away from the French capital, creatives head to the Med for a slower, more affordable way of life.

WRITER
Julia Webster Ayuso

PHOTOGRAPHY
Stephanie Fuessenich

Summer Listing 2022

"Marseille has always sparked an interest in artists," says Véronique Collard Bovy, the CEO of Fræme, which produces the city's contemporary art fair Art-o-rama. We are sitting on a terrace at the Friche la Belle de Mai, a former tobacco factory turned cultural hub where her show takes place every year. From this spot, with its bird's-eye view of the city, it's easy to see why. France's grittiest and most multicultural city might have long-standing issues but it's a place of stunning beauty with a white limestone coastline, turquoise waters and jaw-dropping sunsets. In the past decade a wave of businesses – in sectors ranging from food to hospitality – has helped to turn its reputation around. Now there is a widespread feeling that it is reaching a tipping point in matters of art too. According to the national statistics bureau of France, about 10,500 young creatives move to the city every year, mainly from Paris, seeking low rents and a slower pace of life.

"In the past two or three years, entire classes from art schools across France, such as Nice's Villa Arson, have shown up in Marseille straight after graduation," says Nicolas Veidig-Favarel, the young director of Double V Gallery, which he founded in 2016. "It's very fertile territory for creation because the city is affordable and a pleasant place to live," he says. "At the same time, it's the second biggest city in France and a Mediterranean capital."

Almost a decade since the city served as the European Capital of Culture, the boost that title carried with it is still in the air. In 2013 smart new buildings were erected to house cultural ventures and spruce up the city centre, including Rudy Ricciotti's filigree-clad Museum of European and Mediterranean Civilisations (MUCEM), the Frac Paca art centre, with its Kengo

1. Artist Léa Bigot
2. Bigot's works

1

Kuma-designed chequered glass façade, and the Villa Méditerranée, a building designed by Stefano Boeri to host multilateral summits on Mediterranean co-operation. Despite being held in a tough year, Marseille's staging of nomadic biennale Manifesta in 2020 helped cement the city's arts reputation, with exhibitions taking over landmarks and lesser-known buildings across the city. An ambition to revamp major cultural venues continues today: the cutting-edge Museum of Contemporary Art (MAC) is expected to reopen this year after a much-needed facelift.

Meanwhile, Art-o-rama has steadily grown since its beginnings in 2007 and has taken on a crucial role in promoting the city's art scene on a global stage. Held on the final weekend of August at the Friche la Belle de Mai, the opening brings together about 50 galleries from 18 different countries. This year's edition will also include a new design section with 22 exhibitors.

"[Much of France's art scene] is unfortunately very centralised in Paris, so it was very important for us not to become a regional fair but to establish ourselves internationally in order to exist," says Bovy. Other than hosting far-flung players, the event also acts as a springboard for local artists, with initiatives such as the Région Sud prize – awarded every year to a young graduate from one of the region's art schools, who gets to showcase their work in the fair the following year. Last year's winner, Flore Saunois, stood out with

2

1. 'More Pricks than Kicks' by
   Anastasia Bay
2. Véronique Collard-Bovy
3. 'Holding tight' by Norm Clasen
4. Flore Saunois's installation
5. Artist Sol Cattino
6. Villard & Brossard's 'Rupture Turbo'

3

4

an installation featuring a pink satin curtain that played with the viewer's desire to find out what's on the other side.

With artists and galleries leaving the grey skies of Paris for a spot on the Mediterranean, the demand for exhibition venues and residencies has boomed. Artist-run spaces such as Belsunce Projects, Atelier Panthera and Sissi Club have sprung up across the city to showcase emerging talent and Parisian non-profit Artagon launched a Marseille outpost inside an old Ricard pastis factory to house 25 resident artists. Seeing a rising demand for studio space, last year Marseille-based non-profit Yes We Camp launched Buropolis, a temporary transformation of a nine-floor office building into 253 affordable artist studios. Though the project is not permanent, its success has demonstrated that there is plenty of room for these kinds of experiments in the city – and Yes We Camp are looking for more opportunities for similar ventures.

Maëva Tobalagba is one of the artists who took advantage of the programme. After studying in Lyon, she moved to Marseille where she works as an illustrator. She also co-founded design collective La Rallonge. "Being in Marseille is a big advantage. It's a dynamic city where making connections is very easy," she says. "It's like a village."

Fellow artist Thibaut Caesar, a sculptor who has also directed music videos for British electronic music group Metronomy, lived in Paris, Brussels and Berlin before arriving

5

6

Places to visit:

Artagon
Founded in 2014 by Anna Labouze and Keimis Henni, Artagon is dedicated to promoting emerging artists. After opening their first space in Paris in 2015, the duo launched their Marseille space in 2021 in the former Ricard factory north of the city. Here, they house 25 artists and host exhibitions. *artagon.org*

Pavillon Southway
Former curator Emmanuelle Luciani opened the Pavillon Southway in a 19th-century house in Mazargues. An artist residence and a gallery, it showcases decorative art by collective Southway Studio. *southwaystudio.com*

Voiture 14
This space hosts regular exhibitions and events by the city's emerging talent, whether it's art, music or fashion. It was founded by Myriam Mokdes, who graduated from Marseille's school of fine arts and sought to remedy the lack of central exhibition spaces for its students. *14 Rue des Héros*

Double V Gallery
Double V Gallery is a respected presence in Marseille, representing emerging international artists while supporting the local scene. Its founder, Nicolas Veidig-Favarel, worked at Art-o-rama before setting up his gallery in the trendy 6th arrondissement. *double-v-gallery.com*

Le Cabinet d'Ulysse
Just around the corner from Double V, this gallery opened by Stéphane Salles-Abarca in 2019 offers a sharp selection of artists across diverse disciplines. This summer, it is showing paintings by Marseille-born artist Philippe Fangeaux. *lecabinetdulysse.com*

in Marseille three years ago. "There isn't any space to do anything in Paris," he says. "And I don't mean just physical space. Someone else has already had the same idea as you and done it, whereas here, there is still a lot to be done."

Réunion-born artist Léa Bigot, who spent a decade in Paris before moving to Marseille three years ago, agrees. "It feels like you can do anything, that everything is possible," she says, surrounded by her curvy black and white ceramic sculptures. "It's easier to find your voice here. Not like in Paris, where you're among thousands of artists who are all doing interesting things."

This sense of possibility is echoed by many creatives in town. But others worry that the arrival of so many affluent Parisians is pushing Marseille-born artists out of their home city – which, despite everything, remains one of the most disadvantaged in France. Marseille-born Sol Cattino feels that there is a disconnect. "Art should coexist with the city, not just land for a short time and then leave," says the painter, whose work explores femininity through the southern French stereotype of *la cagole* – or bimbo. "When you're an artist in Marseille, it's important to not forget the inhabitants."

But Marseille-born collector Sébastien Peyret, who inaugurated a location for his project space Atlantis in the northern neighbourhood of La Rose in 2021, believes the arrival of a new wave of artists is helping boost the city's confidence. "There is definitely a renaissance happening. Marseille is becoming more uninhibited," he says. As well as being a collector, he is a pharmacist and the president of Triangle Astérides, a contemporary art centre based in the Friche la Belle de Mai. "I never really believed in myself or my city because from a young age you are told that to be successful, you have to go to Paris. But now we see people moving here and we realise that it's not the case."

Still, there is some way to go before Marseille's art market catches up with the might of Paris's commercial power. But that doesn't seem to scare or dissuade the city's galleries too much. That's why Veidig-Favarel's Double V Gallery, the first Marseille-based gallery to participate in Art-o-rama, recently opened a second, satellite outpost in the capital. "I try to spend most of my time in Marseille and I go to Paris only when it's necessary," he says. "But I don't see this as an

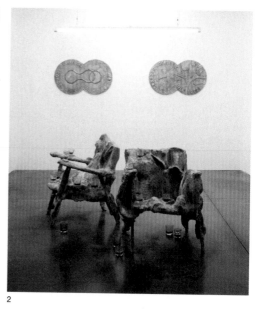

1

2

3

"From a young age, you're told that to be successful, you have to go to Paris. It's not the case"

obstacle; it just means that we need to work within this context."

For others, the solution lies in building a wider, more international customer base. "I don't think that I could run a gallery with an exclusively local market," says Frédéric Bonnet, talking about his sales trips to Mexico and Japan. After 20 years in Paris as an art critic and curator, he moved back to his home city to set up Nendo, a gallery specialising in ceramics. His space on the central Rue Sylvabelle, inaugurated in April, showcases sculptures by the likes of Pep Gomez and Claire Lindner.

After working as a gallerist in Brussels for 20 years, Avignon-born Catherine Bastide also ended up making the journey south. She has poured a lot of energy into revamping La Traverse, a house overlooking the picturesque bay of Anse de Malmousque dedicated to fostering dialogue between various creative disciplines. In its rooms, furnished with designs by artist Régis Jocteur Monrozier and Marseille collective Laissez Passer, Bastide hosts exhibitions, artist residencies as well as dinners with local chefs.

This recent swell of creative energy might feel new and exhilarating but for Veidig-Favarel, all of this is simply a manifestation of Marseille's character. "What has been happening for the past few years is quite exciting," says the gallerist. "But the city has always been this way; it's always been a *terre d'accueil* – a welcoming ground." — Ⓜ

1. Furniture by Regis Jocteur Monrozier at La Traverse
2. Work by James Lewis
3. Dining table and chairs by artist Régis Jocteur Monrozier
4. 'La soupe primitive' by Marie-Sarah Adenis
5. Kitchen at La Traverse
6. Catherine Bastide, gallerist and founder of La Traverse
7. 'Googleos mentales' by Ramiro Quesada Pons at Art-o-rama
8. Terrace at La Friche la Belle de Mai

4

5

6

7   8

Screen time
Global

Far from the bustling, buzzing multiplexes, with their packed screenings and sprawling footprints, these small cinemas offer their own unique ways of watching a movie – and being part of a city's culture and community.

1 2

I.
Cool for cats
Cinema Neko, Tokyo

Yasuhiro Kikuchi is standing in the sunshine, surveying the unusual duck-egg blue exterior of his 63-seat cinema in the far west of Tokyo. "The building is a registered historic property, so we had to stick with the original colour," he says. Cinema Neko (Cinema Cat) opened last summer in an old silk factory in Ome, a town once famed for its lively movie scene. During the postwar years, there were three cinemas close to the station and the streets were plastered with hand-painted film posters by billboard artist Bankan Kubo.

Kikuchi had his heart set on giving his hometown a cinema worthy of its history. The old wooden building had been given a lifeless interior makeover. With architect Ao Ikegami on board, the new project started coming to life.

The bill for the renovation and equipment was ¥100m (€760,000); Kikuchi invested his own money, bolstered it with crowdfunding and the rest was covered by a government subsidy. Ikegami ripped out the plaster ceilings and exposed the roof beams;

he made a feature of the old wooden panelling and let the light pour into the café and lobby through high windows.

The cinema has been greeted with open arms: 700 people have signed up to become members. Kikuchi welcomes school parties, introducing them to the pleasures of cinema. The schedule changes fortnightly with three different screenings a day. The roster is a mix of classics, documentaries, new releases and European arthouse fare. Visitors are also encouraged to make suggestions.

The cinema's name comes from another former feature of Ome: cats. They used to be everywhere, keeping tabs on the rodent population that was attracted by the silkworms. Kikuchi pulled off a coup for the official opening with a screening of Studio Ghibli's classic *The Cat Returns*. "Everyone said it would be impossible to get permission to show it but I wrote a letter to Hayao Miyazaki [Ghibli co-founder] and he said yes."

Kikuchi is passionate about the power of cinema. "We live in an age when you can see films whenever and wherever you like but going to the cinema is a special experience that is detached from everyday life." — FW
cinema-neko.com

3

1. Intimate screen at Cinema Neko
2. Service with a smile
3. Merchandise stand
4. The facade of the Alhambra cinema
5. Sine Pop founder Carlson Chan
6. Eye-catching branding
7. The 48-seat screen

4

2.
Collective impact
Alhambra, Marseille

Could there be a more fitting address for one of Marseille's most storied movie theatres than Rue du Cinéma? Generations of Marseillais have discovered the magic of cinema at the Alhambra. Built in 1928, its façade with ochre-yellow accents is unchanged. The Alhambra was the childhood haunt of film director Robert Guédiguian, whose movies about his hometown have won international acclaim. Retrospectives of his work, as well as showings of films by French directors such as Hafsia Herzi, drew crowds who swelled with local pride.

After closing down in 1980, the theatre reopened in 1990 and is today owned by the city and run by a non-profit organisation. "We see this as much more than a cinema," says its director, William Benedetto. On summer evenings, audiences spill out onto Rue du Cinéma, having an apèro at the bar opposite. Sometimes there is live music or karaoke – and often that means dancing.

Convinced that cinema can change lives, Benedetto has reached out to nearby schools, some of which are in France's most deprived neighbourhoods. "I believe that the collective experience of discovering a movie in a room with other people is even more essential in a world where people, particularly the younger generation, spend more and more time alone," he says. "Young people can discover movies they might not otherwise encounter, including films about their own city."

Cinema can play an important role in fostering social cohesion – and the Alhambra can be a model for communities in Marseille and beyond. — MFI
alhambracine.com

5   6

7

3.
Independent means
Sine Pop, Manila

Ancestral houses in Metro Manila are typically refurbished into trendy cafés but Carlson Chan had a different idea when he acquired a 1948 home from its longtime owners of almost 70 years. He opened a cinema.

Micro-cinema Sine Pop blends the old with the new in its minimalist design, which maintains most of the house's original structure to preserve its storied past but Chan has also added a lush bamboo garden to bring a touch of greenery to the venue. The cinema's austere simplicity is inspired by the Japanese *wabi-sabi* philosophy of purity and deliberate imperfection (though budget constraints also played a role in its sparse aesthetics).

"We want to show that heritage conservation doesn't need to be expensive," says Chan. "We splurged only on the concrete works and cinema equipment."

Sine Pop had its first screening in 2020, showing *Norte, The End of History*, a psychological drama by critically acclaimed Filipino director Lavrente Diaz; the 48-seater cinema makes a point of supporting independent films.

"Micro-cinemas are necessary to maximise the reach of independent local films," says Chan. He is also realistic and resourceful when it comes to keeping the business healthy. "For a cinema our size to survive, we cannot rely on ticket sales and food-service income; we cater to the private-events market, while continuing our advocacy for free public screenings too," he says. — FG
14 St Mary Street, Quezon City, Manila

Artistic intake
Global

From a sculpture park to record shops, these are the cultural hotspots to hit this summer.

EDITED BY
Chiara Rimella

Fondation Maeght
St-Paul-de-Vence, France

Nestled between the French riviera and the Préalpes d'Azur mountain range, Saint-Paul-de-Vence is a small village that has been on the map for art lovers since Calder, Chagall and Miro first flocked to the Colombe d'Or hotel and the Fondation Maeght opened in 1964. Now artists Arik Levy and Zoé Ouvrier are taking appointments for visitors and collectors to tour their bright studio and expansive, verdant garden. "They come and see the dialogue between sculpture and nature," says Levy. "Collectors imagine how a piece would look in their own garden. In the white space of a gallery it takes a lot more convincing that it could work." Levy leads the tours himself.

The house previously belonged to French ballerina Sylvie Guillem and her photographer husband Gilles Tapie. Her dance studio has now been repurposed as a space where Ouvrier can focus on her wood-based paintings and engravings and Levy on his geometric metallic sculptures. "It's a dream for any artist to have this space, with 7 metre-high ceilings and windows

that never end. It's practical and inspiring," says Levy. The house sits on a huge expanse of land, where Levy's pieces, such as the towering "Micro Rocks Copper" and star-shaped "Rock Growth", pop up between cypress, lemon and olive trees.

Levy and Ouvrier moved here two years ago, leaving Paris in search of a warmer climate and proximity to the sea. A self-professed beach bum from Tel-Aviv, Levy started his career painting surfboards and designing wetsuits. Today, other than working on his art pieces, he carries out design commissions for the likes of Swiss company Vitra, US office-furniture firm Coalesse and French lighting brand Forestier. "I learned a lot from design," he says. "Structural materials, physics, technology – I implement it into my art because it's a tool. And vice versa, I enrich design with art." — GCH
ariklevysculpturepark.com

Artipelag
Värmdö island, Sweden

Just as its name suggests, Artipelag is an art institution set in the middle of an archipelago; its main venue sits on the island of Värmdö, in Baggen's bay, a 90-minute boat ride from the centre of Stockholm. The building is embedded in a landscape of pine trees, granite rocks and rugged coastlines.

The works displayed inside are chosen because of how they explore people's relationships with their natural surroundings. "We prefer to showcase art that has a connection to nature in one way or another," says director Bo Nilsson. "Normally you refer to a gallery as a white cube but we call Artipelag the 'green room'; nature tends to ease up the art experience for visitors."

This summer, Artipelag is opening its largest exhibition so far. *Essence-Eksistence*, a solo show by German artist Anselm Kiefer, will coincide with the museum's 10-year anniversary and will present paintings, sculptures and an installation that all reflect on German history and its effect on the environment. "Kiefer is obsessed with the destruction of the landscape. As he was born in 1945, he never experienced the war but as a child he experienced a ruinous landscape in Germany that was slowly turned into a new industrial society," says Nilsson.

Besides an exhibition and event space with stunning views to the sea outside, there is an outdoor sculpture park which includes the recently added "Solar Egg" by Stockholm-based artist duo Bigert & Bergström: a huge, multi-faceted golden egg-shaped sculpture right by the waves. "It guides visitors to the museum like a lantern," says Nilsson. — JDA
artipelag.se

Summer Listing 2022

Offtrack
Singapore

DJ Dean Chew and fellow audiophile Daniel O'Connor opened their listening bar-cum-restaurant Offtrack this year inside a shophouse that used to house a karaoke lounge. On this Friday evening, the free jazz of Alice Coltrane is drifting out of a restored set of hulking La Scala speakers made by US sound specialists Klipsch.

At the heart of this 40-seater venue is a DJ booth, backdropped by an eclectic, genre-bending collection of records; it reflects the wide range of music played by guest DJs and vinyl collectors who come and perform from all around the region. "We are community-centric," says Chew. "This is our version of a social club without being members-only. It's a space for people to meet and get inspired."

It's a full house tonight. Many of the customers are friends: Chew and O'Connor have built a dedicated following over the years through their own independent ventures. While Chew is co-founder of electronic music label Darker Than Wax, O'Connor is behind Ice Cream Sundays, a music collective known for organising crowd-pleasing daytime jamborees. The pair have previously collaborated on gigs and parties, many of which were pop-ups. Having their own venue now feels like a dream come true.

"We want to use this space as an incubator," says Chew. The plan is to bring together people who work across different disciplines and give them room to experiment and share their expertise; workshops on bartending and graphic design are in the pipeline. The team is also working with curator Tulika Ahuja of Singaporean art consultancy Mama Magnet and Yogyakarta-based printmaking studio Krack! to present art shows. "It is about expanding the community so we engage people beyond our own circles," says Chew.

The kitchen at Offtrack whips up pan-Asian dishes such as charred aubergine with red-pepper sambal. Chew has designed the interiors so that the restaurant side of the venue doesn't overshadow its artsy credentials. Japanese screens and custom furniture create an intimate space that encourages people to hang out. "We don't want to become another typical F&B outlet," he says.— YX
offtrack.sg

Lusophonica
Cascais, Portugal

When Pedro Avillez Costa returned to his native Portugal in 2016 following a six-year stint in New York's music industry, he had an idea: to launch a radio station that promoted the music of the Lusophone communities (something the acts in our report on Lisbon's multicultural music scene on page 144 will be pleased to hear). "We wanted to connect Portuguese-speaking countries – compare musical tastes, discover new genres and create a platform for people to interact with," says Costa, who co-founded Lusophonica Web Radio in 2020 with his childhood friend and DJ Nuno Rodrigues. The pair set up base beside the striking Santa Marta Lighthouse by the sea in Cascais. "It's the perfect location – very close to Lisbon but not as urban – and the artistic community here is always developing," says Costa.

The small radio studio is also home to an airy café and, on sunny days, the Lusophonica beats can be heard across the forecourt, where visitors enjoy views of the Atlantic ocean while they sip coffee – the beans, much like the music, are sourced from Lusophone nations. "The main idea was always the radio but we had to figure out a way to pay for it," says Costa. "We wanted to learn from each of the countries directly and give them a voice. I'm proud that we're helping the community thrive." — MPC
lusophonica.com

PHOTOGRAPHERS: Grégoire Bernardi, Pedro Guimarães, Khoo Guo Jie

Summer Listing 2022

Deep
Marseille

"When we had the idea to turn an old newspaper kiosk into a coffee shop, we wanted to stay true to the DNA of the venue," says Tony Collins, founder of Marseille-based coffee roaster Deep. Since March his kiosk, the small sister to Deep's main café near the city's Vieux Port, is supplying the Camas neighbourhood with speciality coffee and independent magazines from France and beyond, including South Korea's surfing magazine *Stoned*, Canadian food title *Serviette* and, perhaps unsurprisingly, the coffee-themed *Drift*. Unlike most newsagents, Deep's kiosk spotlights a different title every month, selling its entire back catalogue (stock permitting). "This gives our customers the chance to get their hands on rare and difficult-to-find past issues," says Collins. This July, French travel magazine *Les Others* is taking centre stage, followed by UK photography journal *Off the Rails*. Pick up a cup of Deep's own cold drip and take your print bounty down to the corniche. — AW
deep.coffee

Rupture Records
Paris

Last year, entrepreneur Alexandre Sap gave fellow Frenchman and architect Pierre Gonalons carte blanche to execute his vision for a vinyl shop in Paris's chic Haut Marais neighbourhood. The result is decor inspired by the luxurious general goods shop Drugstore Publicis in Saint-Germain-des-Prés, with pink parquet, velvet Paradisoterrestre chairs and rich textiles from Hermès's textile division Métaphores, evoking 1970s Paris. "There's a touch of Serge Gainsbourg in the black glass tiles," says Sap. "My record shop might not be the biggest one in Paris but it is the most beautiful," he adds proudly. Rupture is also a café, bar and office for Sap's communications agency and music label, where he receives clients and musicians for an apéro. "Instead of having a boring corporate office, why not create a lifestyle?" he says. Visitors can browse vintage vinyl rarities alongside the latest releases while sipping on a rosé and requesting records to be played on the speakers. Across the road, a Rupture bookshop has swiftly followed and Sap has plans to expand to Venice and Marseille, inside Le Corbusier's Radiant City complex. "I want to make people discover new things," he says. "I don't treat people like algorithms and I can't track them beforehand. I feel a social responsibility to create a link between people and culture." — GCH
rupture.tv

Ypsigrock
Sicily

Ypsigrock, a small but exciting Sicilian event set in the medieval hilltop village of Castelbuono, is celebrating its 25th anniversary this year and is holding on to its reputation as a place to discover the best, cutting-edge independent acts from Italy and beyond. Co-founder Vincenzo Barreca reveals what's on the cards for this year's event. — SMN

What makes Ypsigrock special?
As well as the artists' quality, Ypsigrock mixes an intimate atmosphere with a historic location. All of the performances are within walking distance of each other with ice cream or bowls of pasta in between. The early-morning stage is in the mountainous pinewoods overlooking the town.

What can visitors expect?
A warm welcome, outstanding gastronomy and stunning surroundings.

What are this year's highlights?
We're particularly excited to welcome The Flaming Lips, 2manydjs, Self Esteem and Anna B Savage. We also have some of the most interesting up-and-coming Italian acts. Over the years, we have welcomed artists from Iosonouncane to La Rappresentante di Lista and many more. This year we're also teaming up with UK independent record label Bella Union, who are celebrating their 25th anniversary as well. So it's a double 25th: a *Festa Bellissima!* Ypsigrock runs 4-7 August; ypsigrock.it

Paperground
Madrid

Paperground, an excellent new addition to the independent retail scene in the northern Madrid neighbourhood of Chamberí, opened its doors in May. Inside the striking yellow-fronted magazine and book shop, shoppers can choose from global publications such as Turkish bathing magazine *Hamam* to British slow-news quarterly *Delayed Gratification*. There's also a selection of books focusing on art and design that showcases young Spanish publishers such as Terranova and Dalpine. Behind the shop are Margherita Visentini, a journalist and editor of *Polpettas on Paper* magazine, and Aiser Rua, a photographer who also runs his own publishing business, Rua Ediciones. "Spain's independent publishing scene has really grown over the past few years," says Rua. "Paperground is a way of celebrating that." — HU
Calle de Medellín 4

PHOTOGRAPHERS: Grégoire Bernardi, Alex Créuy Systermans, Victor Garrido

Summer's soundtrack
Global

Monocle's senior culture correspondent has fashioned the ultimate holiday playlist full of fresh releases and timeless classics.

SELECTED BY
Fernando Augusto Pacheco

Summer Listing 2022

Road trip

From breezy Aussie electro-pop to rocky riffs from Texas and smooth French hip-hop, put these tunes on and roll down the windows.

1.
Push It Up
Confidence Man

2.
Supermodel
Måneskin

3.
Steal My Sunshine
Len

4.
Night Drive
Shinichiro Yokota

5.
Le Banana Split
Lio

6.
Nouveau Western
MC Solaar

7.
Hell on Wheels
Cher

8.
Samurai
Cairokee

9.
É Proibido Fumar
Rita Lee and Gilberto Gil

10.
Summer in New York
Sofi Tukker

11.
Teardrops
Womack & Womack

12.
Texas Sun
Khruangbin and Leon Bridges

13.
Soaked
Benee

14.
Summer in the City
Quincy Jones

15.
I Got the Moves
Habibi

16.
Mediterranea
Irama

17.
A Gira
Trio Ternura

18.
I Can't Go for That (No Can Do)
Hall & Oates

19.
Lotta Love
Nicolette Larson

Apéro time

Slow down with Nigerian-Italian funk, Austrian chillout and vintage disco.

20.
Ease Your Mind
Darius feat. Devin Tracy

21.
Bells
DBN Gogo feat. Eltonk SA, DJ Stopper and TNK Musiq

22.
Juice
Muzi

23.
Think About Me
Hammer

24.
Lagos Connect
Aura Safari feat. Villy

25.
Holding on Too Long
Hard Feelings

26.
What Is It Like
Wolfram feat. Pam

27.
Negotiate With Love
Rachel Stevens

28.
Un Millón
The Marías

29.
Perfetta Cosi
Sam Rufillo

30.
Yo Yo
Mika

31.
Count What You Have Now
Vantage

32.
Pourquoi faire aujourd'hui
Lisa LeBlanc

33.
Arpoador
Carwyn Ellis & Rio 18

34.
Ride It
Regard

35.
Mourir sur scène
Dalida

36.
Le Reste
Clara Luciani

37.
Summer Night City
Abba

38.
Space & Sound
Oliver

Afternoon sunbathing

Scorching-hot tracks, from 1990s classics to Cali soul.

39.
Summer Blue
Bread & Butter

40.
Imizamo
Karyendasoul and Blaqrhythm feat. Nana Atta and Teezy Musician

41.
Dreams of Music
Aura Safari

42.
Enty Hayaty
Saad Lamjarred feat. Calema

43.
Vamos a la Playa
Miranda

44.
It's So Nice (To See Old Friends)
Minnie Riperton

45.
Ain't Nobody Straight in LA
Whale Island

46.
Instant Sunshine (Luke Million remix)
Lau

47.
Sheltered Life
Erlend Øye

48.
Western Wind
Carly Rae Jepsen

49.
L'âme-stram-gram
Mylène Farmer

50.
Calma
Marisa Monte

51.
French Waltz
Leon Ware

52.
Só Para Você
Juniper feat. Sango
and Vhoor

53.
Together Again
Janet Jackson

54.
*Se a vida é
(That's the Way Life Is)*
Pet Shop Boys

55.
Breathe
Télépopmusik

56.
Summer Breeze
The Isley Brothers

57.
*Everybody Loves
the Sunshine*
Roy Ayers Ubiquity

58.
Pick Up Your Heart
Paige Bea

59.
Rhythm to Ya Love
Sunni Colón

60.
Sunchyme
Dario G

Euro dance floor

Italo-disco, Cypriot salsa
and Spanish pop tunes to
transport you straight to a
Mediterranean nightclub.

61.
Ciao Ciao
La Rappresentante di Lista

62.
Libre
Angèle

63.
This Girl
Kungs vs Cookin'
on 3 Burners

64.
Slomo
Chanel

65.
Je Survivrai
Régine

66.
Madame
Kings × Trannos

67.
On Your Mind
Doss

68.
You Could Be
Anz feat. George Riley

69.
Bamboo Fighter
Soichi Terada

70.
Cleo
Shygirl

71.
I'm Good
Betta Lemme

72.
Talk About
Rain Radio and
DJ Craig Gorman

73.
Into the Groove (remix)
Madonna

74.
La Nuit
Diva

75.
The Summer Is Magic
Playahitty

76.
Bagno a Mezzanotte
Elodie

77.
IUL
Danny L Harle

78.
I Can't Get Enough
Cazzi Opeia

79.
All Around the World
ATC

80.
Kuuma Jäbä
Isaac Sene

81.
Turn Me On
Kevin Lyttle

82.
Caramela
Eleni Foureira

83.
Live Is Life
Opus

Brazilian sunset

Sultry, tropical beats to
wind down to – expect
moody jazz, samba and
bossa nova from Latin-
America and beyond.

84.
Dégaine
Aya Nakamura
feat. Damso

85.
São Paulo
Julia Jean-Baptiste

86.
Pourquoi C'est Comme Ça?
Jacques

87.
I'm Not in Love
Karen Souza

88.
*Paris Tropical
(Kazy Lambist remix)*
Minuit

89.
Brisa
Iza

90.
Sexy Yemanjá
Pepeu Gomes

91.
Midnight Cruisin'
Kingo Hamada

92.
Sove Lanmou
Zouk Machine

93.
Passarinha
Bala Desejo

94.
Give My Love a Try
Body Music feat.
Xavier Smith

95.
Sensitivity
Ralph Tresvant

96.
Menino do Rio
Caetano Veloso

97.
Darling Come Back Home
Barbara Mason

98.
Freed from Desire
Gala

99.
*Tutto Va Bene Quando
Facciamo l'amore*
Alex Rossi feat. Jo Wedin

100.
Smooth Operator
Sade

To listen to the playlist,
search for Monocle 24's
account on Spotify – and
make sure to tune in
to our round-the-clock
programming.

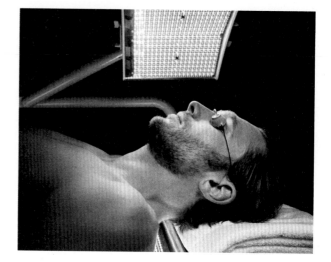

THE KEY TO LASTING WELLBEING

LONG LIVE LIFE

DEFYING AGE, THE RIGHT WAY

How Clinique La Prairie pioneered holistic health

The search for longevity is as old as humankind. When Swiss scientist Paul Niehans developed a groundbreaking cellular therapy to slow down the ageing process in 1931, the world got one step closer in the quest. Today, Clinique La Prairie is keeping Niehans' mission alive in the very same Montreux location where the research was first carried out. With a team of 50 leading medical specialists, it is helping and inspiring people to live a longer, healthier and fuller life.

To take this unparalleled expertise beyond the four walls of the clinic, Clinique La Prairie developed Holistic Health, a range of science-driven, Swiss-made supplements that boost wellbeing from the cells up.

"With our products, we allow people who already feel good to feel better," says Simone Gibertoni, CEO and co-founder of Clinique La Prairie Holistic Health.

Featuring high-diversity natural compounds that even the healthiest of diets can't offer, the supplements in the line are designed to complement a balanced daily lifestyle, thanks to a unique core complex that promotes the natural anti-ageing process.

Because health is so much more than the absence of illness, Clinique La Prairie Holistic Health's ultimate wellbeing solution comes in the form of Age-Defy, the clinic's most comprehensive longevity supplement. Its revitalising ingredients target antioxidation, anti-inflammation and cell regeneration, bringing more than 90 years of transformative rejuvenation into the day-to-day lives of health-conscious individuals.

CLINIQUELAPRAIRIE-HH.COM

2

SIMONE GIBERTONI

CEO and co-founder, Clinique La Prairie Holistic Health

What is wellbeing to you?
We have a holistic approach to wellbeing at Clinique La Prairie. For me and the entire team, it's so much more than a medical concept. Movement, nutrition and mental health play an equally important role. We are firm believers in preventive medicine and lifestyle changes – you come to us not because of health issues but because you want to enhance the way you live. Health is probably the number one prerequisite for quality of life. Anyone who has been ill knows that it affects the entire body, so we have to do our best to incorporate wellbeing rituals into our daily routine to prevent this from happening.

Is this where the idea behind the Clinique La Prairie Holistic Health supplement range came from?
You can start changing someone's life during a stay at Clinique La Prairie but one or two weeks are only the beginning of this journey of transformation to achieve the ultimate results. This is where the supplements come in. We wanted to offer our clients a powerful, complementary tool that scientifically targets the body's functions and cellular regeneration, all year. We could have gone for an existing supplement but we didn't find anything that satisfied our high standards and rigour. It quickly became clear that we had to launch Clinique La Prairie Holistic Health to offer clients the Swiss quality, efficacy and expertise in longevity that our clinic is known for.

Why did you land on four products and not just one?
We knew from the outset that we didn't want a one-size-fits-all supplement because we strongly believe that long-term wellbeing is much more than one thing. So we deliver a strong statement that has cellular longevity at its core: this is Age-Defy, our star product, next-generation longevity formulation, which boosts the immune system and cell regeneration. But we felt that there was a need for other supplements to reach the objectives we wanted to fulfil. With our range we have everything covered, from the body's detoxifying process to better focus and sleep.

What do you swear by in your personal routine?
I meditate twice daily, which has been a real life-changer. It's funny because it's far from being the latest technology but still, all these millennia later, meditation has exceptional effects on the body and our stress levels. It's important to find time in our busy schedules for the things that make us feel good.

EXPERTISE Simone Gibertoni and Clinique La Prairie's Holistic Health products

2 DESIGN: Architecture

Force of nature
Italy

Italy's leading landscape designer Pietro Porcinai,
who brought modernism to traditional gardens,
was passionate about the importance of nature
in design and ensuring that greenery was part
of any built environment. His legacy is more
pertinent than ever.

WRITER
Stella Roos

PHOTOGRAPHY
Andrea Pugiotto

1

2

1

Florence is not known for its modernist landscape architecture. The Renaissance city and rolling hills around it are teeming with grand, heritage-protected homes and any new construction has to clear a thicket of bureaucratic hurdles, if it is not blocked outright. But in among this mix are multiple modernist gardens created by Pietro Porcinai, Italy's greatest landscape designer of the 20th century. One example lies in Fiesole on the grounds of Villa Rondinelli, the former guesthouse of a neighbouring Medici villa. Tucked in to the hillside are two glass-walled greenhouses, camouflaged by vines and a roof garden. They were designed in the 1960s and are officially *limonaias*, winter storage spaces for lemon trees. In practice, they were Porcinai's personal studios.

"Landscape architects didn't exist in Italy before my father," says Pietro's daughter, Paola Porcinai. It is an unseasonably warm May day and she is sitting outside one of the greenhouse studios. "He was the only one working in the field at the time and he single-handedly established the profession." Up until his death in 1986, Porcinai employed more than 50 people who worked in the main house of Villa Rondinelli and helped draw up designs for gardens, parks, piazzas, industrial areas and even highways. Injecting modernism into traditional garden design, he carried out more than 1,000 projects in his career, including 200 in Florence alone.

Paola explains that her father developed his green fingers during a childhood spent in Villa Gamberaia, an opulent Tuscan estate where his dad was a gardener. "From an early age he lived around this paradise of a formal Italian garden," she says. After studying for an agriculture diploma in Florence, the 18-year-old Porcinai hopped on a motorbike and spent a year visiting leading landscape architects in Belgium and Germany, where the profession was more established. Once back in Italy, Porcinai got to work designing what he – quite ambitiously – thought of as earthly paradises. "He would say that the ideal garden was that of Adam and Eve, the garden of Eden," says Paola. "But his design methods were always avant garde." Many of Porcinai's creations are still in use by the families that commissioned them. On a typical weekday at Villa La Terrazza on the southern edge of Florence, members of the Rangoni family while away the afternoon in their garden working, studying or swimming in the pool. From the iron terrace furniture to the custom-designed stone lamps, the garden has remained essentially unchanged

2

"He was critical of the inhumane aspects of modernism. He argued nobody can live well surrounded by cement; greenery needs to be part of any built environment"

since Ugo Rangoni, founder of a shoe-making business, commissioned Porcinai to design it in 1952 before moving into the house with his wife. "As far as I understand, they gave him carte blanche," says their daughter-in-law and current owner Elisabetta Rangoni. "They knew he was the best one, so they trusted him fully."

The centrepiece of the garden is the swimming pool, which is separated from the house only by a terrace, almost becoming a continuation of the living room. It is bordered by round slabs of red Verona marble that are balanced around a water lily pond surrounding the pool. Circular shapes, inspired by Japanese gardens and the paintings of Russian abstract artist Wassily Kandinsky, are repeated in the stepping stones on the lawn and red marble terrace. A tall hedge wrapping elegantly around the garden continues this theme. The impeccable state of the landscape is thanks to Elisabetta, who learned the ins and outs of looking after each plant from her mother-in-law. "We sometimes tried to switch out the plants in our greenhouse or create a new flower bed but they would always die," says Rangoni. "We always had to bring back the plants chosen by Porcinai."

Three years after starting works on Villa La Terrazza, Porcinai was commissioned to design the gardens of Villa Ottolenghi, a 1920s estate perched on a hilltop by Acqui Terme in Piedmont. The estate, which now serves as a wedding venue, restaurant and hotel, includes two swimming pools, a Japanese garden and a curved terrace overlooking vineyards and the city below. All over the lawn grows wild mint, which was planted to cover the sweeter smell of the wisteria overhanging a covered walkway. "The scent gets so strong that it feels like walking in a mojito," says tour guide Chiara Fogliati.

In the summer, the garden is a favourite spot for locals to cool off and enjoy Porcinai's eye for design detail. The base of the shallow pool is covered in rounded river pebbles that massage the feet and aid blood circulation. On the lawn are dotted sculptural stone chairs that face the afternoon sun. Few are lucky enough to own a Porcinai-designed garden but many Italians are likely to have unwittingly visited one. In the 1960s, together with architect Marco Zanuso and sculptor Pietro Consagra, he designed the second half of Parco di Pinocchio in Collodi, near Florence. Here, winding paths among foliage, bamboo and a labyrinth of hedges are dotted with sculptures drawn from the popular Italian children's story. Porcinai also designed the landscaping

1

2

Water cistern at Villa Ottolenghi

1

2   3

around dozens of factories and offices of Italian companies such as Olivetti and Mondadori, providing both white and blue-collared workers access to green space.

Porcinai advocated a design philosophy that he described as "propaganda of the green". He dropped out of architecture school in Florence because he believed that the teaching ignored the importance of nature in design. "He was always critical of the inhumane aspects of modernism," says Paola. "He argued that nobody can live well surrounded by cement and that greenery needed to be part of any built environment." During his career, Porcinai was a regular contributor to *Domus* and other architecture publications. He also co-founded the International Federation of Landscape Architects and persistently lobbied Italian universities to start offering courses in the field.

Today, Porcinai is not a household name but his legacy is felt in the Italian design world. "Italian universities now host Masters and PHD courses related to landscape design and it's thanks to him," says Stefano Boeri, founder of Stefano Boeri Architetti. "Before Porcinai, the realms of architecture and botany were considered separate and it was a tremendous effort from Porcinai to change that."

Boeri explains that his practice – which is known for the Bosco Verticale, two foliage-covered skyscrapers in Milan – is based on the same ideas as those advocated by Porcinai. "When we design a green façade, we first invite botanists to help us select plants that are adaptable to the specific climatic conditions on the site and only then do we start on the architecture," says Boeri. "This idea of a landscape that is not just a decoration but a fundamental part of the design comes from Porcinai. We're always considering this delicate threshold between a natural and artificial settlement and we try to produce an osmosis between the two."

Porcinai's idea to blur the lines between architecture and nature, between indoors and outdoors, is evident at his Villa Rondinelli studio, now Paola's home. A climbing fig has nearly outgrown the hole drilled in the wall through which it reaches inside, covering the entire living-room ceiling with verdant leaves. "It spreads and latches onto everything," says Paola. "I'm always picking up leaves from the floor. Here, you can't forget about nature because it's everywhere – inside and outside – and you're constantly maintaining it. You'll never reach tidy perfection but that's not the point. Taking care of plants brings happiness in itself." — Ⓜ

4

Best of the rest

While many of the landscapes designed by Porcinai have been either lost or are still in private ownership, there are some that are open to the public and well worth a visit. In Italy, take the children to Parco di Pinocchio in Collodi, near Lucca, or head for a relaxing meal and afternoon swim at Villa Ottolenghi in Acqui Terme (call in advance).

When you're passing through Paris, take a closer look at the sloping plaza outside Centre Pompidou, for which Porcinai was a consultant to Renzo Piano and Richard Rogers.

The city of Milan is also currently working on restoring a section of the central Parco Sempione, which Porcinai designed with architect Vittoriano Viganò.

5

Best in town
Global

From architects to street-lighting experts, these firms are keeping our cities liveable.

ILLUSTRATOR
Peter Zhao

Urban development is hard work. Getting your city's infrastructure up to scratch, maintaining it and, importantly, creating a place that citizens enjoy living in takes many minds and multiple skills. That's why we've provided something of a cheat sheet for smart mayors and property developers to help them build, beautify and preserve the perfect city. Who you gonna call? Let us tell you. — Ⓜ

①

Offer the perfect kiosk
Germany

The K67, designed by Slovenian architect Saša Mächtig in 1966, was sold as an affordable, prefabricated structure to be used by newsagents or as parking-ticket booths. Many have been abandoned and fallen into disrepair but Berlin couple Ann-Marie and Martin Ruge von Löw, who operate their own café from a K67, provide businesses with a refurbished kiosk. — SRO
kioski.berlin

②

Jazz up your public transport fleet
Switzerland

Swiss firm Nose uses creative design to add personality and efficiency to transport networks. Its latest concept is the self-driving electric Yumo Shuttle Bus, which plugs the gap by shuttling between remote areas and the closest commuter station. — SRO
nose.ch

③

Masterplan your neighbourhood
Denmark

Bringing character to a neighbourhood is no easy task, which is what makes the work of Danish design agency BRIQ so impressive. Since 2017 the studio has been engaged in projects in Copenhagen's Carlsberg City District, a former industrial area built around the brewery's iconic former headquarters. BRIQ has transformed it into a buzzy residential neighbourhood, where historic buildings sit happily next to modern blocks and towers. Through a smart zoning strategy, a strong retail and hospitality mix, and an emphasis on imbuing new venues with characteristics inspired by the area's heritage, BRIQ is forming a global benchmark for placemaking. — CAG
briqgroup.com

④

Make your city more playful
Chile

If you don't have children you might not notice how many playgrounds your city has. But providing safe spaces for children to socialise and play in is fundamental to any urban environment.

The Bicentenario De La Infancia park is a clever project by Chilean architecture firm Elemental, headed up by Alejandro Aravena, to provide a haven for children from all walks of life in Santiago's northern suburb of Recoleta. An urban walkway on San Cristóbal hill was repurposed with more than 60 slides, fountains, timber huts and a funicular to address a dearth in the city's high-quality public spaces.

In the face of the nation's growing economic inequality, the park is a rare communal area for children from different backgrounds to meet on a level playing field. Parents, meanwhile, will be relieved to know that safety was a priority throughout the development, making the playground as accident-proof as possible. Our favourite features? The perimeter is enclosed by an adventure course and an amphitheatre has been included to host shows for the young *chilenos*. — GCH
elementalchile.cl

⑤

Scoop up those scooters
USA

San Diego's Scoot Scoop is taking e-scooter sharing giants to task for littering our cities. E-scooter operators leave it to customers to park correctly after their ride, which is why scooters are often strewn across footpaths. Scoot Scoop impounds two-wheelers left on private property and charges the operators to retrieve them. — NSG
scootscoop.com

⑥

Green solutions
Brazil

São Paulo has deployed greenery in recent years as a strategy to tackle the spray paint of urban graffiti vandals. The city mayor commissioned a 3.5km (11,000 sq m) vertical garden along one of the city's main traffic corridors, Avenida 23 de Maio, in 2017 to cover up the graffiti. Residents also use the technique, covering their walls entirely with creepers.

Landscape architect Ricardo Cardim is an expert in incorporating plants into commercial and residential buildings in the city, from office towers to shops and schools. He exclusively uses native Atlantic Forest vegetation in a peaceful protest against invasive foreign flora.

His Floresta de Bolso project is also part of his mission, gathering groups of volunteers at weekends to help plant patches of native forest in the city on degraded land as small as 15 sq m. — CPB
cardimpaisagismo.com.br

⑦

Bring farming to the city
Japan

Projects imitating New York's elevated linear park, the High Line, are old news. For a fresher benchmark for regenerating an under-used and under-appreciated part of town, city planners would be wise to turn to the work of Paris-based Japanese architect Tsuyoshi Tane.

In Shibuya, Tokyo, he's transforming a 2.6km stretch of the Tamagawa *josui*, a waterway constructed in the Edo period and later covered over, into a linear park reserved for urban farming. The now-derelict space will become a place where locals can meet, socialise and leisurely grow vegetables that they can sell at farmers' markets.

"It will have urban kitchens and urban markets," Tane tells MONOCLE. "We even want to form rivalries between different farming groups along the river, competing over who is growing the best tomatoes." Truly a multi-purpose project, Tane's farmlands add precious green space to the city, offer leisure areas for citizens and shorten the supply chain in the selling of fresh fruit and vegetables. — NSG
at-ta.fr

8

Shade with care
Thailand

Thai architectural design studio Allzone, founded by Rachaporn Choochuey, is turning to smart shading solutions to keep cities cool. For a recent project in the UAE, it created a porous fabric roof over a courtyard. It repels heat from the ground during the day and transfers it up into the air at night. — CAG
allzonedesignall.com

9

Give public spaces to the people
Australia

Aspect Studios has mastered the art of public space design. The firm's projects invite people to interact with a space but lets them choose how to use it. Its new precinct at Sydney's Macquarie University has water flowing through a terraced seating area. Children splash about, while elderly couples sit back and relax. — NSG
aspect-studios.com

10

Give the best directions
Singapore

Applied Information Group is a London-based firm that specialises in way-finding, creating attractive, clear signage in cities from Singapore to Rio de Janeiro. In the former, an intuitive colour-coded signage scheme was deployed on the city's Sentosa Island, keeping walkers, joggers and cyclists moving in the right direction. — NSG
appliedinformation.group

11

Provide the perfect retrofit
Luxembourg

Cities frequently face a dilemma when it comes to ageing infrastructure, from bridges to buildings. Knock them down or fix them up? In cases involving characterful structures, we're in favour of retrofitting to suit contemporary needs. And to do this, we suggest CBA, a Luxembourgian architecture practice led by Christian Bauer, whose portfolio of retrofitted works is outstanding.

In recent years CBA has transformed an old factory into a smart hotel, refurbished an 18th-century listed building, and turned a dilapidated warehouse into its own office space. The standout, though, is the recent retrofit of Luxembourg City's Pont Adolphe bridge. Built in 1903 the structure has, for more than a century, served as a key route for vehicle and pedestrian traffic but its capacity couldn't keep up with modern demand. Rather than build a new bridge, the city commissioned CBA to design a new, lightweight platform for pedestrians and cyclists to sit subtly beneath the vehicle deck. This protects the structure's heritage, while ensuring that it meets today's transit needs. — NM
cba.lu

13

Make buildings to bring people together
Dubai

Dutch architects OMA's projects include a new performing arts venue in Taipei that draws street life into the centre, a historic former post office in Houston transformed into a culture, food and shopping venue, and an inviting pavilion (replete with a park on its roof) for a Los Angeles temple. In Dubai, the firm cleverly applied wide, foldable polycarbonate doors onto a transformed warehouse, which now operates as a cultural centre named Concrete. The flexible design means that when the walls fall away, the building becomes something entirely different. A public forum opens up outdoors for events such as performances and talks, with the backdrop being the beautiful interior of the arts building itself.

Flexible architecture is increasingly needed in cities where space is tight and this Dubai building's ability to morph for many purposes makes it a meaningful benchmark. — NSG
oma.com

14

Host a festival
Spain

The Spanish city of Logroño didn't come up much in urbanism conversations until 2015, when Javier Peña Ibáñez launched Concéntrico, a yearly festival that allows designers and architects to take over the city with installations.

While putting Logroño on the design map, the festival is also an opportunity for residents to see their hometown through fresh eyes and think more critically about the spaces around them. "We want to give the tools to help understand how cities can change," says Ibáñez. The result? Citizens care more about their hometown's development and good urban planning can be better appreciated. — NSG
concentrico.es

15

Give cyclists security
Switzerland

In almost any city, locking your bike outside a train station can be risky, leaving it vulnerable to both the elements and people with sticky fingers. A secure, smartly designed bike garage can help, something that Swiss architecture firm Amplatz is particularly adept at creating.

We suggest taking to two wheels and pulling your own cycle into one of the 570 parking spaces at its recently completed garage in Winterthur. Located outside the city's main station, a gently curving ramp carries bike riders from the street into the colonnaded, pavilion-like structure, ensuring smooth transport connections and safety for cycles. — NM
amplatz.ch

12

Light your city at night
Spain

When it comes to combating light pollution in cities and making them more enjoyable in the evening, we turn to Santa & Cole's urban lighting and furniture arm, Urbidermis. The Spanish brand's products are designed so that light is diffused and directed towards the ground, ensuring that it doesn't obtrusively light up the night sky – or your date's face. — NM
urbidermis.com

In plain sight
Geneva

A sensitive city hall revamp opens up this storied building to foster dialogue and democracy.

WRITER
Nic Monisse

PHOTOGRAPHY
Leo Fabrizio

1

"We want it to be a place where people will feel at home because the idea is that this is a 'house for everyone'," says Julia Zapata, co-founder of Geneva-based design studio Bonhôte Zapata, as she leads MONOCLE through the newly renovated Geneva City Hall. "What we really wanted to give this building is a feeling of solemnity – to represent the activity taking place here – but also a feeling of comfort and a sense of domesticity."

Zapata and her team have just finalised the update to the 16th-century building, which has endured a hodgepodge of largely uninspiring alterations over the years. The latest efforts are the most ambitious, with a brief aiming to make the government building a place that goes beyond setting policy for the Swiss city of more than 500,000.

The project is about opening the space up, which is felt most profoundly in the main council chamber. In the lofty hall, Bonhôte Zapata added an eye-catching multifaceted, oak-slatted structure, which covers the space. It reaches up towards the roof, where a new skylight fills the room with natural light, a glow that is complemented by an elaborate lighting system from Lebanon's PSLab

1. City hall records are kept in a beautifully lit meeting room
2. Finn Juhl FJ 51 walnut armchairs in an open layout

"We want it to be a place where people will feel at home because the idea is that this is a 'house for everyone'"

hidden within the oak structure. The theme of transparency continues with the removal of existing windows – stained-glass numbers, which, while beautiful, didn't allow for much natural light to flow in. They've been moved to another state building and replaced by translucent panes that now allow the deputies to look out at the metropolis that they're responsible for, while allowing their electorate to look into the building when the parliament is in session.

"We wanted to create a strong visual connection with the city," says Zapata. "When there's a sitting here, people on the streets and by the lake can feel like they're in session." The personal responsibility of every deputy is also enhanced by the fact that, rather than sitting along a bench – as is typical in many parliaments – each has their own desk and chair: a Finn Juhl FJ 51 walnut armchair. Upholstered with blue fabric (such a perch is only found in one other location, the UN headquarters in New York), the stately pieces have been exclusively supplied to the Geneva council by Denmark's House of Finn Juhl. Significantly, the chamber was also reconfigured into a semicircular seating plan, a much friendlier layout than the previous face-to-face seating, which placed politicians opposite each other.

Moving beyond the main hall, the Bonhôte Zapata team also revitalised a number of other rooms in the building, including the welcome chamber, where it uncovered and restored the room's original shape, and the parliament's café, chancellery and administration offices. They also renovated the parliamentary restaurant, transforming what was once a dining hall catering to diplomats into a popular, public-facing spot.

Each room has distinct characteristics and, says Zapata, "each of these rooms has a whole history of its own". And now these different spaces are beautifully united by a consistency of materials. A robust selection of green marble, brass, oak and walnut has been deployed throughout. "We very carefully selected a small palette of materials," she says. "We decided to work with them in a modular way, using them throughout the building to give the spaces continuity."

The result is a cohesive environment that's representative of good government: open and transparent, efficient in the use of resources and built with the long-term in mind. But it is also a place that, thanks to the abundance of natural light and the warmth of the oak and walnut, feels incredibly welcoming, calming and set up for dialogue and diplomacy. This is the kind of intuitive design that allows for good governance – something we hope that the politicians sitting here respond to with enthusiasm. — Ⓜ

2

1

② DESIGN: Architecture

Keep cool
Palma

In the island sun sits an innovative
new apartment block that could
reshape the city's design ambitions.

WRITER
Andrew Tuck

PHOTOGRAPHY
Ben Roberts

Running up from the sea, dissecting the town, is
Paseo Mallorca, the smartest avenue in Palma,
Mallorca's capital, where wealthy residents
have rambling old-school apartments. There
was once an ancient wall here but when most
of it was removed on this flank of the then-
bursting-at-the-seams city in the late 19th century, it made space for new, desirable housing.

Today the *paseo* has a water course running down its centre, a rather busy road on the
western side of this stream, a more pedestrian
and al fresco dining vibe on the other. With
the bridges that skip across the water, it's picturesque, if a little architecturally strait-laced.

But now a new 10-apartment block –
Paseo Mallorca 15 – has been completed here
by local architects Ohlab and it has the potential to shake things up; be a cooler guest at
the urban party. Ohlab, run by husband-and-
wife team Jaime Oliver and Paloma Hernaiz,

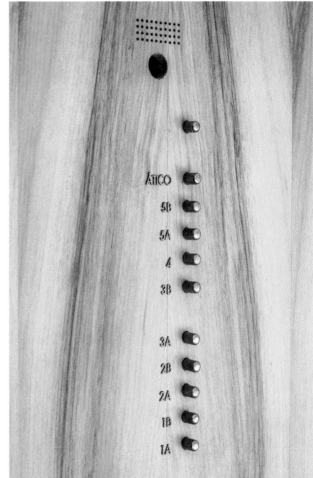

ÁTICO
5B
5A
4
3B

3A
2B
2A
1B
1A

2

3

3

has made a name for itself with a series of buildings that sit at ease with their environment, limit the need for air-conditioning and heating, and use modest tactile materials and muted colour palettes in extraordinary ways. The outcomes of this considered approach have won numerous plaudits: a compact home, the MM House, that they made in 2016, when starting their practice, for a retired teacher and doctor has already been given listed status by the island's government.

Mallorca, like many parts of the Mediterranean, is taking a hit from global warming. This year the spring was oddly cold but then May brought a blast of heat of an intensity that would be more normal in August. So wise architects and clients know that not only are shade and cooler inner sanctums needed but buildings should be designed to be less energy-hungry, to do their part to fix this problem and cope with seasonal uncertainties.

Like that small MM House, Paseo Mallorca 15 has been built to meet Passivhaus standards; a set of criteria that can lower energy consumption by up to 90 per cent. One of the ways this has been achieved here is with the addition of sliding timber-slatted panels – inspired by those seen on island homes – that help slice and soften even the harshest summer sun and give the building a striking and dynamic façade.

"We feel a responsibility to use less energy and to convince clients that this is important," says Oliver. "When you live on an island, you are even more aware of the scarcity of resources and the need to protect them."

Hernaiz stresses that being sustainable does not mean sacrificing beauty; over the past decade they have become more radical in their choices of materials and been clearer about the benefits of using products that help cut energy consumption. "And we learn more with every project," she adds.

But let's get Jaime and Paloma to walk us through. At the entrance they ask MONOCLE to note the detailing of the postboxes and brass-buttoned intercom buzzers, before opening the door and guiding us into a small lobby within. There's a trick of the eye at play here because the modest lobby garden extends to a shaggier outdoors one – and you barely notice the glass wall that divides the two spaces. The grounds are the work of the British landscape gardener Jonathan Bell (known for his collaborations with John Pawson) and provide shade to mediate the heat. We linger a moment while Oliver looks at every branch and stem to make sure all the foliage is in fine fettle. Hernaiz points out the central void that runs throughout the building, giving the apartments more

3

"When you live on an island, you are very aware of the scarcity of resources and the need to protect them"

Previous page
1. Communal area
2. Intercom with timber and brass detailing
3. Façade with moving panels by Grupo Habita

This page
1. View of penthouse from external garden
2. Paloma Hernaiz and Jaime Oliver of Ohlab
3. Staircase detailing

3

1. Stone washbasin
2. Landing and stairwell
3. Penthouse kitchen with lime-mortar walls
4. Using simple materials well is the mantra throughout
5. Car lift built by Malift

1

2

filtered light, and explains how the greenery also descends – alongside a cooling, cascading water feature. At the base of the void is a gym and stone-lined swimming pool that has Peter Zumthor-levels of calming asceticism. And hidden below all of this are three subterranean levels of parking, reached by a glass car-lift at street level that's lined with a wall of cane. It's a Bond-like twist – being virtuous in your design choices doesn't mean ditching all the fun stuff.

The apartments are shaped and informed by the same materials as the exterior. While on the external façades stone has been gauged and grooved to sit alongside all the soft-looking slats, inside bathrooms have stone washbasins that look as though they have been heaved directly from the mountain (there's a lot of hidden metal work preventing these heavy beasts crashing to the ground). And the use of timber internally includes impeccable cedar cabinetry, with shelves manoeuvred up and down using a series of simple grooves – all made by island carpenters.

"We want to use materials that show their age but still look great," says Hernaiz while Oliver explains how they placed lime mortar on the walls, which not only smells great but means that no toxic paint was used. "These are materials that are about timeless techniques," he says.

Ohlab had as their client on this project a passionate developer, José Miguel Ramis, who comes from a long line of builders on the island. He has been deliberately slow to market the homes, not wanting them released until they were finished to his exacting demands (he hopes that most of these residences will be occupied full-time by the same sort of people who have always settled on the *paseo*). "He's a great client," says Oliver. "He wanted to build something remarkable, and we entered this positive loop where we were pushing each other to do ever better things; to build to the highest standard."

"With food, people understand that you have to spend a bit more to eat healthily," says Hernaiz wisely. "We need the same attitude in architecture if people want to be part of this sustainability story."

It might just be a 10-apartment building but it's clear that this project has the potential to shake things up in a world where white walls, plate glass and dodgy art too often define the Mediterranean vernacular of grand residences. Paseo Mallorca 15 offers the city an alternative vision: a groundbreaking residential development that moves away from old tropes to focus on environmental needs, craft with restrained beauty – building that plants a flag for change. — Ⓜ

3

4

5

The Monocle Shop

From homeware to beachware via a very accurate clock, here's our selection of products you simply can't live without. These beauties will make your world better, trust us.

Photography
Michael Bodiam

(+) Find all of these and more in Monocle Shops or online at *monocle.com*

1.
Niwaki × Monocle hinoki wood chopping board

€85

Niwaki is a purveyor of exemplary Japanese DIY, homeware and gardening essentials, from stepladders to telescopic pruners. Created by timber artisan Sekikawa-san, this engraved chopping board is made from hinoki, a wood loaded with moisture-repelling oils to ward off bacteria. It's the perfect example of craftsmanship and minimalism, values that Niwaki and MONOCLE share.

MATERIAL: Hinoki wood.
DETAIL: Engraved MONOCLE and Niwaki logos.
MADE IN: Japan.

2.
Selected by Monocle Twemco calendar wall clock

€360

Twemco has perfected automatic digital calendar clocks. They are found in banks and government buildings worldwide. The Hong Kong brand's timekeeping products are as dependable as they are beautiful. This one hangs in MONOCLE's bureaux across the globe and will guide you with the same accuracy that a journalistic floor needs to break news around the world.

MATERIAL: ABS black.
DIMENSIONS: 305mm × 380mm × 75mm.
MADE IN: Hong Kong.

3.
Sebastian Marbacher × Monocle salt and pepper mills

€170

With an emphasis on using natural materials, Sebastian Marbacher's studio designs minimalist and practical products and furniture. MONOCLE's design team took inspiration from his Salz Pfeffermühle series of wooden grinders, when creating this salt-and-pepper set in collaboration with his studio. Made in Switzerland from certified domestic ash and with a high-quality mill from Strässler, it offers a contemporary twist on a classic look.

MATERIAL: Ash.
COLOURS: Ash, salmon, yellow and navy.
MADE IN: Switzerland.

4.
Monocle Irish linen

€80 tea towels, €85 napkins

Linen brand Thomas Ferguson's work is steeped in its Irish heritage. While more than a century has passed since the company was first established, its bed, bath and kitchen linens remain coveted by the discerning – a reminder that quality craft traditions can always find a place in contemporary homes.

MATERIAL: Linen
COLOURS: Natural, grey, navy and moss green.
MADE IN: Northern Ireland.

The Monocle Shop

1.
Nikari × Monocle Ita stool

€450

For our 15th anniversary, we have recommissioned the iconic Ita stool from our friends at Nikari, made in Finland's oldest machinery workshop. The oak stool has a unique shape that makes it easy to stack and comes with a MONOCLE engraving.

MATERIAL: Oak.
MADE IN: Finland.

2.
Heath Ceramics × Monocle Bud vase

€95

These rounded vases will bring Californian sunshine to your sideboard, bookshelf or table. The Bud is a chic teardrop-shaped design created by Heath in the 1980s. There is also the Bulb, a striking, swollen form.

MATERIAL: Ceramic.
COLOURS: Yellow, olive or sage.
MADE IN: USA.

3.
Selected by Monocle Marset Bicoca portable lamp

Price: €190

Spanish brand Marset's lightweight portable lamp can be used to set a scene with intimate illumination or, thanks to its tilting lamp shade, can create direct lighting for focused work.

MATERIAL: Polycarbonate.
COLOURS: Yellow and anthracite.
MADE IN: Spain.

4.
Mad Lab × Monocle High Wing Air

€110

We enlisted designer Borja García of Madrid studio Mad Lab for this collaboration. What these helicopters and planes lack in flying power, they more than make up for in character. The vehicles are carved from oak and accented with brass details.

MATERIALS: Oak and brass.
MADE IN: Spain.

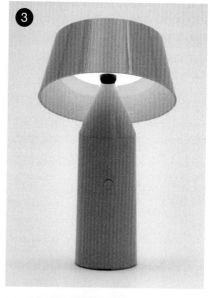

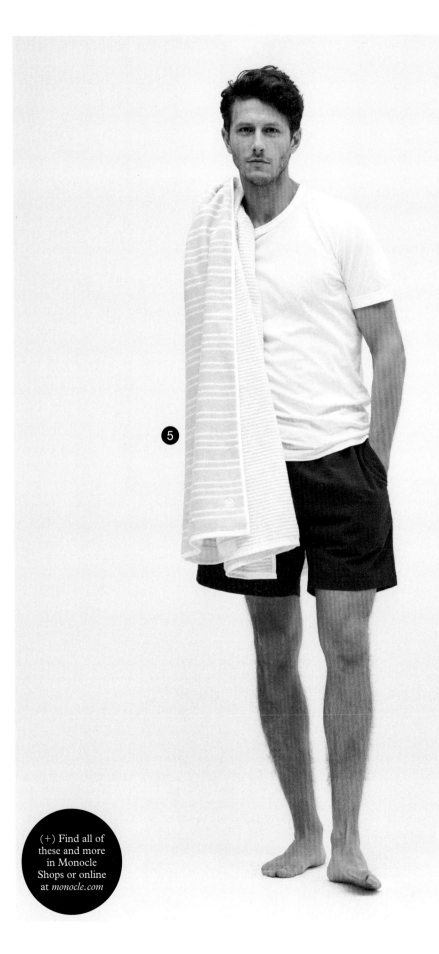

5.
Monocle beach towel
€55

You'll have the brightest sunbathing patch on the beach thanks to our towels, which come in vivid sky blue and canary yellow. Designed in-house and made in Portugal, these cheery terry numbers are super-soft and expansive, so you can stretch out as you leaf through a magazine or take a nap.

MATERIAL: Cotton.
COLOURS: Sky blue or yellow.
MADE IN: Portugal.

(+) Find all of these and more in Monocle Shops or online at *monocle.com*

The new wave
Global

Surfwear, footwear, city shorts and relaxed shirts – summer holidays are all about breezy, effortless dressing. From Bali to Brazil, we've found the new generation of retailers selling the best summery brands.

Spread across sunny spots all over the world, these retailers are detached from the mainstream fashion industry and bring new points of view on modern dressing. Working hand in hand with independent designers and artisans in their communities, they are experts in offering summer staples, crafted to perfection using high-quality, environmentally friendly materials. But their edits go beyond beach essentials to unique design pieces that work year-round, while also holding on to the happy memories of your holiday. — Ⓜ

2

3

1.
Hotstep it
Escalier, Bali

Escalier at Bali's famed Potato Head Beach Club mixes internationally acclaimed names such as Los Angeles-based Bode and Japan's Sacai with local labels including Buru Studio, Ofninety and Zodiac. The multi-brand boutique is where Bali's most discerning travellers go for inspiration and to discover the latest names. "We pick brands that are quite unheard of or have the potential to become huge," says Emmelyn Gunawan, who co-founded Escalier (part of the broader Potato Head group) in 2009 with two friends. The owners have an eye for breakout hits: they brought Simone Rocha, JW Anderson and Jacquemus to Indonesia some seven years ago, before they were global brand names.

The shop's buying, which extends to jewellery and home accessories, is overseen by Gunawan and co-founder Resida Irmine, who make a point to keep the brands they stock on rotation. The likes of Comme des Garçons are among their longest-standing partners but the owners will still not hesitate to skip a season or two before reintroducing labels back in shop. As a result, regular customers,

1

2.
Holiday heaven
Diária, São Paulo

Diária is a multi-brand shop in São Paulo's leafy Pinheiros neighbourhood, dedicated to what it calls "vacation lifestyle". Founders Raphael Dias, who grew up further south in the city of Curitiba, and Raffaele Asselta, who is a Pinheiros native, designed their shop for anyone who has travel in mind. From beautiful artwork to the perfect pair of shorts, Diária prides itself on selling independent Brazilian brands. "We are always trying to find new names from local makers," says Dias. As well as stocking surf-wear labels such as By the Sea and Lyria, they also have their own brand, Nøgen, which is Danish for "naked". It's known for its simple pieces in earthy or pastel tones.

Although Brazil has been living through turbulent political and economic times, Dias says that the creative scene is resurgent in the city. "I see lots of new business, especially in our neighbourhood of Pinheiros but also in places such as Barra Funda and Santa Cecília," he says. "Those places are becoming vital for the independent fashion, art and gastronomy scenes in Brazil." — FP
casa.diaria.co

whom Gunawan describes as "the collector type", can always expect a surprise when they walk in. "They have hobbies; they buy records; they ride skateboards even in their late thirties and forties," she says. "They still wear their old Stüssy tees and they probably only buy their Converse sneakers in Japan."

Escalier likes to collaborate with Balinese creatives too. In-house label Vacation, which makes Hawaiian shirts, is produced with pop-culture-inspired prints from illustrator Angela Judiyanto. "It's seriously out of this world and I think that's why we have a cult following," says Gunawan of the sellout in-house collections. — YX
escalier-store.com

1. Escalier customers
   visit for inspiration
2. Global and local brands
3. Tie-dye T-shirts with a twist
4. Verdant store entrance
5. Raphael Dias (on right)
   and Raffaele Asselta

1
2
3 4

3.
Wear craft
Agora, Ibiza

"It's like a magazine telling stories about responsible fashion – and everything happens to be available to buy," says Tiffanie Darke of Agora, a concept shop she co-founded with Daniela Agnelli in the north of Ibiza. Their boutique is part of the new Six Senses resort and mirrors its bohemian flair and commitment to environmental responsibility.

The pair have created a shop where stories of handcraft and provenance are front and centre in their sunny edits. They stock a selection of vintage and upcycled clothing, as well as fashion made from new materials such as Tencel (a sustainable fibre). Many of the brands on show are under-the-radar names producing collections made by people from around the world who are skilled in traditional crafts.

Agnelli, now a permanent Ibiza resident, points to the men's label SMR Days, known for breezy linens that are handwoven or tie-dyed by Indian artisans. Wooden sunglasses by French label Nordic Wood and shawls by Wehve, made by women in rural Uruguay, are other highlights. "We need to support communities that have been thriving on artisanal trade for generations," says Darke. — NT

1. Sandals made using traditional methods
2. Open-toe option
3. Agora in Ibiza
4. Inside the concept shop
5. Summer's Stéphane Sultana
6. Splash of colour
7. Welcoming interior

5

6

4.
California dreaming
Summer, Arles

A slice of California might seem out of place in the South of France but husband and wife Stéphane and Sophie Sultana have channelled the Golden State's laid-back spirit into their shop Summer. The brand's first shop opened in 2012 in their hometown, Lyon, and after a decade of success they've expanded into a new outpost in Arles. Offering a mix of Japanese, French and Californian skate and surf brands, the Sultanas are doing their shop's name justice. "We spent a lot of time in California; for us our shops should be symbols of all things sunny," says Stéphane.

Specialising in menswear and lifestyle clothing, Summer mixes minimal linen pieces with brighter graphic T-shirts. "Our customer can be the guy working in the

"We spent a lot of time in California, so for us, our shops should be symbols of all things sunny"

7

restaurant nextdoor, an artist visiting exhibitions or a tourist exploring the city," says Stéphane. Popular brands include Common Projects and Japan's Auralee. Arpenteur and Reception, two new Lyon-based brands, were added recently. They also invite neighbouring restaurants and florists into their world with a variety of creative projects, including co-branded capsules, and host a programme of events. "We want it to be more of an exhibition and social space," says Stéphane. "We're working with French photographers and planning events to coincide with the photography festival Les Rencontres d'Arles this July." — FMA
summer-store.com

1

5.
Beautifully surfed
+351, Lisbon

Lisbon has become a popular stop-off in recent years for people who want to look good riding the waves along the Portuguese coast. One of the shops that caters to this surfing community, as well as anyone else on the lookout for laid-back summer staples, is +351. Located in the city's waterfront district of Cais do Sodré since 2019, this is a warm, inviting space created by the designer Ana Penha e Costa, a Lisbon native and avid surfer.

The shop offers a mix of Penha e Costa's own designs for her +351 label alongside a selection of accessories from other brands. "The vibe is very relaxed here in the shop," says Penha e Costa, who has surfing in her blood and previously worked for labels such as Osklen and Billabong.

> "The idea was to capture our enviable lifestyle here in Portugal, where we can work in the morning and head to the beach in the afternoon to chill or challenge the waves"

"I often have surfing friends, some of whom hail from as far away as Colombia and Italy, coming by."

Clients are drawn to the +351 collection of T-shirts, sweatshirts and polos made in the north of Portugal using supersoft organic cotton. "I love designing great basics; essentials pieces done in fabrics that feel cosy," says the designer, pointing to two-tone board shorts and long-sleeved cotton terry shirts as some of her must-haves. She has also collaborated with Portuguese footwear label Sanjo, incoporating +351's soft signature fabrics.

The shop is housed in a former hardware store and Penha e Costa uses the back room as an office and stockroom. References to the sea abound: there's a fibreglass shark by Portuguese artist Sebastião Lobo suspended from the ceiling and striped cotton canvas beach chairs by local brand Lona. "The idea of the shop was to capture the mood of our enviable lifestyle here in Portugal, where we can work in the morning and then head out to the beach in the afternoon to chill or challenge the waves." — IC
plus351.pt

1. Ana Penha e Costa
2. Deckchairs outside +351
3. Soft cotton polo shirt
4. Summery slip-ons
5. Bright and spacious interior

1 Smart sandals that will take you everywhere

SANDALS by *Myrqvist*

2 Splash out on comfortable shorts

SWIMMING TRUNKS by *Bather*

3 A sunhat that can't be crumpled

HAT by *Trunk*

5 Put it all into a trusty tote

BAG by *Haulier*

4 It's cocktail hour somewhere...

SPIRIT PIONEER EDITION WATCH by *Longines*

7 Keep things cool and comfortable

SHORTS by *La Paz*

❷ FASHION: Summer break

Pack it in
Global

Pop some sturdy sandals, no-nonsense trunks and cool stripes into your holdall and you're away. Just add a crisp white for the cooler box (and don't forget the corkscrew).

PHOTOGRAPHY
Tony Hay

STYLIST
Kyoko Tamoto

6 Look leisurely in linen

SHIRT by *Ripa Ripa*

8 The only accessory you really need

COOLER BOX by *Yeti*

9 Fresh feet for your morning run

TRAINERS and SOCKS by *CQP Sport*

10 For hunting, fishing and impromptu picnics

SWISS ARMY KNIFE by *Victorinox*

11 Crisp tees for sunny days

T-SHIRTS by *Asket*

12 Packing a case has never felt so good

SUITCASE by *Proteca*

13 Make a statement pool or beachside

BEACH TOWEL by *Hommey*

14 Elegant shades that transcend fashion

CLEAR SUNGLASSES by *Monc*
GREEN SUNGLASSES by *Ahlem*

Ebb and flow
Paris

The Canal St Martin offers a chance to contemplate.
And when Paris empties in summer, you'll have it all
to yourself. Get comfy, stay cool and head to the water.

STYLIST
Daphné Hézard

PHOTOGRAPHY
Trisha Ward

THIS PAGE: JUMPER by *Bompard*,
TROUSERS by *Edwin*, SANDALS
by *APC*, WATCH by *Swatch*

OPPOSITE: JACKET by *American
Vintage*, SHIRT by *Berluti*,
TROUSERS by *Tod's*, SOCKS by
Celine by Hedi Slimane, TRAINERS
by *Pataugas*, WATCH by *Swatch*

THIS PAGE: POLO SHIRT by *Tod's*,
TROUSERS by *Hermès*, SUNGLASSES
by *Persol*, WATCH by *Swatch*

OPPOSITE: JACKET by *Brooksfield*,
T-SHIRT by *Sunspel*, TROUSERS
by *A Kind of Guise*

THIS PAGE: SHIRT and TROUSERS
by *Hermès*, GLASSES by *Persol*

OPPOSITE: SHIRT by *Lemaire*, T-SHIRT
by *Sunspel*, TROUSERS by *De Bonne
Facture*, SOCKS, SUNGLASSES and
TRAINERS by *Celine by Hedi Slimane*,
TRAINERS and WATCH by *Swatch*

THIS PAGE: T-SHIRT by *Sunspel*,
TROUSERS by *JW Anderson*,
TRAINERS by *JM Weston*

OPPOSITE: POLO SHIRT by *Hartford*,
T-SHIRT by *Sunspel*, SHORTS by
De Bonne Facture, TRAINERS *De Bonne
Facture* × *Novesta*, WATCH by *Swatch*

THIS PAGE: PARKA and TROUSERS
by *Fursac* TRAINERS by
Celine by Hedi Slimane

OPPOSITE: JACKET by *American Vintage*,
JUMPER by *Bompard*, TROUSERS by
De bonne Facture, WATCH by *Swatch*

THIS PAGE: SHIRT by *Altea*, SHORTS and SUNGLASSES by *Celine by Hedi Slimane*, SANDALS by *John Lobb*, HAT by *Hélas*, WATCH by *Swatch*

OPPOSITE: T-SHIRT by *Sunspel*, SWIM SHORTS by *Ripa Ripa*, GLASSES by *Ray Ban*, WATCH by *Swatch*

HAIR & MAKE-UP: *Yolette Bouchar*
MODEL: *Alexis Petit*
LOCATIONS: *Baptiste Viry*

Cool running

Criss-crossed by slender iron bridges, Paris's Canal St Martin is a place for morning jogs, lunchtime strolls and early evening apéro; locals linger on its banks with spontaneous *pique-nique* into the evening, legs dangling over the water below. Flanked by small brasseries, chic boutiques and lively nightspots, this 19th-century waterway connects the Canal de l'Ourcq and Bassin de la Villette with the Seine via nine locks. Though much of the canal was covered by Baron Haussmann's reimagined scheme for Paris in the late 19th century (and flows beneath the city in a long, cavernous tunnel) it is a cool, breezy, tree-lined haven during hot Parisian summers. Jump off at metro Oberkampf or Republic to meander – or sprint – along its banks. — Ⓜ

SUMMER STAYS & HOLIDAY FASHION

KONFEKT

Inspiring itineraries, debates & recipes

SUBSCRIBE NOW —— KONFEKTMAGAZINE.COM

July/August 2022

A monthly round-up of all you need

Inventory

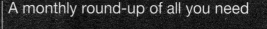

1

INVENTORY: Travel

Taking to the waters
Baden

The Swiss city of Baden is named after its baths but only recently has it embraced its curative waters and revived the riverfront. We dive in to find out how.

Writer
Jessica Bridger

Photography
Dan Wilton

2

Some like it hot; some like it cold. The postcard-pretty city of Baden in Switzerland offers both: a cool, rapid-flowing river runs through it while warm geothermal waters bubble up from beneath. "The hot water will come no matter what," says Andriu Deflorin, co-founder of Bagno Popolare, Baden's independent bathing advocacy association. "We have to use it." He is bobbing in a stone thermal bath on the banks of the Limmat below a streetscape of townhouses and grape

vines. Technically, he's in Ennetbaden, a village of 3,600 on the eastern bank of the river. It's a suburb of the city of Baden, home to 19,400. As an organisation, Bagno Popolare is partly responsible for the return of public bathing in a city named for it. While Baden's bathing history dates back to Roman times its fortunes have ebbed and flowed. Its heyday was in the early 20th century, when people would flock here to sample the area's supposedly curative waters. Eventually, though, Baden's baths drifted into obscurity and the last one closed in 2012 after decades of neglect.

Now, though, the city has returned to the water. Three new thermal baths, two public and one private, opened in 2021, all of them a 10-minute walk from Baden's main train station.

The two public baths, Heisse Brunnen Baden and Heisse Brunnen Ennetbaden, face one another across the Limmat. For reasons that few people remember (something to do with tax law) the village of Ennetbaden separated from Baden 200 years ago and a friendly competition persists. Baden's bath is bigger and no stranger to a popped cork or late-night dip. Meanwhile, the Ennetbaden side is arguably prettier and set under old chestnut trees, as well as being sheltered from the river promenade. Loyalists tend to favour one or the other. "Our bath is better," says one bather, when pressed. Luckily the city is big enough for a little friendly rivalry.

Sitting above the two public baths is the Fortyseven private bath. Designed by Mario Botta, the complex is a draw for tourists and architecture enthusiasts alike. The stone structure crowns the revived Bäderquartier (bathing quarter) with pools that glow by night and steam by day. It is a 160 metre-long, CHF190m (€185m) investment by a local foundation snappily titled Stiftung Gesundheitsförderung Bad Zurzach + Baden. The name Fortyseven comes from the temperature of the mineral-rich water, which is accessible for a fee of CHF39 (€38). The two smaller public baths are free to access.

Previous page
1. Fortyseven thermal bath
2. Surf slalom on the Limmat

This spread
1. 'Bäderquartier' (bathing
    quarter) area in Baden
    and Ennetbaden, with
    new thermal baths

Baden's waterways have not always been a site of leisure. The Limmat river once powered Baden's industrial ambitions, giving rise to companies such as engineering firm Brown, Boveri & Cie (now ABB). In turn the electricity industry boomed and firms such as GE and Axpo made Baden their Swiss base. Today the city's focus has shifted from heavy industry to quality of life. In 2020, Baden won the Swiss Wakker prize for urban reinvention, in recognition of its well-designed public space. Reconnecting the city to the water is next phase of development.

"Finally, we can fully enjoy this heritage again, as the spa area has been returned to the public," says Baden's mayor, Markus Schneider. "*Einzigartig*," is a term he uses often. It means "unique", "unrivalled" and "singularly excellent" all in one neat word. And he's right. While many Swiss cities have cleaned up their waterways to create spaces where you can cool off in the summer, Baden's warm waters are a year-round draw.

The development of the new baths brings people together in a shared space but it took time for it the idea to take root. After years of hosting pop-up baths, Bagno Popolare ignited public imagination and inspired permanent ones. "A big difference is that up there," says Deflorin, nodding to the private bath complex, "people can be private but here they have to get along – and there are all kinds of people from all over the world." Despite some friction, there's enough demand for both public and private bathing facilities here.

Both Heisse Brunnen baths were approved and financed by the public. Befitting Swiss direct democracy, Ennetbaden residents held a public vote on theirs in the village square in 2019. They approved the public bath nearly

1. Kayaker on the Limmat
2. Heisse Brunnen Ennetbaden
3. Geothermal water
4. Baden's mayor, Markus Schneider
5. Swimmers at the slalom

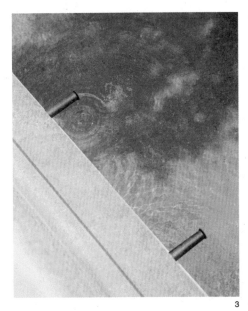

3 4

Residents held a vote in the village square. They approved the public bath nearly unanimously, waving voting cards in the air

unanimously, waving voting cards in the air. Baden followed in a slightly more formal fashion when council members gave the nod, 82 votes to eight.

If the baths draw a diverse public, so does the river. Here you'll spot a slalom course dotted with kayakers and surfers. The course was designed by forestry engineer Tom Hänggli, who kayaks on it most days. "A lot of people think it's natural but it's not. It's completely man-made," he says. He has tended the area for more than 30 years and has seen watersports boom.

You don't have to get wet to enjoy Baden's waters, however. The Oederlin Areal, a former ironworks, houses artist studios, small design firms and craft brewers. At its edge is what's known simply as "the island", an almost hidden idyll atop a dam in the Limmat. Here you'll find a tasteful mishmash of Vitra, Hay and Embru outdoor furniture, gifted by a resident furniture dealer. On summer nights Oederlin tenants, kayakers, bathers and lucky invitees barbecue in the shade as the river rushes by. — Ⓜ

Baden and Ennetbaden address book:

To bathe:
Fortyseven *Baden*
Located a 10-minute walk from Baden SBB station, which is 15 minutes by train from Zürich.
fortyseven.ch

The Heisse Brunnen *Baden*
Lies directly below Fortyseven on the Limmatpromenade. The Heisse Brunnen Ennetbaden is directly across the river.
bagnopopolare.ch

To eat:
Il Brunello *Baden*
Perfect for a morning coffee or a sundown spritz, seated on cheery coloured chairs.
ilbrunello.ch

Brasserie Schwanen *Ennetbaden*
A stunning Jugendstil dining room from 1897 turns out solid Swiss classics.
brasserie-schwanen.ch

Pepe Nero *Ennetbaden*
A well-turned-out Italian features excellent pasta and grilled meats served under vast red parasols.
pepenero.ch

To stay:
Limmathof *Baden and Ennetbaden*
The original grand hotel building from 1834 is across the Limmat from its more recent extension.
limmathof.ch

5

Sleep easy
New York

Three new hotel openings are offering a multitude of reasons to stay in Manhattan. They've made the beds, so now we lie in them.

Writer
Mary Holland

Photography
Max Burkhalter

1. Guest room at Park Lane
2. Harry's Bar
3. Plate expectations
4. Managing director Prince A Sanders
5. Sun and service
6. Comfy corner

1
Park Lane
Central Park South

This 46-storey property on Central Park South was built in 1971 and was in dire need of an update when design studio Yabu Pushelberg moved in. Long the shabbiest space in this exclusive enclave, the hotel now looks right at home in the area that's sometimes referred to as Billionaires' Row.

Ritz-Carlton alumnus Prince A Sanders is managing director on behalf of owner Highgate. "You feel like you're still part of the park," says Sanders, gesturing to the plant-motif murals in the rooms as he shows us around. And it's Central Park that rightly takes centre stage. Many rooms have great views over the green

"The designers wanted to play with the fact that the hotel opened in 1971"

4

5

6

space but the best ones are from Darling, a rooftop lounge that's filled with plants and dotted with rattan chairs.

Another theme is the building itself. "The designers wanted to play with the fact that the hotel opened in 1971," says Sanders as we pass a plush velvet tub seat. There are mid-century chairs, patterned carpets and murals everywhere. "It's a nod to the past and it honours that retro feel."

To breathe new life into the food and drink on offer, Sanders tapped restaurateur Scott Sartiano (of Zero Bond club and several downtown restaurants) to oversee the menus and bring his culinary chops uptown. The hotel's flagship restaurant is Harry's Bar, tucked away on the second floor. With its blue panelled walls and intimate booths, there's nowhere better for a late-night martini or cosmopolitan. "We wanted a throwback to that old New York charm," says Sanders.

Downstairs is Rose Lane, an all-day French bistro-inspired café that transforms into a buzzy bar by night. In the early evening, patrons grab seats at the gas fireplace or along the bar, where cocktails such as the central park south (gin, Campari, melon de Provence, sweet vermouth and lemon) are served with aplomb, alongside a small selection of New York-style pizza from the oven.

Perhaps what's most striking about Park Lane, however, is how accessible it feels. In an area known for its exclusivity, the hotel is the sort of place you can saunter into, no questions asked.
parklanenewyork.com

3

1

2

Civilian
Midtown

A few steps from busy Broadway is a quiet gem: Civilian. Unlike the lit-up theatre buildings and flashing signs that dominate this stretch between West 48th Street and 8th Avenue, the Civilian is unassuming; walk past the narrow brick building and you might even miss it.

For Jason Pomeranc, founder of hotel group Sixty Collective, and architect David Rockwell, the property is a tribute to New York's theatre district. "It was a real labour of love," says Rockwell, who conceived the hotel with plenty of nods to its neighbourhood. Inside, the space is licked with deep reds and dramatic bright blues and no shortage of Broadway paraphernalia. In the lobby, guests are greeted by a row of theatre-style seating and a spiral staircase surrounded by drapes, which leads up to the bar where models of the current Broadway show sets are on display. The nearby Blue Room, a jewellery box of a lounge, is lined with glass cabinets containing histrionic curios.

The theatrical theme doesn't stop there. The wallpaper that lines the halls is by costume designers Isabel and Ruben Toledo and in the interior of the elevator is bedecked with sketches from

4

the show *Hamilton*. In the street-level restaurant the sconces include drawings by scenic designers that represent 41 theatres along Broadway. There's even an analogue board displaying all the current shows should guests care to step out for a performance after checking in.

The 203 guest rooms are reasonably roomy, with some featuring velvet-draped four-poster beds and costume-trunk-inspired closets. Sumptuous seats and floor-to-ceiling windows that look over the storied street continue the theatrics.

The hidden-away nature of the place is a big part of the appeal – you wouldn't guess you were a few blocks from busy Times Square. It's exactly what you need from a hotel here: a bit of a show, with none of the drama.
civilianhotel.com

5

3
Pendry Manhattan West
Hudson Yards

On a Friday evening, Bar Pendry is humming and a seat is hard to come by in a way that was scarcely imaginable a year ago. That said, even before the pandemic, Manhattan West – on the Hudson River – was something of a forgotten part of town.

Pendry Manhattan West hotel is a newcomer to Hudson Yards, an area blighted by underwhelming reviews when it opened in 2019 but that has been steadily gaining footfall thanks to the nearby High Line. This hotel is one of the more exciting additions to an area that includes restaurants by star chefs including Danny Meyer.

The property's undulating edifice is designed by architecture studio SOM (responsible for One World Trade Center) and fits in with the district's glass and steel vernacular. "It's meant to capture the energy of the area," says Danielle Choi, SOM's director of sales and marketing. But behind the somewhat chilly façade it's all sunny finishes: a nod to Pendry's sunny Californian origins. "It's an opportunity for us to bring the things that inspire us as a brand to this iconic and electric city," says Michael Fuerstman, co-founder and creative director of Pendry Hotels & Resorts.

Pendry is a more contemporary brand from hospitality group Montage Resorts, which has a number of resorts across the US, including California. To transport a slice of the West Coast to the east, the team worked with Gachot Studios. The lobby is filled with light wood as well as a fireplace and simple mid-century-style sofas. There's an abundance of plants and strip lighting inspired by the work of artists from the Light and Space movement, such as James Turrell. The ground floor is home to the glowing Bar Pendry with its gold-plate ceiling, and Zou Zou's, an Eastern Mediterranean restaurant where ingredients such as sea bass and artichokes are cooked over an open fire. Upstairs is cocktail lounge Chez Zou, which is modelled on a 1960s speakeasy in Beirut. The rooms are a quieter affair. Featuring panelled wood with a Japanese aesthetic, they have floor-to-ceiling windows, oval baths and beds from which guests can look down at the city but, luckily, won't hear it.
pendry.com

6

7

"It's an opportunity for us to bring the things that inspire us as a brand to this iconic and electric city"

1. Upstairs bar at Civilian
2. The Blue Room
3. Civilian guest room
4. Street leve
5. Guests in the bar
6. Bar Pendry
7. Table at Zou Zou's
8. The light-filled restaurant

8

INVENTORY: Picnic recipes

Let's go outside
Global

Swiss chef Ralph Schelling shares his tried and trusted recipes for perfect outdoor dining, from savoury nibbles to tasty bakes and even a tipple or two. As soon as the sun's shining, grab your picnic basket and load it up with plates, cutlery and some of these irresistible goodies.

Writer
Ralph Schelling

Illustration
Xihanation

There are few greater pleasures than eating alfresco. Whether you're unfurling a crisp gingham blanket between iffy clouds or basking under an azure sky with a heavy wicker hamper laden with delights, there's an inherent optimism to the act of picnicking – something primal and pleasing.

First you're implicitly hoping that the weather holds – never assured in certain latitudes. Second, and perhaps more meaningfully, you're actively choosing to share your space with your fellow citizens – to leave the safety of dining tables, terraces and menus behind, and simply make do with just what you are able to carry.

Whether you've found a scrap of urban greenery or set up in a nook enjoying the view of a secluded lake, you're completely committing to the experience – wind, rain or shine. It's what makes proper packing so important. And remember some simple rules: certain foods don't travel well, others are hard to eat standing up and yes, someone *will* spill something. Bring wipes, cutlery that will cut it and some plates and cups that can stand a stiff breeze.

Here we've tapped Swiss chef Ralph Schelling for his picnic favourites. Like the act of eating outdoors, our list isn't fussy. We've suggested simple, crowdpleasers that reward experimentation and won't take a chef to perfect. Now, shall we tuck in? — Ⓜ

To drink

Classic chelada
Serves 4

The name of this refreshing Mexican number is believed to be a contraction of "*mi chela helada*", something like "my cold beer". It's a simple version of that, which is good for barbecues or hot days. "You don't necessarily have to use a Mexican beer, just pour your favourite," says chef Ralph Schelling. "In Switzerland, for example, I like Appenzeller or Flühgass."

Ingredients:
Juice of 2 limes
Thinly sliced red chilli as a garnish (optional)
Chilli salt (or Mexican condiment Tajín)
12 ice cubes, crushed
3 330ml bottles of lager
4 lime slices
200ml pineapple juice (optional)

Method:
1. Moisten the rims of medium-sized glasses with lime juice and chilli salt.
2. Fill up with ice, beer and remaining lime juice and garnish with lime and chilli.
3. Adding 50ml of pineapple juice per glass adds a fruity kick. Refill at leisure.

To drink

Strawberry shrub
Serves 4

Shrubs are non-alcoholic and can be diluted with water to make refreshing summer sippers. Usually made with vinegar and sugar, they have plenty of kick. You can also vary the fruit – try elderberry or blueberry – or add a shot or two of white rum to create a strawberry mojito shrub.

Ingredients:
500g strawberries in pieces, stalks removed
200g cane sugar
200ml apple cider vinegar
600ml mineral water
Ice cubes
Mint leaves or lemon verbena (optional)

Method:
1. Mix the strawberries with the sugar and vinegar. Cover and leave to macerate at room temperature overnight.
2. Purée the strawberries and pass through a sieve, and refrigerate until ready to use.
3. Funnel into a bottle to bring to the picnic, and mix with water and ice cubes to a ratio of one part purée to three parts water.

Ralph's tips:
1. The vinegar adds an extra kick of freshness.
2. Simply pour the base for the picnic into a clip-on bottle.
3. I love to add a few leaves of mint or lemon verbena.
4. In spring, add one or two stalks of rhubarb and you can do without about a third of the vinegar.
5. I can confirm elderberry or blueberry shrub is also pretty cool.
6. And, yes, I like to add some white rum to create a strawberry mojito shrub. Tasty!

Main

Chicken Waldorf sandwich
Serves 4

A humble sandwich? Perhaps. "This is the Waldorf-Astoria's classic recipe to-go," says Schelling. "I recommend the best seeded bread you can get, lightly toasted."

Ingredients
2 chicken breasts, cut into pieces, cooked
1 apple, cored and diced
2 stalks of celery, diced
Handful of grapes, halved
Handful of walnuts, crushed
3 tbsps mayonnaise
3 tbsps Greek yoghurt
1 tsp Dijon mustard
2 tsps lemon juice
Salt and pepper
8 slices of bread
Lettuce leaves or purslane (optional)

Method:
1. Mix the mayonnaise with the yoghurt, mustard and lemon juice in a bowl and season.
2. Mix the chicken pieces and the rest of the ingredients well in the sauce and divide between the bread to make sandwiches. It's that simple.

Main

Tramezzini with cucumber and pea
Serves 4 people

These Italian-style sandwiches are usually cut into triangles and are perfect picnic fodder. "I often add fresh radish and cress," says Schelling. "Pink pepper always goes well too."

Ingredients:
350g peas (fresh or frozen)
1 sprig of fresh mint
½ cucumber
1 clove of garlic
1 lemon (juice and zest)
3 tbsps olive oil
Sea salt
Pepper
8 slices of bread

Method:
1. Cook the frozen peas in salted water according to packet instructions. Drain and leave to cool. Set aside 100g of the peas. Finely slice the cucumber.
2. Blitz the garlic, mint, 200g of the peas, juice and zest of the lemon, olive oil, salt and pepper in a stand mixer until it's lump-free. Now stir in the remaining whole peas.
3. Spread the purée on one side of each slice of bread and add a few slices of cucumber. Cut the tramezzini into triangles or into any shape you fancy.

Side

Feta with filo, thyme, honey and almonds
Serves 4

These tasty little bites are a perfect mix of salty and sweet. "For the picnic, I recommend spreading a little honey together with the butter on the pastry at the beginning and you can also do without sesame or almonds, or sprinkle them with black sesame seeds as you prefer," says Schelling. "Don't worry about the mess – you can always lick your fingers."

Ingredients:
4 filo pastry sheets
4 tbsps melted butter
Thyme (fresh or dried)
180g feta
Honey
Handful of roasted almonds or sesame seeds

Method:
1. Preheat the oven to 180C.
2. Unfold the filo pastry and spread with melted butter and sprinkle with fresh or dried thyme.
3. Cut the feta into small triangles or cubes of 3cm or so and wrap in the filo pastry, brushing it with a little butter so that it folds better and holds together.
4. Brush the parcels again (and sprinkle with the almonds or sesame seeds). Bake the parcels for 15 minutes until they are golden brown and the kitchen smells of thyme. Drizzle a little honey over them before you serve.

Side

Korean cucumber salad
Serves 4

This simple pickled salad keeps well for a few days in a mason jar and is a brilliantly bright and spicy addition to a barbecue line-up.

Ingredients
2 small cucumbers
50g salt
1 fresh chilli pepper
2 spring onions
1 tbsp soy sauce
1 tbsp sesame oil
1 tsp brown sugar
1 tbsp rice vinegar
1 tbsp sesame seeds (roasted)
10g coriander

Method
1. Cut the cucumbers into 1cm thick rounds. Place in a bowl and salt generously. Mix well and leave to stand for 30 minutes.
2. Now finely dice the chilli and cut the spring onions into 2mm rings.
3. After half an hour, drain any liquid from the cucumber pieces and rinse with cold water. Mix the soy sauce, sesame oil, sugar and vinegar in a bowl then add the drained cucumber pieces, chilli, spring onions and sesame seeds. Mix well. Season to taste and add fresh coriander.

Hummus with lemon za'atar
Serves 4

This needs a little prep the day before but you can speed things up by using cooked chickpeas. "My friends in Lebanon taught me a trick for an unbelievably smooth hummus," says Schelling. "Mix a few ice cubes into the hummus at the end to make it lighter and airier." This goes well with some celery for dunking.

For the hummus:
300g dried chickpeas
2 litres water
50g tahini (sesame paste)
1 lemon, juice only
5 tbsps olive oil
1 tsp salt
2 cloves of garlic

For the lemon za'atar:
1 tbsp sesame seeds
½ lemon, zested
1 tbsp dried thyme
1 tsp fleur de sel

Method:
1. The day before, put chickpeas in the cold water and leave them to soak overnight.
2. On the day of preparation, drain the chickpeas, cover with water and bring to the boil. Cook the chickpeas for about an hour until soft.
3. Meanwhile, for the lemon za'atar, toast the sesame seeds until golden and put them in a mortar. Finely grate the lemon zest. Coarsely crush everything. Mix in the fleur de sel and thyme leaves.
4. Drain the chickpeas, saving a cup of the cooking water. Put the rest of the chickpeas in a tall blender jar with the tahini, 4 tbsps lemon juice, a little oil and salt. Add the garlic. Blend everything into a purée, adding from the cooking water until the desired consistency is reached.
5. Season the hummus with lemon juice and salt. Pour into a bowl and make a well with a spoon. Drizzle oil into it and sprinkle with a little za'atar.

Fish skewers with lemongrass and oats
Serves 4

This simple skewer – served on a lemongrass stick – can be whipped up quickly and eaten without cutlery. Ralph's recipe calls for pike perch but other fish work equally well.

Ingredients
400g pike-perch fillets, deskinned and deboned
1 egg yolk
150g single cream, ice cold
1 tsp ground ginger
2 tsps salt
6 lemongrass stalks
150g oat flakes
3 tbsps vegetable oil
½ lemon (juice and zest)

Method
1. Cut the fish into fine 2cm by 2cm cubes.
2. Blitz in a blender with the egg yolk, cream, ginger and salt to form a coarse mixture.
3. Remove the outer layer from the lemongrass. Chop 1-2 tbsp of the fine, lower part of the lemongrass stalks very finely and stir into the fish mixture.
4. Now cut the lemongrass stalks in half lengthwise. Press the fish mixture around the lemongrass stalks.
5. Roll in the oat flakes to cover
6. Heat the oil in a frying pan. Fry the skewers for 5 minutes, turning occasionally, until golden.
7. Grate lemon zest, squeeze lemon, mix zest and juice. Drizzle over the fish kebabs and serve.

Ralph's raw vegan lasagne
Serves 4

This vegan take on the Italian classic involves no cooking whatsoever. "I am not necessarily a fan of raw vegan food but my lasagne made an Italian nonna cry," says Schelling. (In a good way, we hope.) "I served it at a recent party in Portofino and we served it as a family dish to share in old terracotta plates like a real lasagne from the oven." You can also add grated pine nuts on top to simulate parmesan or a layer of pea pesto for a fresh kick.

Ingredients:
220g cashew nuts (soaked in water for at least six hours)
1 tsp salt
2 cloves of garlic
1 tsp yeast powder
2 tsp apple vinegar or lemon juice
200g dried tomatoes
100g walnuts
50ml best cold-pressed olive oil
2 courgettes thinly sliced lengthwise
2-3 handfuls of spinach
10g basil
Pine nuts, to taste (optional)

Method
1. Drain the cashew nuts and mix with salt, garlic cloves, yeast, vinegar and a little water (little by little) in a powerful blender to form a thick béchamel-like cream. Refrigerate until ready to use.
2. Now mix the dried tomatoes, walnuts and olive oil in a blender to a coarse paste (something like minced meat). This is your ragú.
3. In a platter, or Tupperware if you're off for a picnic, layer the courgette and spinach alternately with the vegan béchamel and ragù alternative, and serve with basil and a drizzle of olive oil.

Dessert

Swiss cheese selection
Serves the whole gathering

Alpsbrinz, hard
From Switzerland, the raw milk is partially skimmed, processed in copper vats and curdled at a temperature of 32C and matured for 30 months. It's worth the wait.

Schwellbrunner, medium-hard
Cheese from the only Appenzell dairy that still makes it from raw milk that's flavoured with the rich grasses and flowers of the nearby mountain pastures.

Jersey Blue, soft
Schelling's favourite of Willi Schmid's cheeses, the Jersey Blue is exported all over the world and popular with top chefs. It combines the taste of rich Jersey milk with a tang but is creamy, nutty and smoky too.

Dessert

Swiss granola bar
Makes about 15 bars

These simple, sweet anytime bars are sure-fire family favourites. "The mixture can be varied according to your own preferences, with nuts or berries," says Schelling. "For an easy granola you can also crumble the bars over yoghurt, kefir or almond milk."

Ingredients
150g oat flakes
5 tbsps hemp powder
5 tbsps hemp nuts
5 tbsps pumpkin seeds
5 tbsps linseed
5 tbsps barberries
5 tbsps sunflower seeds
½ tsp cinnamon powder
½ tsp cardamom powder
½ tsp ginger powder
2 pinches of salt
5 tbsps apple syrup or honey
3 tbsps walnut oil

Method:

1. Preheat oven to 160C.
2. Mix all ingredients and place in silicone moulds (or about 3cm high in two cake tins lined with baking paper). Press the mixture down firmly.
3. Bake for about 18 minutes, then remove. While still warm, cut into bars or into shapes of your choice and leave to cool. If kept dry and sealed, the bars will keep for about two weeks.

Dessert

Almond madeleines au beurre sale
Makes 12

These tasty bakes can be made nuttier by browning the butter first or fresher by serving with wild strawberries. You could also add matcha powder (1½ tsp per 50g of flour) or create a gluten-free take on things by using cornflour instead. You'll need a madeleine mould plus a little extra flour and butter. Enjoy.

Ingredients
130g caster sugar
50g almonds, peeled
50g plain white flour
100g butter, liquid
100g egg (about three large ones)
2 pinches of salt
Matcha powder (optional)

Method
1. Preheat the oven to 220C degrees.
2. Blitz the sugar, almonds and flour in a blender to combine.
3. Add the butter, eggs and salt to form a liquid dough.
4. Butter the madeleine moulds and fill to the brim with the mixture and bake for about 10 minutes until golden brown.

And to drink...
Wine to complete the picnic

Wine writer Aimee Hartley suggests some bottles to accompany you on your outing.

Sparkling

Davenport
Limney Estate Organic Sparkling, Sussex, England 2015
A rich and elegant English fizz that's designed to give champagne a run for its money – and does.

Rosé

Morgado do Quintão
Palhete, Algarve, Portugal 2019
A unique blend of red and white grapes makes for a refreshing rosé-inspired wine with Portuguese charm and character.

White

Sybille Kuntz Riesling Qualitätswein
Trocken, Mosel, Germany 2020
A refreshing and deliciously dry riesling from a biodynamic, family estate in the Mosel Valley. *Sehr gut!*

Partida Creus,
BN Blanco Natural
Catalonia, Spain 2020
A crisp, salty white that's ideal for langorous sunny days, made by one of Spain's most celebrated natural wine producers.

Red

Pierre Cotton
Ygueule, Beaujolais, France 2018
From a rising star in Beaujolais: chill down this fresh, quaffable gamay for a picnic-perfect companion.

Orange

Ca' de Noci
Notte di Luna, Emilia-Romagna, Italy 2019
A heady blend of floral grapes – muscat blanc, malvasia and spergola – with skin contact for added texture and sunshine. *Cin-cin.*

About the writer:
Aimee Hartley is the founder of wine magazine *Above Sea Level*. She also runs Twelve Noon, a creative studio for food, drink and hospitality projects.

A spate of recent hotel openings has given Madrid a kick of confidence despite last year's slump in visitor numbers. The once museum-like Ritz (purchased by the Mandarin-Oriental for €130m) underwent a makeover that included a new subterranean marble-walled spa. The 200-key Four Seasons landed in the capital following a slow-motion journey through the bureaucracy. Earlier this year, the Villa Magna hotel was reimagined by Rosewood (*see issue 150*), while Philippe Starck is currently remaking a 1920s building on Calle Gran Via into a Brach hotel.

And, in the midst of all this ribbon-cutting, comes The Madrid Edition. Marriott's behemoth (it's the 13th Edition, with more on the way) enlisted Studio 54 co-founder Ian Schrager back in 2008.

The ambitious three-year fit-out of an old building perched between Puerta de Sol and Plaza Mayor was undertaken by architect John Pawson and Paris-based François Champsaur. The statement marble staircase swirls people up to the cream-coloured retro-future lounge and lobby. Restaurant Jerónimo, headed by Enrique Olvera, is not to be missed.

"The architecture we inherited – a modern building with a baroque portal – was the conceptual starting point," says Pawson, who describes the entire project as a lively conversation with place. "Schrager and I talked about combining the energy and optimism of La Movida Madrileña with the sensory richness of a Velázquez painting. This is the energy we wanted to flow out to become part of the wider cultural and social life of this part of the city." Last but not least is the roof where Peruvian chef Diego Muñoz's Oroya restaurant sits alongside Madrid's biggest rooftop pool. Surely this will be Madrid's most coveted sunbed this summer. — Ⓜ
editionhotels.com

INVENTORY: New opening
Checking in Madrid

Bringing a sense of fun and colour to Spain's capital, the newest Edition hotel is revitalising hospitality in Madrid. Oh, and it has the city's biggest rooftop pool.

Writer
Liam Aldous

Photography
Ben Roberts

1. Thirst-quenching sipper
2. Madrid's biggest rooftop pool
3. Time for a game
4. Take a seat
5. Tempting dish

Now hear this
Global

The sounds of summer are upon us, so this issue we focus on the best ways to listen to music anywhere – but especially outdoors.

Writer
David Phelan

Photography
Tony Hay

Bang & Olufsen
Beoplay EX

The latest in-ear headphones from Bang & Olufsen feature great sound in a fully waterproof design, so suitable for beach or poolside. The design comes in three colours: anthracite oxygen, gold tone and black anthracite. The charging case is brushed aluminium. The earphone itself is small, despite having a 9.2mm speaker driver, giving impressive sound while still being small enough to fit the ear comfortably, even for a long time. It also works well for making and receiving calls, thanks to three microphones on each earbud which efficiently reduce background noise.

The latest Bluetooth tech means it can connect to two separate devices, so you can listen to tracks from a music player but take calls when your phone rings.
bang-olufsen.com

Loewe
We Hear 1

We is the name of a new affordable sub-brand for Loewe audio-visual products. In the first launch is an eye-catching portable Bluetooth speaker. The cylindrical device has speakers at both ends, though tiny feet at one end tell you which way is up. The audio is excellent, with plenty enough volume for the great outdoors, but strong accuracy and a good balance of midtones and bass. Choose from storm grey, cool grey, aqua blue and coral red. There's also a larger model in the same colours, called We Hear 2, with an extra three hours' battery life.
we-by-loewe.com

Sonos
Roam

The problem with Bluetooth speakers is while you want them to be as small as possible for convenience and portability, audio quality usually suffers. The Roam bucks this trend. It's small enough to carry easily in one hand, about the size of a water bottle, and light at 430g, but it sounds terrific. It's also tough enough to handle a drop or two of rain, or even survive unscathed after being submerged in water a metre deep for half an hour. Because it's a Sonos, it's smart enough to know when you are in range of another Sonos speaker and will switch to wi-fi automatically, with the press of a button transferring to the next speaker. Sonos includes Trueplay in its latest products, which means it adjusts the sound according to the environment, often with dramatic improvement. Here, Trueplay is done automatically. And just in time for summer,

Sonos has added great colours to the range which was previously just black and white. Choose from a calming blue (wave), luscious green (olive) or a perky red (sunset).
sonos.com

Sony
WH-1000XM5

When it comes to noise-cancelling headphones, you can count the brands that get it right on one hand: Bose, Apple and Sony. Of the three, Sony's noise-cancellation is the most enjoyable. It's better than ever in this latest, fifth, edition of its over-ear headphones. Even with noise-cancelling switched off, the audio is improved with

better bass thanks to a new internal design. The sleeker look is the biggest change yet for Sony's headphones. Smart effects include Speak to Chat – that sounds tautological but just means that when you start talking, the headphones automatically pause playback so you can hear the person you're talking to. The only downside is you can't sing along to your favourite track with this feature turned on.
sony.com

Join the MONOCLE community

1 Truly independent journalism **2** In a fresh-look magazine **3** With bigger reads and deeper dives, and **4** Ideas that inspire **5** That's truly global

Plus: we have a new print-only subscription that gives you 10 issues of MONOCLE straight to your door.

Join the club today at *monocle.com/subscribe*

EXPO

WRITERS
James Chambers, Grace Charlton, Carolina Abbott Galvão, Kati Krause, Monica Lillis, Louis Harnett O'Meara, Carli Ratcliff, Carlota Rebelo, Chiara Rimella, Natalie Theodosi, Junichi Toyofuku, Andrew Tuck, Fiona Wilson

PHOTOGRAPHY
Gaia Cambiaggi, Rodrigo Cardoso, Terence Chin, Amara Eno, Luigi Fiano, Thomas Humery, Iris Humm, Yiorgos Kaplandis, Jake Naughton, Felix Odell, Evgeniy Rein, Arata Suzuki, Kohei Take, Kenneth Tsang, Saskia Wilson, Dan Wilton

Summer is all about taking a break and doing the things that enhance your quality of life. And we've devised a modest checklist of ideas to set you on the right course – to make life just a bit nicer. So grab your swimmers and sunnies – we have places to go.

25 THINGS TO MAKE YOU HAPPY

01.

Move to a sunny neighbourhood

From community hubs to independent shops, several man-made components help to make a good neighbourhood. That said, some locations have a natural advantage: sunshine. In recent years, La Condesa in the Cuauhtémoc borough of Mexico City has enjoyed an influx of international residents attracted by the alfresco drinking and dining options, good shopping and jungle-like greenery that flourishes in the city's warm climes. Stroll between its art nouveau-inspired buildings up to Bosque de Chapultepec park on the northern edge. Or stick around on a balmy evening to enjoy a cocktail or two at Baltra, one of the city's best bars.

02.

Rock a good hat

Tucked away in the narrow cobbled streets of Monastiraki in central Athens, Giorgio Hatter looks unassuming: stripped back interiors, long industrial shelves and neatly arranged piles of hats. But a sense of warmth envelops the place thanks to owners George and Vasiliki Polychronopoulos (*pictured*). The pair are always on hand to greet customers and share their passion for hat-making, passed down from their father Elias, who opened the shop in 1978, and grandfather Georgios, who used to create hats for primary school students in his village of Kalamata. Today, Giorgio Hatter remains one of the city's best-kept secrets for summer hats, from cotton bucket styles to fedoras handmade using natural straw. Place one on your head – it will add confidence to your stride.

03.

Hit the dance floor

It doesn't matter if it's at a cool club, chilled beach bar or naff haunt that only plays music worthy of a wedding playlist, letting go on a dance floor should be embraced. Turn that timid shimmy into a proper shake, command the room, do that extra fist pump if the song calls for it. On the dance floor, as in life, there really is no point holding back. You're more likely to be praised for some out-there moves than judged for half-arsed ones. Too many love stories have begun inside nightclubs packed with wriggling bodies (or in their smoking room, Cupid's favourite playpen) not to believe in the romantic potential of sweat-glistening skin. Founded in 1929 by Achille Franceschi as a little shack on the beach that played music on a gramophone, La Capannina di Franceschi (*pictured*) evolved into a storied nightclub in the Italian resort town of Forte dei Marmi. Its afternoon aperitivo still turns into a live DJ set every weekend. Forget about tomorrow and stay out a little later – the next track is always a great tune.

04.

Have a morning routine

We're all partial to pressing the snooze button a few too many times but when it comes to the mornings, studies have shown that consistent routines help. That means that the minutes between rolling out of bed and leaving the house count. Luckily, the way we see it, the recipe for a good morning is simple: start in the shower with Haeckels' broccoli shampoo, then moisturise with Lumene's Glow Reveal line and top it all off with a hefty scoop of Malin+Goetz SPF. Been out dancing the night before? Dr Barbara Sturm × Aquazzura's foot spray is just the thing. Then a spritz of Perfumer H's Bergamot fragrance and you're out the door.

05.

Wear a favourite T-shirt

Why is it that you find yourself reaching for the same T-shirt again and again, even snatching it from the dryer before it's really dry? Perhaps it's the softness of the cotton or that it defies the tumbling cycle to keep its shape. Whatever the reason, we all need a reliable T-shirt partner. And a classic white T-shirt is probably the most essential piece of clothing in your wardrobe. We recommend going for a lightweight one that feels soft to the touch. You can't go wrong with something by Auralee (*pictured*), Harris Reed, Organic Basics, Lady White Co, Asket or Sunspel. Maybe a little oversized if you're feeling adventurous. Trends come and go but you'll never go wrong if you stick with the basics.
auralee.jp, harrisreed.com; organicbasics.com; ladywhiteco.com; asket.com; sunspel.com

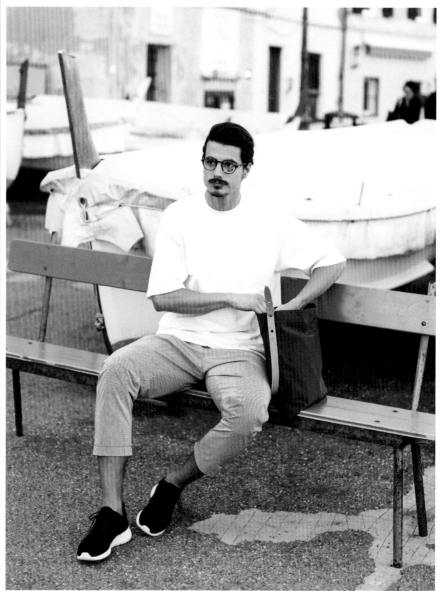

07.
Find a wise architect

Everyone wants to live in their dream home but getting there isn't as simple as it sounds. Meeting the right architect is a good place to start. We suggest looking for someone with a couple of years of experience under their belt, who understands that all great homes need a personal touch. "It's about getting to know clients and understanding the everyday moments they value," says Sydney-based architect Shaun Carter (*pictured*). "That can be as simple as preserving the place where the owner drinks a cup of tea every day." A good architect should be interested in your life too, so make sure they get to know you. It'll help you get the best outcome. And you might even make a new friend.
carterwilliamson.com

06.
Surround yourself with colour

It's easy to let the world make you feel grey, especially if you're based in a cloudy city. But there is a simple antidote to the blues. Studies have shown that colour can dramatically alter how you feel, think and even behave. Putting on that bright jumper or looking at an eye-catching painting can instantly provide a mood boost. The players at Pigalle Duperré basketball court in Paris (*pictured*) have an unfair advantage. A collaboration between Parisian creative agency Ill Studio, fashion brand Pigalle and Nike, the court's rubber floors are saturated with vibrant blue, yellow and fuchsia. Done judiciously, as here, flashes of urban colour can brighten the day.

09.
Have a dish to impress

Everyone should have a go-to summer dish. Not something that demands you spend hours in a kitchen or searching the city for an elusive ingredient – but something that delights diners (and perhaps makes them a little envious). Nobody understands this better than Ruth Rogers, who helps us out here. At The River Café, her restaurant in London, her team, including Sian Wyn Owen (*pictured*) grows their own herbs and leaves – mint, rocket and courgette flowers all sprout here. "Today we picked them to make the salad," says Rogers of this treat of broad beans topped with *mozzarella di bufala* and River Café greens. "Eating good food is comparable to seeing a piece of great art," says Rogers. So what's your go-to?

08.
Mix a cocktail

Everyone should know how to make a good cocktail. Like everything in life, it's important to start with the basics: an old fashioned often does the trick. "Say you're at a party and you've decided to make a cocktail for your friends," says Giovanni Dellaglio, a bartender at London's Beaumont Hotel, as he pours 60ml of Maker's Mark bourbon into a glass. "Sometimes the time you spend making it is even better than drinking the final product." If you're a beginner, definitely stick to a recipe (*The Savoy Cocktail Book*, Eddie Clarke's *Shaking in the 60s* and Phaidon's *Spirited: Cocktails from Around the World* are all good places to start). While taking the time to fix someone a drink is hardly common in the hustle and bustle of everyday life, a small act of kindness often goes a long way. So bottom's up!

10.

Take care of your knees

If it's good for your knees, embrace it. The ability to meander for hours, to head out for a joyous run at dusk or dance till dawn is a beautiful thing. So do all you can to move with grace and ease – because once you start creaking you'll yearn for that 5K dash, throwing some dance moves. What should you do to stay lithe? We asked MONOCLE's (and *Konfekt*'s) favourite medic, Dr Vera Stucki, for some advice. Here's her verdict.

"The good news first: even intensive sport does not harm the joints; the process of degeneration is not simply a question of the quantity of the impact. On the contrary, regular exercise and physical activity have a positive effect on the knee joints.

The secret to avoiding degenerative arthritis is simply mechanical: the hip, knee and ankle joints must be kept in their optimal axis. This is achieved through well-trained hip and femoral muscles, which stabilise and control the joints' movements. Concave soft-shoe inner soles can exacerbate deviation of the axis; running shoes should balance out any deficits, so get some advice.

A Mediterranean diet rich in omega-3 fatty acids can have a positive effect on inflammatory processes and help prevent obesity. So far, there is no evidence that any dietary supplements can regenerate the cartilage layer. Most important: invest in strengthening your muscles and never stop moving."
Thanks Dr Stucki!

11.

Help out

It is said that the happiness you gain from giving is more meaningful than any instant gratification could ever be. Moral superiority is never in vogue but an appreciation for a sense of purpose, social connection and helping a cause greater than yourself can do wonders for your morale. In London, Walworth Garden, an organic community garden, operating for more than 30 years, is always looking for volunteers. And from participating in workshops to planting herbs, there's a lot that horticulture enthusiasts can do to lend a green hand. But you don't need a special occasion; just be the kind of person who offers their hand.

12.

Jump

It doesn't need to involve a bungee or a mad leap into unknown waters (breaking a limb is never a great addition to your quality of life) but jumping into a lake, off the end of a pier or the edge of a boat is good for the soul. Too often we dither and ease ourselves into the chilly sea. But sometimes it's better to let out a scream, a mad holler, and just go for it. While we might not have the skills of the divers who leap from Pigeon Rocks in Beirut, the MONOCLE posse has been seen leaping into the sea along the coast at Sporting Club. But whether from a Copenhagen dockside (*pictured*) or Greek-isle-anchored cruiser, take a leap (with care) this summer.

13.

Have big-screen nights

We've all spent way too much time scrolling through endless lists of titles on a streaming service for our own good. An evening at the cinema is a simple way to achieve many joys at once. Whether you're going on your own, with friends or a new date, making the deliberate choice to get yourself a ticket and bucket of popcorn will always turn casual viewing into a memorable occasion. There's something supremely comforting about knowing that you can rely on a small cinema with solid programming to pick up the independent films that would otherwise slip past unnoticed. Once the lights go out and the mobile phone gets switched off, the world outside disappears for a bit. Being surrounded by people who laugh (and cry) at the same time as you provides the quickest and most powerful shortcut to a sense of community – and it never fails to ignite a childlike wonder. If the set-up is complete with plush velvet chairs, brass side tables and a grand hall, just like Stockholm's Capitol Bio (*pictured*), then it'll be impossible to resist the pull of the big screen.
capitolbio.se

14.

Have a party trick

Whether it's dinner at someone's house or a picnic in the park, a delicious cup of coffee or homemade family dish, there are lots of ways to entertain a party – but singing a big song is perhaps a more surprising trick. Look no further than Japan, the karaoke kingdom, for professional instructors who help you polish your skills. Kazuhide Kinoshita (*pictured, on left*), a singer-songwriter and composer at Clip Music in Tokyo, does exactly that, giving lessons to everyone from businessmen and women who hope to impress their clients to parents who want to sing at their children's weddings. Even Buddhist monks come to him for voice training to chant the long sutras. No need to pull a rabbit out of a hat. Just sing!

15.
Take a long walk

Hiking might be what everyone is calling it nowadays but don't be put off by the lofty nomenclature. A long walk can be as simple or strenuous as you want to make it, from city strolls along the river and rambles through the countryside to an alternative commute, such as the one taken by James Chambers, our Hong Kong bureau chief (*pictured*), that cuts across the mountains. Not every step needs to be mapped out (in fact, ditch the map) and there's no need to get carried away with expensive kit. Long walks make for good conversations and we find that they work particularly well as a digestif. Get the most out of this change of scenery by leaving the tracking gadgets behind and be sure to share a friendly greeting with any fellow walkers you pass along the way.

16.
See friends

Having your own back only goes so far. At the end of the day, there's nothing like being able to rely on someone – and knowing that they can count on you too. Studies show that spending time with friends can enhance your mood, boost happiness levels and reduces stress (we're talking about the real deal here by the way, not social media). Most people are constantly being bombarded with emails and texts. But how often do you take the time to see someone face to face? "Interestingly, friendships appear to be most important for those that are the most vulnerable in society – those who have risk factors for poorer health and well-being," says Bill Chopik, a professor of psychology at Michigan State University, who specialises in personal relationships. "In this way, having more and better-quality friendships is something that can improve nearly everyone's lives." So make plans to see old friends this summer. Go for that drink or dinner you've been meaning to set up. In the grand scheme of things, taking the time will do you some good.

18.

Find your shady spot

Anyone can benefit from spending a little time in the shade. In need of a good spot? Try Lisbon. The Portuguese capital is known for its sunny disposition and it also has a healthy tree canopy providing much-needed cover. The urban heat island effect is rare in Lisbon as it boasts more than 90 parks and gardens, community tree-planting programmes and a new project called Life Lungs that is reseeding some of its wilder spots. Ensuring that neighbourhoods have shade and greenery is crucial to making resilient cities. Plus, it makes for a pretty view – just stroll down Avenida da Liberdade when the jacaranda trees are in full bloom to see it for yourself.

17.

Befriend a gallerist

Buying a work of art to hang in your living room is a fulfilling way to make your home feel as though it really is an expression of your taste. But it can also be an intimidating prospect if you've not been hanging out at trade fairs or at vernissages for half your life. That's why having a gallerist for a friend to help you navigate the intricacies of the art world can change everything (and dispel a few myths about what everything "means" with down-to-earth conversations too). At his gallery in Paris's Le Marais, Jérôme Poggi (*pictured*) takes his time to talk and patiently explain his artists' work to whoever comes in – and he might stick around for a post-meeting glass of wine. "Friendship is at the core of art," he says. "I can say that the most engaged collectors in the galleries are real friends, in the most noble meaning of the word: we are sincere, faithful, intimate in our relationship to art. We are sharing something very personal."
galeriepoggi.com

19.
Get it repaired

As cool shops come and go, it's the people who know how to create things last that make the difference. In Berlin, Mitte's savvy residents have long understood that every neighbourhood needs a good repairman (or woman). From clarinet technician Boris Schoenherr (*pictured, right*) to furniture fixer Artur Drozd (*pictured, below*), the district is teeming with shopkeepers who specialise in making old objects new again. In his workshop, trainer repairman Hagen Matuszak fixes 400 to 500 pairs of shoes every month – nearly all of them everyday footwear items. The son of a cobbler, Matuszak (*pictured, below right*) worked as a shoe-maker in Zürich before opening Sneaker Rescue in 2018 to focus on sustainability. "What I do isn't extraordinary but my work is meaningful," he says. "There are thousands of creative agencies in Berlin but cobblers are a dying trade."

20.
Own a dog

Come on – by now you must have noticed that MONOCLE is pro-hound. You'll find the handsomest mutts lingering with their owners outside our café in Zürich and curled up under editors' desks in London and Tokyo. (We are just as fond of donkeys and goats but have found that they are less office-friendly – the goat kept climbing on the desks). The reasons for owning a dog are simple: they change the mood, turn the sternest of folk into softies and offer loyalty and kindness when you need it most. Featured here are a couple of our favourite friends (with four legs), Luna and Macy.

21.
Grow your own

No one should be afraid of change: as the seasons come and go, we all need a little room to grow (and yes, we mean that in the literal sense too). Milan-based architecture firm Piuarch, which in 2015 built a vegetable garden on the roof of its office, knows and understands this well. After all, urban agriculture has always been central to the Milanese experience. "We grew up eating the cherry tomatoes that our mothers planted on their balconies," says principal architect Francesco Fresa. "So it was nice to bring back a part of our culture that we had lost." Fresa believes that Piuarch's garden could start a broader trend in cities around the world. In 2021 he devised a scheme to help potential rooftop urban gardeners follow his firm's lead. In that spirit, we urge you to find your own patch this summer. Plant something and watch it bud. Come autumn, you might already be reaping the rewards.

23.

Drink a summery rosé

Whether on a sun-soaked patio or a terrace, a glass of rosé tends to hit the spot. The ideal blend should be crisp and snappy; something that lasts on your palate. According to our resident wine expert, Chandra Kurt, L'été avec Deux Frères, the latest release from Swiss wine-makers Florian and Gian Grundböck, ticks all the boxes. A blend of grenache, syrah and other white-grape varieties, the wine conjures up the feeling of an afternoon spent in the sun. That's because crafting that mood was essential to the brothers' creative process. "For me, a good rosé should taste like summer," says Gian Grundböck.

22.

Write a diary

The simple act of filling a notebook with your scrawl makes the day clearer and resets priorities. But more than that, it's there when you need to remember the name of that place by the lake where you met, the thrill you felt when you opened the door for the first time, what it was like when they were no longer here. A diary is not about dates and events, it's about catching a snapshot of who you are every day, committing it to ink and paper. Making the fleeting, well, less fleeting. So start today; soon the task will become a habit – and then a pleasure.

24.
Get lost in a book

Having a bookseller like Jack Rollo to hand can transform your approach to beach reading. He navigates the shelves at our London neighbour Daunt Books and when he dispenses advice, it quickly becomes clear that he has an astonishing ability to find you the perfect read. We tasked him with picking a haul of books for summer, when you need chilling poolside thrillers, sunny short stories and smart non-fiction. Long afternoons on the lounger are also when you finally have time to tackle hefty classics. Here's what he's come up with to respond to our demands: something tropical, a bit magical realist? That'll be Violet Kupersmith's *Build Your House Around My Body*. A forgotten 1940s European noir? Take your pick between Patrick Modiano's *Missing Person* and Ulrich Alexander Boschwitz's *The Passenger*. There's an aquatic-themed look at art history, the tale of a fearless aviator and scorching Mediterranean coming-of-age stories in our stack (*pictured*). Take your pick – or pack them all.

25.
Take the slow train

Before bullet trains and domestic air travel became commonplace, Japanese travellers used to cross the country by sleeper train. These days, sleepers have all but disappeared but for a more stately view of Japan, we recommend an overnight trip on the Sunrise Express. It leaves Tokyo Station daily at 22.00 and heads west to Okayama, which is more than 500km away, pulling in at 06.27. There are a variety of sleeping arrangements, from the open-plan *nobinobi* compartment (good for heavy sleepers) to a single deluxe cabin. The Sunrise is no Orient Express – expect a shower cubicle and vending machines – but clean functionalism is something that Japan does well and travellers load up with snacks and bento boxes before they board. Once in your private cabin, you can slip into the *yukata* cotton robe and slippers, switch off the light and enjoy the nightscape unfolding before your eyes. One piece of advice: travel light because there isn't room in the cabin for a chunky suitcase. Oh, and enjoy the journey.

MAKE MY DAY 10: A diddy drink

Cold comfort
Porto

Founded near Porto in 1927, Super Bock is a Portuguese brewery which knows that less is sometimes more. Its miniature 200ml brown-glass bottles are a perfect summer staple for beaches, picnics and terraces as they stay cold longer than their larger cousins. It's the same idea as the smaller schooner glass used in Australia (a pint would get too hot) but rather cuter in execution. Now, a toast to the warm weather and keeping cool as the mercury rises. — Ⓜ

PHOTOGRAPHER: *Rodrigo Cardoso*